Researching Your Own Practice

Central to all caring professions, including teaching, is the need to be sensitive to – to notice — the experiences of students, colleagues and 'clients'. Starting from this position, *Researching Your Own Practice: The Discipline of Noticing* demonstrates that in order to develop your professional practice, you must first develop your own sensitivities and awareness. You must be attuned to fresh possibilities when they are needed and to be alert to such a need through awareness of what is happening at any given time.

At once an explication of this theory and a guide to its implementation, *Researching Your Own Practice: The Discipline of Noticing* provides:

- a practical approach to becoming more methodical and systematic in professional development;
- a sound basis for turning professional development into practitioner research;
- advice on how noticing can be used to improve any research, or as a research paradigm in its own right.

The Discipline of Noticing is a groundbreaking approach to professional development and research, based upon noticing a possibility for the future, noticing a possibility in the present moment and using what has been noticed in order to prepare for the future. John Mason, who derived and developed noticing as a discipline, provides a clear, persuasive and practical guide to understanding and using our inherent powers to notice and to be awake to possibilities.

John Mason is Professor of Mathematics Education at the Open University, where he was, for some 15 years, Director of the Centre for Mathematics Education. The Centre's ways of working were informed by John Mason's contact with the experience of J.G. Bennett in the 1970s, which crystallised his lifelong interest in fostering and sustaining mathematical thinking in others. He is the author of a number of books on teaching mathematics.

Researching Your Own Practice
The Discipline of Noticing

John Mason

Routledge
Taylor & Francis Group

LONDON AND NEW YORK

First published 2002
by Routledge
2 Park Square, Milton Park, Abingdon, Oxon, OX14 4RN

Simultaneously published in the USA and Canada
by Routledge
270 Madison Ave, New York NY 10016

Routledge is an imprint of the Taylor & Francis Group

Transferred to Digital Printing 2008

© 2002 John Mason

Typeset in Sabon by
M Rules

British Library Cataloguing in Publication Data
A catalogue record for this book is available from the British Library

Library of Congress Cataloging in Publication Data
A catalog record for this book has been requested

ISBN 0–415–24861–2 (hbk)
ISBN 0–415–24862–0 (pbk)

I cannot change others;
I can work at changing myself

Contents

Preface

Noticing is something we do all the time. For example, as you read this, you may become aware of the fact that you are holding a book, and also of the fact that you are reading it. You can also simultaneously become aware of sensation in your hands and feet, and of noises around you. In order to notice each of these, you have to distinguish them from the background (or in the case of background noise, distinguish them from the foreground!) yet you can, with practice, hold all of them more or less simultaneously in your awareness. It is unlikely, however, that you would have noticed any of these features while reading this unless the text drew your attention to them specifically. Of course, if you are very tired, you may have noticed sensation in your feet anyway; if it is unusually noisy you may have noticed that, and so on.

Already by now you will probably have been struck by a certain informality of style in this writing, and a reference to lived experience through an invitation to check something out in your own experience. These two features are indeed characteristic of this book as a whole, and also of what the book is about: turning ordinary noticing into a tuned and powerful approach to professional development and to various forms of research.

As a professional, you are sensitised to notice certain things in professional situations. To develop your professional practice means to increase the range and to decrease the grain size of relevant things you notice, all in order to make informed choices as to how to act in the moment, how to respond to situations as they emerge. Thus to develop professionally requires two things: to increase sensitivity to notice opportunities to act, while at the same time, to have come to mind in the moment when they are relevant, a range of possible appropriate actions.

However, developing your practice is no easy matter: how often have you set yourself to do something differently, even just to do something, and then realised later that you had forgotten all about it? Even when you know of a strategy for dealing with or exploiting a particular situation, the action may not come to mind when you need it.

The Discipline of Noticing provides a way of working against the tendency to forget, to not notice, to be so caught up in your own world that you fail to be sufficiently sensitive to possibilities. It develops entirely natural acts into a collection of practices which assist in professional development, indeed which lie at the heart of any approach to professional development. Furthermore, since all research depends, at heart, on noticing, the Discipline of Noticing can assist in improving almost any kind of research. Even more, although most researchers research other things or other people, it is also possible to research yourself, to enquire into your own lived experience. Working to develop your own practices can be transformed into a systematic and methodologically sound process of 'researching from the inside', that is, of researching yourself.

The first three parts of the book are entirely practical, providing a range of tasks through which to experience the practices and perspectives associated with noticing, and to encounter the structures which become the Discipline of Noticing. Part IV provides practical ways of working with professional experiences, whether your own, with colleagues, or in a leadership capacity supporting others. Part V then moves into research, analysing what makes research different from professional development, how noticing fits into all research in some way, how it can be used to enhance most research, and how it constitutes a research paradigm in its own right when used to research from the inside. It ends by addressing some of the common practical and philosophical issues which arise when people embark on practitioner research in general, and especially when researching their own practice in particular.

The fundamental hypothesis of this book is that change is not something that you do to other people, but something you do to yourself, following the maxim that 'I cannot change others, but I can work at changing myself'. Growth and development is seen as a maturation process, a process of transformation, not a process of tinkering as if adjusting the settings on some machine.

Although noticing is natural and fundamental to all enquiry, the development of the Discipline of Noticing leads to radical proposals concerning the nature of validity and the role of research in improving practice. If you undertake the tasks proposed in the book reasonably diligently, and if you ponder the claims made which can only be validated in your own experience, then you will certainly find here ways to improve the efficiency and effectiveness of your professional practice. You may even find yourself drawn into researching your practice. If you are drawn in any deeper, then you may find yourself embarking on a lifelong process of personal professional development or 'research from the inside'.

> *Only the wisest and the stupidest of men never change.*
> Confucius, 551?–479? BC

Acknowledgements

The inspiration and basis for this work was a three year period centred around a year spent with J. G. Bennett learning to notice. When, some seven years later, I came across the notes of his lecture which I had attended, I was pleased to find that I had reconstructed all but one paragraph. The imperfect expressions and missed opportunities in this version and approach are mine; the basic idea can be traced back as far as recorded history.

I am extremely grateful for the tolerance shown to me by very many colleagues over the years who have tried to engage with tasks I have set, and whose responses and insights have informed my articulations. Among them I must mention particularly Joy Davis, Dick Tahta, and Dave Hewitt who understood intuitively what I was on about and helped me bring it to expression, colleagues at the Open University who encouraged me to carry on trying to articulate a way of working which we had developed, and my wife Anne Watson, for continuing to question and challenge. The responses of the masters students in Edmonton in May 2000 led to the writing of Chapters 10 to 12, and those of the masters students in Cape Town in August 2000 led to Chapter 7. I have drawn on many of their accounts for my examples.

Introduction

I consider anyone working with others in some caring or supportive capacity which draws upon the exercise of professional expertise, to be a teacher. The people with whom they work cannot be 'fixed': they have to engage in some personal change for themselves, and hence they can be thought of as students in the most general sense of that term.

This book provides practical ways in which teachers can move from concern about their students and what they are learning, concern about their teaching, or even concern about other practices such as managing, conducting and participating in meetings, to doing something about it in a practical and disciplined manner. At the heart of all practice lies noticing: noticing an opportunity to act appropriately. To notice an opportunity to act requires three things: being present and sensitive in the moment, having a reason to act, and having a different act come to mind. Consequently one important aspect of being professional is noticing possible acts to try out in the future, whether gleaned from reading, from discussion, from watching others, or from personal reflection. A second important aspect is working on becoming more articulate and more precise about reasons for acting.

The mark of an expert is that they are sensitised to notice things which novices overlook. They have finer discernment. They make things look easy, because they have a refined sensitivity to professional situations and a rich collection of responses on which to draw. Among other things, experts are aware of their actions in ways that the novice is not, whether teaching, researching, attending meetings, administering, supporting colleagues, or preparing for any of these.

Professional Development is about becoming more expert. It is about questioning and perhaps changing habitual reactions which were developed in order to cope in certain situations. Thus professional development is a form of personal enquiry in order to broaden and deepen professional sensitivities to notice and to act. Noticing can be developed into a disciplined contribution to any enquiry, and it can be used as an approach research. You can use it to augment some chosen research method, or as a method of enquiry, best suited to working on your own practice rather than that of others.

The book is in six parts.

Part I offers a range of activities to help locate issues of particular concern which as a professional teacher, you might wish to enquire into in your own practice. It distinguishes between the reflective practitioner, the professional concerned to develop their practice, and practitioner research.

Part II is a practical introduction to the core notion of *noticing* which underpins all professional practice, whether as teacher, teacher–researcher, or researcher. It takes common sense observations about how people experiment with and modify their practice, what could be called the epistemology of *just plain folks* (Lave 1988, Lave and Wenger 1991), and casts this in a precise form designed both to make professional development more effective, and to provide an approach to doing effective research. Part II breaks off at the vexed question of validating what one finds as a result of enquiry. When undertaken systematically, noticing becomes the Discipline of Noticing, and this forms the basis for *researching from the inside* which is developed in Part III.

Part III highlights the practices which, if used in a disciplined manner, become the Discipline of Noticing, and completes the discussion of noticing as a form of enquiry by suggesting one way of validating and reporting findings in a manner consistent with the spirit, practice and experience of noticing.

Part IV highlights particular uses of aspects of the Discipline of Noticing which are particularly relevant in most research methods, and in leading professional development for others.

Part V marks a transition from professional development to research, summarising different approaches to research with particular emphasis on commonalities and differences with other forms of qualitative research, and thus placing the Discipline of Noticing in a wider context of action research.

Part VI treats problematic issues associated with practitioner research in general, and the Discipline of Noticing in particular.

Part VII provides a background theory for the psychological details of the Discipline of Noticing, presented appropriately as conjectures to be tested in experience.

The book ends with a brief epilogue and some appendices containing various prompts to personal reflection and discussion with colleagues.

An essential feature of the Discipline of Noticing is that it requires its practitioners to treat all assertions as conjectures to be tested in experience, either in order to make sense of the past or to inform action in the future. This means that nothing offered here should be taken as obvious or true by virtue of being written.

One of the features of individual development is that sensitivity to notice is different at different times. Things which seem obvious now may have been invisible in the past, and things invisible now may become blindingly obvious in the future. Thus if part of what is written here does not seem to be relevant or appropriate, or even accord with experience, this does not invalidate the rest. The important thing is to locate what is true for you now.

As Fisher (1998: 20) put it, 'We notice something insofar as it is unexpected . . . The act of noticing it and of itself gives pleasure . . . surprise, the eliciting of notice [is] the very heart of what it means to have an experience.'

Each of the sections in Parts I and II ends with practical tasks to try for yourself, to assist you in making sense of the text. But be warned: there is more to trying things out than merely thinking about it while you are reading! To get the most out of them, you really must try them yourself, not once but several, even many times, suitably modified in order to fit with your situation.

Part I

Enquiry

This book is about transitions:

from being a sensitive practitioner awake to possibilities, perhaps dissatisfied with aspects of the status quo;

through reflective practices,

to engaging in productive and effective personal professional development;

through drawing on published research and colleagues' experience,

to contributing to the professional development of others;

through being systematic and disciplined in recording,

to undertaking research and participating in a research community.

Its aims are, therefore, pragmatic and, although the soundness of the approach will be validated (or not) in your own experience, practice alone is merely practice; doing is merely doing. The whole thrust of this book is that the natural and intuitive actions of any teacher can be developed, made more systematic and more disciplined, to good effect. This process involves both the adoption of appropriate alternative or modified practices, and the development of criteria for deciding what constitutes appropriateness. The two go hand in hand. As Maturana (1988) observed, 'Reason drives us only through the emotions which arise in us.'

The single chapter in this part is about practice, about the various acts which are essential for any teacher who is doing more than going through the motions. Certain elements will then be extracted in Part II to constitute noticing.

1 Forces for development

Every practitioner, in what ever domain they work, wants to be awake to possibilities, to be sensitive to the situation and to respond appropriately. What is considered appropriate depends on what is valued, which in turn affects what is noticed. Thus every act of caring and supporting depends on noticing: noticing what students are doing and what they are likely to need in the near future in order to achieve their goals (Langer 1989). Every act of teaching depends on noticing: noticing what children are doing, how they respond, evaluating what is being said or done against expectations and criteria, and considering what might be said or done next. It is almost too obvious even to say that what you do not notice, you cannot act upon; you cannot choose to act if you do not notice an opportunity. Of course we all would like to do so much more than we do, even though there is not the time in which to do it. It is not always possible to devote enough time to listening and observing, to planning and preparing. The Discipline of Noticing provides a way to select and work at one or two aspects at a time. It focuses attention on enhancing awareness by sharpening and enriching those moments when you get a taste of freedom as you participate in a creative moment. It focuses attention on changing what can be changed, if it is deemed appropriate to change, not fussing about what cannot be changed for social, cultural, or institutional reasons.

We have to develop implicit theories of action in order to make professional life tolerable. There are too many variables to take into account all at once, so we develop routines and decision habits to keep mental effort at a reasonable level. To change the routine or question the theory is to reverse the process, to draw attention once more to myriads of additional variables, and to raise the possibility of paralysis from information overload and failing to cope (Eraut 1994: 34). Not to change, modify, experiment is to be stuck in the rut of habit, ending up where those habits lead. As the sage put it, 'If you don't change your direction, you may end up where you are headed.'

Each act of teaching, of caring, of supporting, is also an act of learning: learning about the students, learning about the situation, and learning about oneself. Or at least that is the myth which is promulgated. If it were true, then there would be a lot more variation in practice from day to day than there actually is, a lot more experimentation, and a lot more pleasure from teaching. A good deal of pleasure in any of the caring professions, comes from seeing those being supported change and develop. But there is more. An important source of pleasure comes from participating in a moment of choice, by making an informed decision to act non-habitually, to respond professionally rather than just react. But the practical facts of the matter are that there is too much to attend to in any inter-action, too much to be aware of, too much to notice. So we get through as best we can. Although it is a common and often quoted sentiment that 'Experience is the best of schoolmasters', or 'you learn from experience', it is also often questioned. For example, Benjamin Franklin (1758) suggested that 'Experience keeps a dear school, but fools will learn in no other, and scarce in that'. Far from learning from experience moment by moment, we react, just managing or coping.

> One thing we do not seem to learn from experience,
> is that we do not often learn from experience alone.

A great deal can be learned from getting in and doing things, but after a while the learning is supplanted by ingrained habits 'learned' from experience. Supporting and caring for others, whether as teacher or in some other way, is such a complex activity that it is essential to develop stratagems and tactics for dealing with common situations, which then become habitual. We cannot afford to think out a response to each emerging incident. Habits must be developed in order to free our attention to keep in mind our over-all goal. The trouble with habits is that 'habit forming can be habit forming' (Shigematsu 1981 no. 341).

Instead of responding sensitively to situations, we frequently react according to established patterns. We may even find ourselves quickly classifying people and situations in which we are involved and then reacting to those stereotypes before we realise what has happened. So we continue to believe we act freshly all the time, when in fact much of the time we react rather than respond.

By contrast, in those few brief moments when we feel we have participated in an informed choice, when we have acted freshly and appropriately, there is a sense of freedom, of meaning, of worth-whileness and self-esteem. It is these moments of personal freedom which keep us going.

The details of caring in general and of teaching in particular necessarily involve noticing. We notice that the people being cared for are restless or their attention is elsewhere, so we switch our own attention to match theirs. We notice that a class is losing concentration, so we switch the mode of interaction from whole class to groups or individuals, or introduce a fresh task; we notice that some students are working quickly while others are not, so we try to give more attention where it seems needed, challenging each in ways we feel most appropriate for the individual. If we notice that some technique which we hoped they had mastered is suddenly problematic again, we may choose to switch tasks and rehearse the technique again before proceeding.

Noticing requires sensitivity. I cannot notice that some students are bored if my attention is focused on my own nervousness or insecurity. I need to become aware of the ebb and flow of energy in the classroom (and each class is different in this respect).

To notice an opportunity requires two things. I have to be awake to the situation at the moment, and I have to have alternative actions prepared which will also come to mind in the moment. For example, I cannot invoke a technique like 'circle-time' if I have never heard of it or never imagined myself using it. And even though I may decide in advance of a lesson that I want to generate some discussion, I may get so caught up in the flow of events that I forget all about it during the lesson.

So on the one hand we notice all the time, make choices, and get through the day. On the other hand, there is so much more that we could notice, so many more options we could choose between.

Personal forces

Students often just do not seem to learn despite having been shown, taught, and having apparently learned: the cry from the heart that 'I did fractions with them all last half-term, and today they still couldn't do it' must be familiar to every teacher. The topic could be anything: some element of grammar, some aspect of writing, some scientific principle. You explain patiently, build up from examples, use apparatus and diagrams, carefully work through techniques, and yet still they don't remember. You reduce it all to a few simple rules and try to get them to memorise them; still no significant success. You look around for some other approach, some other materials. If you find a possibility, you work at that for a bit, and for a while you feel better. Then even that begins to pale and you look around again.

Development is a cyclical process; sometimes exhilarating and positive, often frustrating and negative. No description is likely to be complete, but there are usually cycles of

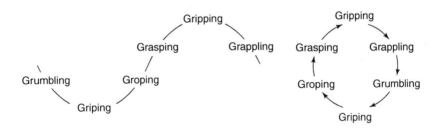

Grumbling	about how things are, leading to
Griping	about specific frustrations, leading to
Groping	for some alternative, leading to
Grasping	at some passing possibility, which with luck leads to
Grappling	with some issue and proposed actions, developing into
Gripping	hard to 'something that works', then finding further
Grumbling and Griping as the substance seems to leak out.

A new cycle begins. This book is about breaking out of a cycle of frustration with the Grs.

What triggers a new phase of personal development? Most frequently there is some form of disturbance which starts things off. It may be a surprise remark in a lesson, a particularly poor showing on a test, something said by a colleague, something asserted in a journal or book, or a moment of insight. Whatever it is, something startles me out of my current habits.

Disturbance can have positive and negative aspects: a small disturbance can usually be encompassed, while a large disturbance may be disruptive. An idea for doing things differently can be seen as an opportunity, or as a pressure. If the disturbance is experienced as negative, then I need some mechanism for dissipating the energy which comes with noticing, and this is achieved in characteristic ways such as blaming others or myself, or justifying my actions by showing how I could not actually have done otherwise. Often these justifications take the form of inner monologues, and sometimes they creep out into conversation. The disturbance itself is eliminated or ignored.

Whatever their form, blame and justification, explanation and judgement only dissipate the energy which could otherwise be turned to good use, setting up the possibility of acting differently in the future. This is what the discipline part of noticing is all about.

If the disturbance remains, if something positive attracts my attention, something different to try which I hope or believe will make a difference may come to mind. So I pursue it in detail. I try 'it' out for myself.

Account 1: Trying it out

I read that in a survey many children answered 0.3 × 0.3 with 0.9 Would my pupils do that? I try it out to see. Does it make a difference if I offer them a choice between 0.9 and 0.09 or just ask them for the answer, or ask whether 0.9 is correct? If I tell them that some other children incorrectly answered 0.9, will mine be stimulated to say what they think the others might have been thinking?

Probing someone else's thinking is difficult at the best of times when there is one researcher and one 'subject'. The way you pose the question, your tone of voice, your body posture, and the context in which the probe arises, all influence the response.

What might lie behind the answer of 0.9, if it does turn out to be prevalent? One day I hear a child saying 'oh point five times oh point five is oh point twenty-five' and suddenly I hear in my head

'oh point four times oh point four is oh point sixteen, oh point three times oh point three is oh point nine'.

What wonderful mathematical thinking! A pattern has been seized upon and extended. What a pity it is applied to inappropriate data! By inappropriately pronouncing decimal numbers, children may be led into an inappropriate generalisation. Now I have been sensitised by my following up of the 0.3 × 0.3 = 0.9 answer and come across a reason. Now I can make a distinction: I can praise the thinking while criticising the answer. Next time I can offer a pupil a disturbance and some praise at the same time.

Account 2: Repeating back

I suddenly caught myself repeating back to the class what one student had just said. I recognise that I do this a lot.

There is nothing wrong with repeating back. No judgement is being made whatsoever. But if I recognise that I do it all the time, that it has become a habit, I might decide I want to gain the freedom not to repeat back sometimes. One useful thing to do is to make a list of positive and negative features of repeating back:

Positive	Negative
• I am sure everyone hears • I gain time to think about a response or to locate another child to respond • I give the speaker a chance to rethink about what they said and perhaps modify it before others comment • I keep control • I can rephrase it more succinctly and memorably	Especially if it becomes a habit: • Students may become used to listening only to me because I will repeat anything of importance • I maintain control as the central pivot for class discussions • I may be seen as the (only) source of certainty and validity • Students my become dependent upon my contribution

The point is not that 'repeating back' is good or bad in itself, but rather whether I am choosing to do it, or whether it chooses me so that 'repeating back' happens automatically.

Reflection

What has just happened? Two examples have been given. But of what are they examples? I hope that at least one of them struck a chord in you.

Take for example the 'They still can't do fractions' syndrome: in order to recognise the force behind such a quotation, you have to have experience of classrooms. If you found that quote meaningful, then you may be able to recall recent specific instances where you felt or said something similar; alternatively, you may have a general sense of recognition without any specific instances coming to mind. Similarly with 'repeating back'. In order for my description to be meaningful to you, you need to recognise that you have seen others doing it, and perhaps even, now that I mention it, recognise it in your own practice.

In either case you are demonstrating the way all true professionals operate. They draw upon both specific and generalised experience to recognise or reject assertions made to them. The idea of noticing is to refine the details of this process, to become a little more systematic and disciplined, and in the process, to turn practice into professional development into research to whatever extent you wish.

In summarising his experiences while writing a master's thesis on critical moments, John Chately (1992: 143–145) wrote:

> Central to my work for this thesis has been my own observation of myself as teacher, head of department, and researcher. As a result of this work I have become much more skilled in the process of observation and so have developed higher expectations of myself as a teacher and manager as well as being able to analyse the significance of situations more readily.
>
> Looking at oneself is not easy, reflecting accurately on the way one has worked and thought, objectively, is particularly difficult, and . . . would have been much more difficult without the documentation of the journal. This has taken my own experience and initial reflections a step removed from me personally . . . it is only by doing the kind of examination I have of my own work that I have gained access to greater understanding of what I did and how I did it. . . .
>
> For the purpose of this [work] it has been necessary to recall (and where possible re-enter) situations as accurately as possible with complete honesty. . . .
>
> I have, by my own reflection, . . . become more skilled at helping others to reflect on their own experience. At times similarities to my own experience, or sharp contrasts become apparent and it is then useful to help others to identify the roots of the situation they find themselves in and the possible roots leading from it.

Reading about critical moments is useful only up to a point. What is much more useful is to experience and use them for yourself. Here are some possibilities. In order to appreciate what is being offered, it is vital that you try some version of these or similar tasks.

Some things to try now

Mentally imagine softly saying 'should' followed by strongly saying 'could'. Repeat this three or four times in succession. Whenever you hear the word 'should' in conversation, try mentally replacing it with 'could'. If you like the substitution, try inviting colleagues to make the same switch. See how it feels.

Imagine yourself with a group of children, and suddenly becoming aware that you are repeating back what one has just said (or that you are about to do so). Imagine yourself doing something different (e.g. asking another child for their version of what the first child just said).

Imagine yourself in a classroom. Focus your mind on just one thing that you want to say to them. Now try to 'see' or experience what posture and gestures you usually adopt. Are they consistent with what you want to say? Imagine changing some aspect of posture or gesture so as to support what you want to say.

The real test is whether these ever occur to you in the midst of a lesson, and whether they help you to see something that you had not seen before. The discipline being developed here will offer ways of working at becoming aware in the moment when a decision is possible.

Social forces

As a professional educator, I am part of an institution which extends well beyond its physical walls, for it is embedded in a larger system of forces and demands. I want my focus to be on the children or other clients and their development, but there are pressures and strictures from those who claim to be stakeholders: parents, colleagues, heads, inspectors, local and national bodies, and politicians. I may want to do something different but find that there is no money, no time, no support, even no interest. I feel constrained and confined. My frustration may partly be due to a strong desire to change 'everything' at once rather than selecting something I have the power and the resolve to alter.

I may find that the statutory requirements of a National Curriculum Statement serve as a useful skeleton, a scaffold around which to structure my teaching. However, I may also experience them as a straitjacket which precludes any variation. I may excuse myself by observing that there are already excessive demands on my time and attention, or by fearing to step outside of specified structures. Part of me may want to be innovative, but at the end of each day I am too tired to take on anything new. Part of me may react against the de-professionalising force of governmental documents; part of me may be more concerned about my particular children than about general statements intended to apply to all children.

One response is to work on delineating the forces acting on me. The grumbling–griping cycle can be focused on the personal level as suggested in the previous section, or it can be turned outward, switching from blaming others, to describing political and institutional forces, how they arise, how they manifest themselves in my work, and how they change. This may draw me into the political domain, into sociological commentary and critique or, by appreciating how the forces work, enable me to locate a domain in which I feel I can contribute. The direction taken in this book is to work on what I *can* work on in spite of all these forces, namely myself, for as George Eliot (1860) said, 'Our deeds determine us as much as we determine our deeds.'

Whichever direction is taken, outwards or inwards, psychological or sociological, any attempt to understand the situation and to make changes requires energy. It is all too easy to dissipate energy in making judgements. A theme to be developed later is that when I am caught up in making judgements, whether blaming or explaining, the energy is not available for transformation, for initiating further action. If I can be descriptive rather than judgemental, I can divert the energy of noticing into clearer sight and into alternative action, thereby investing that energy in the future.

Some things to try now

Some terms for forces acting are displayed in the following diagram. Write them on individual slips of paper and arrange them so that their position (and size?) reflects your impressions of their importance for you. Add others of your own. If possible, compare displays with colleagues and try to experience what it would be like to experience the relative importance the way they do.

<pre>
  Media   Politicians
           Government   Institutional Tests
           Agencies
      Parents   Governors
                            Head
           Inspections   Departmental
                                or School
                                  policies
                  Children's Behaviour
         Preparation   Lesson Plans   Marking
</pre>

Consider how you feel about the various forces acting upon you, and the roles which they force you to play. Use the words provided as stimulus to locate words which best describe those roles. You will find yourself playing different roles at different times depending on circumstances.

Tool	Responsible leader	Autonomous agent	Accountable deliverer of other people's agendas
Agent for others	Independent agent	Dependent follower	Responsible member of supportive structure
	Record-keeper		

Try to identify what it is about different circumstances that lead you into different roles, and how you feel about playing them.

Reflection

Reflection is a much used word, with meaning varying from 'vaguely thinking back to or commenting on an incident' to detailed written records of as much as can be recalled of an event. Schön (1983, 1987) popularised the term *reflective practitioner* to describe the expert who is awake to, and aware of, their practice, not just immersed in it. He described a number of different professions and gave examples of the range of activities which might characterise professional reflection, and coined the terms *reflection-on-action* (thinking back afterwards) and *reflection-in-action* (being aware of, even exposing to others, inner thoughts while engaging in a practice such as talking out loud, or using a diagram to externalise relationships), to which one could add *reflecting-through-action* (becoming aware of one's practice through the act of engaging in that practice).

Even these distinctions are rather vague. *Reflecting-on-action* could mean anything from vaguely thinking back over what happened, to recalling some specific details, trying to re-enter specific moments mentally, describing something to someone else, making notes about any of these, writing a narrative account with or without theorising and expanding on insights arising from the narration, looking for patterns and generalisations, calling upon theories to explain or justify, and so on. *Reflecting-in-action* (Schön's paradigmatic example is an architect thinking aloud while making sketches at a student's desk) could also mean experiencing a heightened sense of awareness of oneself acting professionally in the moment. *Reflecting-through-action* could include deliberately choosing to act in slightly novel ways (using a different hand, standing or sitting differently, not using certain words) in order to heighten sensitivity to notice while engaging in practice. For example, it is said that the brilliant and accomplished pianist Artur Rubinstein would deliberately choose, for a particular concert, not to use a particular finger, in order to keep himself awake and sensitised to his playing. For applications of mindfulness to social psychology, see Langer (1989).

Reflection is also sometimes used to describe the result of attention flowing outwards from an incident to the broader socio-cultural–historical– political forces which are acting to constitute and constrain the individual and the group to act, speak, and work in particular ways.

Thus systematic reflection can be located at any of a number of different levels. The ground of enquiry, as promoted through noticing, is the professional incident. Attention can also be focused on psychological– historical–structural aspects of a specific topic or practice, on processes of learning–teaching, on institutional forces in which I am embedded, or on socio-cultural–political forces and structures which constitute the encompassing system. Communication of insights and analyses will be enhanced if they start from reflective accounts of incidents or examples recognisable by the readership. Only then can the quality and appropriateness of the analysis and insights be considered.

Valli (1993) uses the useful phrase *scope of reflection* to indicate that there are many possibilities. For example, trying to be more efficient and effective in 'covering' a curriculum has a much more narrow scope than considering how the curriculum comes to be specified and what economic and political interests it serves. More complexly, one can reflect upon and work away at details of how to design and use tasks aimed at affording children access to percentages as a useful tool, and one can try to work at a more general level of how to get children to master or gain facility in using important techniques such as percentages. One can also reflect upon wider questions of why percentages are considered important, the role of parental and governmental pressure to master percentages, and the ways in which percentages format (in the sense of a computer disk) social institutions, particularly in the measurement of wage changes, cost of living, inflation and productivity. Each level can be worked at independently, but working on several may enrich work focused on any one. However, if you want to act differently in the classroom, then you need to focus on what you can do, what you can change.

As with any slogan, there is great danger that what starts as a description (what professionals do), will turn into a sequence of specific acts which are required and inspected, and which therefore become mechanical. For example, at a very local level, establishing an ethos in which children greet a teacher ('Good morning Miss . . .') can very easily slip into an empty form in which some children vie with each other to exhibit scorn in their tone of voice. At a more global level, the virtue of planning out a term's work can turn into a requirement for lists which predict for weeks ahead what children will be asked to do. The same applies to reflection. Thinking back over a session and picking out one or two salient moments is a useful thing to do, but it can all too easily turn into an empty and useless mechanical process.

There are close analogies with other domains in which people care for and support others. What starts off as good ideas to prompt people to take responsibility for themselves and to act in ways which speed their development or recovery can be converted into a list of instructions for a series of behaviours. In a caring setting, patients are expected to be patient and to do what they are told, and somehow that alone is sufficient to heal them. Yet the most important thing to engage is the patients' will to recover. 'Keep taking the pills' fails to make use of the most powerful resource.

Similarly with learning. 'Keep doing the work' is not sufficient to ensure learning. What starts off as good ideas to enable students to make contact with important concepts and processes, to awaken the kind of awareness that an expert has, is usually converted into instruction as a series of tasks to be undertaken. In an instructional setting, students do what they are asked to do by the teacher, and expect that that alone means that they are learning. Completing tasks becomes the aim and end of lessons. Yet we all know that it takes more than the mechanical and superficial carrying out of tasks for most learning to take place. The student has to participate in an action, not merely go through the motions. So too with reflection, professional development, and research.

This perspective can be summarised in two terms derived from French research into mathematics education: the *transposition didactique* (Chevellard

1985), and the *didactic tension* arising from the *situation didactique* (Brousseau 1984).

> *Didactic transposition*: the act of constructing teaching materials and of giving instruction transforms expert awareness into training in behaviour.

> *Didactic tension*: the more clearly and specifically the teacher indicates the behaviour sought from students, the more easily they can display that behaviour without generating it from understanding.

Giving people rules and mnemonics, and making them practise these to gain facility can usefully augment their understanding of what the techniques do, why they work, and to what sorts of problems they can be applied. However, it can also dominate attention by displacing the very understanding which performance on tasks is supposed to represent or indicate.

The same is true of reflection. Writing autobiographical and other notes, keeping a journal, and mentally re-entering salient moments can assist professional development and be integral to research; they can also be carried out mechanically and ineffectively. As Francis Bacon (1605) put it, 'Though men often look in a glass, yet they do suddenly forget themselves.'

Not all reflection need be deeply personal. MacIntyre (1993: 44) draws attention to three levels of reflection in his professional development research programme. The levels he identifies reflect his particular concerns with, and emphasis on, socio-political critical theorising.

MacIntyre's first level is technical. People are drawn to professional development through concern with specific but distant goals, such as assessment or equity, classroom or departmental management, or the teaching of a particular topic. The effective attainment of specific practical goals is the dominant concern.

Developing out of this first level is a second level which questions the assumptions, predispositions, values, and consequences, with which actions are linked. 'What makes me so confident that that is an appropriate thing to do in this circumstance?' The dominant concern is with placing the practical issues in a wider context of hidden assumptions and dispositions.

The third level is characterised as being critical or emancipatory. It is concerned with wider ethical, social and political issues, including crucially the institutional and societal forces which may constrain the individual's freedom of action or limit the efficacy of those actions. How do institutions come to exert their influence? Where do institutionalised practices originate, and who benefits from them? What blocks people from changing what they do?

McIntyre's orientation is thus a movement outwards from practice to forces, and might therefore appropriately be referred to as social-reflection. By contrast, noticing, or what might be called psychological- reflection, starts with the same first level but then moves inwards towards sensitising oneself (with the aid of colleagues) to notice situations in which alternative actions are possible, and then changing practices by choosing to act differently. These movements, outward and inward, are represented diagrammatically:

Of course, nothing is as simple as the distinction outward–inward implies. When working on specific practices, it is useful to identify and question underlying assumptions and values which the practice may signal, and when questioning assumptions and values it is useful to examine specific practices which manifest these. Nevertheless, this book concentrates on the inward rather than the outward movement.

Energies

A process as complex and self-referent as 'research into one's own practice' does not proceed as smoothly and directly as written descriptions seem to imply. There are periods of frustration, of low energy and absent motivation, of high energy and desire to act or to communicate with others, and so on. There are periods when it is easy to talk about what you are doing, and times when it all seems to slip away, to evaporate. That is part of the nature of any research, and particularly of investigation from the inside, of yourself for yourself.

Sometimes you feel as if you are noticing all sorts of fresh things; the world seems alive and communicative. Other times nothing seems to stand out, and attention drifts or is caught up by events. Recognition that these are natural phases is an important awareness that can assist you through such periods in your own work. Indeed it is an example of self-reference, for by being sensitised to ebbs and flows of energy, you may become more accepting of changes in energies, in what seems possible for you at any given moment.

Getting started

To do more than cope with events as they unfold, moment by moment, it is necessary for part of you to draw back from the situation, to *mark* rather than 'barely-notice'. For example, the child who is caught up in their anger cannot do anything but be angry. They cannot separate part of themselves to reflect-in-action on that anger, and may not even be able to reflect-on-action later. In some ways that is one of the glories of childhood. Fortunately young children have short memories for these intense states. As they reach adolescence these states are harder to shake off. By contrast, teachers often stress that the anger they show in school is with a child's behaviour and not with the child; there is part of them which is free of the anger, and which continues to respect the person while criticising the behaviour. They are able to reflect-in-action regarding the effect their 'anger' is having and to modify their behaviour accordingly as the situation unfolds. They can switch out into pleasantness in an instant. The 'state of anger' is not preserved because there is part of them which remains separate. Children are unlikely to become aware of the possibility of such a separated state themselves unless they experience it explicitly from adults.

Anyone caring for people who may become caught up in a flood of emotion needs to find a quiet calm place from which to shelter from any tide of emotional energy and from which to act dispassionately, that is, to develop a part of themselves which remains separate from the emotions of the moment, what has been called an inner witness. Teachers have two reasons to want an inner witness: as a safety valve for themselves, and as a role model for children. The inner witness watches without participating, without being caught up in the doing, and so provides both a refuge against turmoil in others, and a source of advice and comment. That is what the Discipline of Noticing aims to achieve.

When caught up in the flow of an event or when stuck in and on a problem, it is helpful to pause and try to describe your current state. The act of describing, particularly when restricted to describing only what others would recognise were they present, while avoiding explanations, judgements, theories and implicit assumptions, is very effective for forcing an inner split between actor and observer. It helps to foster the growth of an inner witness, who remains separate from immediate problems. That is why so many authors who promote reflection also promote writing as a means of personal development (Boud *et al.* 1985; Schön 1987; Brookfield 1995).

To get to the point of wanting to write is already the beginning of an inner separation from being totally caught up in the flow. It requires some energy, some desire. Once writing begins (brief notes about why I am stuck and what seems to be blocking me, or more extensive descriptions of feelings, frustrations etc.) the writing may even displace the problem as something to be totally caught up in. As such it becomes a displacement, but may nevertheless release some obstacles and enable you to be more open to possibilities.

But describing incidents and events can do much more. It can serve as a backdrop or control against which to locate changes and developments in the future. Because we live through the changes, it is often difficult to see what significant alterations do take place over time. It can also be salutary to see how little really does change.

To this end it is worth engaging in some or all of the following position-locating activities. If you feel at all daunted or reluctant, then recall the proverb: a journey of a thousand miles begins with a single step.

Try these now

Autobiography: describe briefly-but-vividly significant moments from your life involving teaching and learning your subject.

Personal Inventory: carry out a personal enquiry of concerns, attitudes, and goals along the lines suggested in Appendix A. It would be wise to respond on a copy of the probes so that you can use them again another time.

Other Inventory: ask colleagues and pupils to comment on aspects of your work from their perspective, along the lines suggested in Appendix B.

Analysis: having described your particular professional situation (as teacher, teacher–educator, researcher, administrator), make a list of what is positive and what is negative about the situation; what is blocking you from acting differently, and what is available as support.

These formats are all intended to provide a sort of snapshot of the current state of affairs (bearing in mind that there is a richness which can never be captured in a few words), but different people find different tasks difficult, challenging or straightforward. It is more valuable to work at one task which is challenging than to spend time responding easily and without challenge to several.

When first asked to keep personal accounts in a journal, there are three standard formats which people employ in different mixtures:

- incidents recounted detail by detail, including actions, feelings, thoughts as a narrative diary of events;
- incidents summarised in a few, often rather general words; and
- incidents recorded as dialogues.

Furthermore, incidents collected together can be in the form of isolated fragments, as in a diary, or connected together by a narrative, even to the extent of an autobiography. In Part II attention is given to keeping brief-but-vivid accounts, but it is worth noting where your own propensities lie. A tendency to dialogue suggests that dialogues are replayed in the head after an event, perhaps even over and over. But there are other important details to pay attention to, including gesture, posture and tone. General summaries tend to mean that over time contact with the incident is lost as all that is available are generalities. Excessive detail and attempts to justify or explain can block access to significant development.

Writing an *autobiographical critical moment* is a means for bringing to the surface ideals and beliefs which may be submerged in the exigencies of moment-by-moment coping. Most people seem to find it easier to recall negative incidents than positive ones. Positive ones tend to leave a flavour, whereas negative ones leave a specific taste. (If you haven't already, see if you can find examples or counter examples to these conjectures. To get the most out of this book you need to be constantly pausing and inspecting your own experience to see whether you can find incidents which fit with, or conflict with, what is proposed.)

The *Personal Inventory* provides an opportunity to make explicit to yourself how you perceive your current state, your goals, aims, desires, etc., and your assessment of the support and resources and possibilities for action of which you are aware. This is likely to involve expressing frustrations as well as delineating historical, cultural, and peer-group forces which seem to be inhibiting your actions, so they can be externalised and their influence thereby reduced. The

Other Inventory acts as a 'reality check' by revealing what others are aware of (and willing or able to record) about how you operate. Comparing your perceptions with the observations of friends and colleagues may reveal differences in perception and differences in criteria for what constitutes 'good enough' participation. It is very hard for professionals to be satisfied with 'good enough' performance, yet it is precisely the demanding personal criteria which lead to so much frustration (Winnicot 1971). All of these forms of position-locating are about exposing a description of your current state and contrasting it with desires and goals.

It is worth working at position-locating with some diligence, because it is more than just a dredge of memory. There is an underlying structure. The gap you are aware of, however subconsciously, between your current-state and your goals can be seen as an axis of development. The gap may seem huge or tiny, or somewhere in between. Hopefully, as you work at being more explicit, you will find the gap widening to the point that it puts you in tension, disturbs you sufficiently to want to do something about it, yet not so wide as to be off-putting.

It is also useful to consider the means by which such a development might take place. To this end, it is worth considering what sorts of resources you have to draw upon (material resources, time, personal energy and commitment, support of colleagues, friends, even students) and what sorts of tasks you are willing to undertake. There is usually a broad spectrum between material resources at one end, and your collection of tasks or acts that you are willing to undertake at the other.

The following diagram (Bennett 1964a) provides a framework for making entries under these headings, and can be used to analyse any activity.

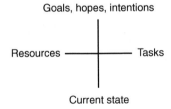

All four poles consist of your perception of them at some given moment. Your perceptions and interpretations may easily change over time, or even as a result of taking the time to bring them to the surface. *Goals* might include what I want for my pupils, my institution, my self. *Resources* might include previous research by others, colleagues, personal energy and commitment etc. *Tasks* might include undertaking reading, writing, taping of classroom incidents, analysis, undertaking suggested reflective practices, working with colleagues, involving pupils, involving colleagues, etc. *Current State* might include finding out what students and colleagues think I do and how that differs from what I think I do, a description of the forces acting upon me which block me doing 'what I want to do', and any dissatisfactions or uncertainties that I am aware of currently. It could be extended to a list of my most frequent habits, gambits, and quirks in the classroom.

The virtue of using a spatial layout is that the positioning of the four terms suggests looking for balance, that is, testing proposals for appropriateness. If the goals are well beyond the reach of the resources or the tasks, then adjustment is needed. If the goals are too close to the current state, or if they are unrelated to the resources available, then nothing much is likely to happen. If the tasks I am willing to undertake are incommensurate with the resources available, or if the current state does not immediately lend itself to exploiting available resources then again little is possible. The purpose of this book is to provide suggestions and structure through which you might form an overview of your own practice, as well as contributing to the resources and suggesting tasks, but these have to be modified and mediated by your personal circumstances.

Exposing primitives

We all have words which we use without questioning their meaning. They are *primitive* in the sense of being the foundations, the building blocks of our own meaning and thought, and for the most part are difficult to define. In education, words like *learning*, *understanding*, *task*, and *activity*, are typically in this category. In order to clarify details of my own practice and to locate problematic areas for more detailed investigation, it helps to expose some of these primitive terms and to enquire as to what I really mean by them. Of course, if we tried to question everything all the time we would never be able to say anything! But sometimes such primitive terms hide confusions and lack of clarity. Often when colleagues appear to agree but then later disagree, it is because they have different meanings for primitive terms. Sometimes there are several meanings and we slide from one meaning to another even in one discussion.

One way to work on a term is to set yourself not to use it for a particular period. If you catch yourself using it, then restate what you said without using that term. It is surprisingly revealing: sometimes it simply means using a longer phrase, but other times it is as if someone has removed a fundamental component! These are the primitives worth pursuing.

Words are of course used in context, both when describing certain situations, and in relation to other terms. Most words which are used in a technical sense are part of an extended metaphor. For example, the words

- deliver, as in delivering skills, care, or the curriculum;
- give, as in giving an idea;
- grasp or get, as in grasping or getting an idea, or getting a point or an idea across;

all contribute to a metaphor of learning as obtaining a package, and teaching as packaging and delivering. Lakoff and Johnson (1980) developed this as the 'container' metaphor for teaching, which pervades educational discourse as a delivery metaphor: skills, training and services are delivered to a waiting clientele. An alternative metaphor might draw on gardening, or some other nurturing image.

The rich meaning we sense for words often comes from metaphor embedded, even frozen into our language. Suggesting that chairing a meeting is like trying to corral a flock of sheep, or that teaching a particular class for the first time is like 'the unwary leading the unwieldy' uses simile (*X* is like *Y*), which is the basis of metaphor. When 'like' turns to 'is', metaphor has arrived. For example, Lakoff and Johnson (1980) pointed out that *argument is war* is an underlying metaphor for argument. To see this, try attending to the words people use when in or talking about an argument, and you will find that many of the descriptive words are derived from battle in some way. Similarly, a great deal of educational discourse is based on a metaphor of parcel delivery.

Metaphors creep into our language and then into our thinking, even when we are not entirely happy with the import. For example, words like *effective* are now applied to teaching, learning, assessment, and even schools themselves, and clichés like *bottom line* and *end of the day* add to the accountancy image of profit and loss, value for money, and efficiency. They support and conform with a cause-and-effect model of how education and caring take place, and in so doing, cut out or render difficult the possibility of alternative images of growth, development and nurture, as in a metaphor of teaching as gardening or of learning as biological evolution (Varela *et al.* 1992). On the other hand, excessive use of a nurturing metaphor may draw attention away from the initiative which learners must take in order to learn successfully. Metaphors usually have both strengths and weaknesses: in stressing some features they ignore or distort others. While capturing one way of perceiving, they may block or rule out others.

For example, the word *support*, which is used in education and in many other caring professions, has many metaphoric connections, from clothing to engineering, from economics to social psychology, but all involve doing something for others, usually because they cannot do those things for themselves. But once you start doing things for someone, it is very hard not to fall into the trap of doing more and more for them, because it is apparently more expedient. The nurse moves a glass because it will take a long time for the patient to do it and it might be spilled, the teacher does a calculation because it will take some students too long to do it and then they will lose the thread. 'Doing for others only what they cannot yet do for themselves' can act as a wake-up slogan or label to sensitise you to pause and ask yourself whether it really is in the person's best interest to do something for them which they could, sort of, perhaps slowly or inefficiently, do for themselves. Education and caring are about creating independence, not training in dependency, and the more you do for someone, the easier it is for them to let you do it and to come to depend upon you continuing to do it.

A similarity between teaching and other caring professions revealed by using a common metaphor (support) offers fresh perspectives, by seeing caring as a form of teaching for (relative) independence, and teaching as based on providing just what is needed and no more. As with all metaphors, it is easy to get carried away with one. Multiplicity is usually much more useful. Teaching seen as caring, nurturing and gardening, as well as delivering, enriches one's perceptions and opens up new ways of thinking and speaking about one's aims and desires, and ultimately about one's practices, with a resulting enriching of the student–patient's experience.

Deliberately altering the words we use by intentionally adjusting the underlying metaphor can have a liberating effect, at least for a while. It is not that one metaphor is better or worse than another, although one may seem more attractive and apposite, at least until deficiencies are pointed out, but that metaphors tend to become embedded in our thinking, or perhaps our thinking becomes encrusted with metaphor. It is much more exciting and informative to be flexible, to be able to change metaphor and investigate the consequences.

Over a period of time, meanings and uses tend to shift, often radically. It is worth making a list of primitive terms and then taking opportunities to look up their etymologies, search out how the use has changed, and look for different uses by colleagues, authors, etc.

Some things to try now

Pick two or three technical terms used in your practice, and look up the root meanings and sources. How has the usage changed over time, and what forces might have influenced those changes?

Pick an aspect of your practice which you feel deserves more attention, perhaps because you are aware of some underlying tension or difficulty. For example, perhaps colleagues are not responding to your suggestions in meetings in the way you would like, or perhaps you are less than satisfied with a particular aspect of your teaching or your way of interacting with students.

Use the sentence format '. . . is like . . .', where the first gap has some particular practice, and the second some sort of image or common experience. For example, 'Suggesting something in meetings *is like* plunging into a deep cold pool of water', or 'Chairing a meeting *is like* being a sheep dog', or 'Teaching students to solve problems *is like* pulling teeth'.

Now elaborate the simile into an analogy by picking aspects or features of the *is like* . . . (e.g. chairing a meeting is like a sheep dog trying to round up sheep) and then find correspondences in your chosen practice (what corresponds to barking, to wayward sheep suddenly running off, to circling the flock, to lying low watching the flock, to gates, to the pen, etc.). It is important to be as un-evaluative as possible, and not to succumb to superficial resemblances. Try to enter each aspect using mental images of yourself in typical situations. [Tasks inspired by Olive Chapman (1997, 1998)].

Set yourself to notice and record words about teaching, learning, and students which you hear colleagues using, which you find yourself using, or which appear in the media. Do the terms you identify contribute to or support a particular metaphor of teaching or learning? As the list starts to grow, try to distinguish between substantive use and jargon. It is not always so easy to tell whether the user has thought about the words or not!

Make a table of names of nine children that you teach like the following:

$$
\begin{array}{ccc}
A & B & C \\
D & E & F \\
G & H & I
\end{array}
$$

Use some process to make the choices of students reasonably random. Now use the rows, columns and three diagonals to select nine triples: ABC, DEF, GHI; ADG, BEH, CFI; AEI, DHC, GBF, and for each triple, find some quality of the children's behaviour which distinguishes one of them from the other two. Thus, child A might be more assiduous in doing homework than either of B or C. The point is not to label the children, but to use the task to locate the kinds of words which you find yourself using in order to make distinctions between children. When you have located five or six different words, write them down and describe what you mean by each of them in a sentence or two. If possible compare notes with a colleague: do they use similar words? In the same way? Do they make similar distinctions but use different words? What sorts of metaphors do they imply?

Make a list of nine different tasks that you have assigned children recently. Go through the same exercise of forming triples, and finding some term or terms to distinguish one of each triple from the other two in that triple. Again the purpose is to bring to awareness the kinds of words that you use to talk about the sorts of tasks you set children. Having located five or six words at least, try to specify what those words mean to you, and if possible, compare notes with colleagues. Do they recognise those terms? Do they use them the same way?

Summary of Chapter 1

There are many forces for change and development acting on each individual. There are external forces coming from institutional and political agencies, and there are internal forces coming from personal desires, dissatisfactions and criteria. This book is about working with forces to develop one's own personal professional practices through increasing one's sensitivity to notice and then to choose how to act, moment by moment as an event unfolds.

Reference has been made to the ambiguity of the term *reflection*, even when distinctions are made between *reflecting-on*, *reflecting-in*, and *reflecting-through*. Reflection is widely acknowledged as an important component of intentional learning, and it is the aim of this book to go beyond the mere word, and to offer detailed, structured, systematic practices which can serve to develop an inner witness. To this end some activities were suggested, and it is vital to undertake them for a fuller appreciation of what is being offered.

Part II

Noticing

In Thornton Wilder's classic play *Our Town*, Emily is permitted to relive some events from her life before entering the afterlife. She remarks that life 'goes so fast' there is no 'time to look at one another'. She did not realise all that was going on – 'she never noticed'. In many ways it is a relief that classroom life goes by quickly, but in many ways it is a tragedy. For the more you probe what happens, for example, by listening to audio-tapes of yourself or watching video-tapes, the more you realise that so many decisions are made on the fly with incomplete, even erroneous information. The more you listen to students working together in groups, the more you realise the complexity of 'being taught'. The more you probe children's thinking, the more you realise how sophisticated and powerful children's thinking can be. Experience of life in general and of classrooms in particular can become much more full and satisfying when there are occasional moments of complete and full attention, producing moments which can be re-entered, savoured, and used to inform future practice.

Experiencing and exploiting moments of complete and full attention is the aim and essence of the Discipline of Noticing. Part II introduces its components as a pragmatic approach to enquiry. Further elaborations are given in the later Parts.

2 Forms of noticing

We all notice all of the time, or at least so we believe. In fact we do notice a great deal, but we certainly don't notice everything. When we do notice, it is often mixed up with evaluation, judgement, or self-justification. Impartiality is rare. Italo Calvino (1983: 55) remarked that, 'It is only after you come to know the surface of things that you can venture to seek what is underneath. But the surface of things is inexhaustible.'

Intentional noticing

The core idea in this book is *noticing*. At first glance it seems a simple notion, and rather obvious. But in fact it is much more complex and far reaching than first appears. In the domain of our own practice, we notice many things in the course of a day, though we may mark relatively few of them and probably record virtually none until we set about this practice intentionally, and of course there are far more incidents and objects which we fail to notice at all. Since what we fail to notice is unlikely to have much influence upon our actions, certainly at any accessible level, it follows that in order to alter our actions it makes sense to work at broadening and deepening our sensitivities to notice different aspects of our professional practice.

Immanuel Kant suggests that a succession of experiences does not add up to an experience of that succession and indicates why intentional noticing is necessary. Something more is needed in order to become aware of the succession of experiences. *Reflection* is the vogue term for intentionally learning from experience, but it is more talked about than carried out effectively. For example, it is widely acknowledged that of the four phases of mathematical problem solving distinguished by George Polya (1937) (understanding the problem; formulating a plan; executing the plan; looking back), the reflective phase was the least often carried out, the hardest to do and the hardest to foster in other people. Schön (1987: 311) noted that reflective practice requires 'living in' and not mere occasional attendance. With an increase in interest in life-long learning, *experiential learning* has become a domain of investigation in and of itself (Boud *et al.* 1985, Boud *et al.* 1993). Experiential learning is based on learning from experience, but this requires more than mere experiencing. *Noticing* as used here is a collection of practices both for living in, and hence learning from, experience, and for informing future practice.

In a slightly different domain, professional noticing is what we do when we watch someone else acting professionally (teaching a lesson, working with a client, leading a workshop, delivering a lecture or training session) and become aware of something that they do (a task they set, a pattern of speech they employ, a gesture they use, a question they ask) which we think we could use ourselves. Perhaps when reading a book or article, something is described or suggested and we can see ourselves 'doing that' in our own way in our own context. But all too often when we put down the book or leave the session, the thing which seemed so salient and important at the time recedes into distant memory, perhaps never to re-appear.

Account 3: Learning from experience

While watching Eduard De Bono give a lecture, I noticed the way he used a pointer with the overhead projector. His movements were slow and deliberate so that I could follow the movement of the end of the pointer, and I was struck by a contrast with the jerky and haphazard way many people jab at their slides. Then he commented that by moving the pointer slowly and deliberately he made it possible for us to keep our attention on the end of his pointer, and, because of the movement, very likely that we would. Consequently he knew what we were attending to, and that our attention was focused.

I resolved to learn from this experience. But it was some time before I managed to remember to make myself a nice pointer that would not roll around, and even longer before I remembered to use it.

Something more is needed if we are to learn effectively from experience. Noticing as an intentional stance towards our profession is enhanced by various practices which serve to support both 'picking up ideas' and 'trying them out for ourselves'. Indeed, the cornerstone of noticing as a method of enquiry is trying things out for ourselves rather than taking them on trust as a result of some statistical study, logical argument, or authoritative assertion.

The essence of this book is to take the apparently simple notion of noticing, to elaborate various features of the kind of noticing which happens as part of carrying out professional practice, and then to turn this into an intentional activity, a disciplined and practical approach to enquiry and research. The basis of the approach is that it is possible to sharpen sensitivity to notice. But the most one can ever do is to increase the likelihood of noticing.

Noticing itself is something that happens to us, not something we do deliberately, or at least, not something that the deliberate and conscious parts of us can decide to do. You can 'decide' to notice some thing or some feature, but it may or may not happen. For example, you could, right now, decide to notice the sensation of sitting, the temperature of the room, the movement of your eyes as you read, whether you are enjoying reading at the moment, the act of reading itself, what you are doing with the ideas as you read, and so on. The stimulus coming from this text may indeed prompt you to notice some of these physiological, affective, or cognitive aspects of what you are doing. But these are in reaction to the text which triggers shifts in the locus and focus of your attention.

If you suddenly say to yourself 'Tomorrow I shall notice . . .', the decision to notice in the future can at best facilitate noticing. It only makes a contribution to the likelihood of noticing. You cannot guarantee it. Furthermore, despite the apparent simplicity of 'deciding to notice', developing the sensitivity to notice particular things, and to notice them when it would be useful to have noticed (and not merely later, in retrospect) requires effort. Disciplined noticing is really about making that effort.

Try these soon

Set yourself to notice when you walk through doorways, and to mark it each time by saying to yourself something like '*I am walking through a doorway*' with stress on the 'I'.

Arrange to have with you two colours of pens, and to choose which colour to use (perhaps alternating) each time you reach for a pen.

Set yourself to notice the moon whenever it is in the sky, or to notice the different types of symbols used to denote the hours on various analogue clocks.

Set yourself to notice instances of some phenomenon associated with your professional expertise. Compare your success rate with setting yourself to notice something not associated with your professional expertise.

The term 'set yourself' is the key element in these tasks. How do we 'set ourselves' to do something? How can we improve the efficiency of this intentionality? Most people find that they remember at most once or twice, then forget all about such a task. Even when the thing you want to remember is important to you, such as remembering to buy something at a shop, to do some annoying little task, or to put your glasses in a standard place, it takes effort. People commonly resort to making lists, or asking someone else to remind them. Setting yourself to notice something you are already professionally sensitised to (for example as a nurse, the way someone deals with a confused client; as a scientist, an occurrence of the use of a scientific principle to make something work; as a teacher, the way adults interact with children in the supermarket) does not take as much effort as trying to sensitise yourself to something you are not in the habit of attending to. Some specific proposals will be made in a later section about 'setting yourself to . . .' which can increase the likelihood of noticing in the future.

Essence of noticing

As multi-sensate beings, we are inundated with sense impressions all the time, but only some of them ever register in conscious awareness. We may think that we are widely aware of what is going on around us, but in fact attention is highly selective, and for good reason. We could not cope with all the impressions pressing on us at every moment. We need to be selective in order to survive. What gets through into awareness (conscious or subconscious) is what we notice, at whatever level.

Take for example connections between posture, gesture and speech. If posture is welcoming but gestures are dismissive, then whatever is said will be perceived, however subliminally, as at best confused. If what is said conflicts with posture or gesture, then again a mixed message is likely to be communicated. By contrast, if all three modes are consonant, then a more coherent and less fragile message is more likely to be communicated. Adults vary considerably in their conscious awareness of posture and gesture, but subconscious reading is part of learned social interaction.

Since children begin life interpreting gestures before they decode and master language, they may be more sensitive to them than adults. If we do not notice conflicts between our actions and our speech, there is nothing we can do about them. If we are unaware of gestures when attending to someone else speaking, then we may be swayed by the subliminal rather than the overt. Goldman (1994) provides a range of useful exercises for becoming aware of body language, both in yourself and in others.

Try these soon

Write down a short statement of something that you believe passionately. Now adopt a declaiming stance (perhaps sitting leaning forward, elbows on knees or on a table, or perhaps standing with one foot slightly forward and a slight forward lean, fore-arms pointing forward at least slightly) and assert your statement out loud. Now adopt a defensive or apologetic stance, and make the same assertion. See what it feels like to have the verbal and the gestural matching and then what it feels like to have them contrasting.

Observe a colleague or friend while they are talking, and note some of their gestures, stances, voice tones. Later, try using those while talking either to the same people or to others.

With prior agreement with a friend, engage in conversation with them, and try mirroring their gestures. Then reverse roles.

Try adopting a different posture from your usual one as you are about to address students or colleagues, perhaps in a meeting, in conversation, or even in class. Try adopting a philosophical or ethical position that you don't agree with while in conversation with a friend, doing your best to produce-reproduce relevant arguments. (Adapted from Goldman 1994: 8, which contains numerous exercises; see also Davis *et al.* 2000.)

One effect of exercises such as these is to enhance your sensitivity to your own gestures, postures, and argumentative positions. It may seem obtuse, even impossible to argue against a position which you hold strongly, but despite commitments, there are usually two or more sides to any dispute. Unpleasantness arises when people are too inflexible to see that other views are equally tenable (even if unjustified!), and it is easier to convince others with different views if you can appreciate their point of view.

Noticing, marking and recording

To notice is to make a distinction, to create foreground and background, to distinguish some 'thing' from its surroundings. This may not be conscious. For example, one mark of an expert is that their sensitivity to notice certain things is integrated into their professional functioning so that all they are aware of is a possibility to act, but not necessarily of the distinctions which trigger that act. Thus *to notice* can be taken to mean the same as *to perceive*, even *to sense* in the most general 'sense' of that word. What is critical is that a distinction is made by virtue of the fact that some change is registered in our perceptual apparatus, whether this is primarily physical, emotional, or cognitive.

We notice all the time, but on several levels.

Account 4: Did you notice?

As I walked into my office one morning, someone asked if I had noticed the sign at the gate. Suddenly I could see the sign in my mind. But until I was asked about it, I had no explicit awareness of it. I certainly could not have introduced it into a conversation.

It is useful to distinguish between *ordinary-noticing*, or perceiving, in which sufficient memory is established accessibly to be jogged and reconstructed by what someone else says, and *marking*, in which not only do you notice but you are able to initiate mention of what you have noticed. Ordinary-noticing is easily lost from accessible memory. It is only available through being re-minded (literally) by someone or something else. To *mark* something is to be able to re-mark upon it later to others. *Marking* signals that there was something salient about the incident, and re-marking about it to someone else or even to yourself makes the incident more likely to be available for yet further access, reflection and re-construction in the future. Thus *marking* is a heightened form of noticing. Intentional marking involves a higher level of energy, of commitment, because it requires more than casual attention.

Ordinary-noticing, or perceiving, provides the rich backdrop of experience on which learning depends, but in itself is insufficient. It is distinguished from *noticing* which refers to all aspects of moving from ordinary-noticing or perceiving, to marking and recording, and to various practices which support these. Marking provides specific data to work on. But even incidents that are marked may be overlaid by or merged into subsequent events. There is a third level of intensity or energy in noticing which fuels *recording*. The desire to make a note, to *record* in some way, may be a product of our written-visual culture, but it does play a significant role in personal development. Recording could use words as in a list, journal, or creative writing, but might be expressed in some other medium including performance. By making a brief-but-vivid note of some incident, you both externalise it from your immediate flow of thoughts, and you give yourself access to it at a later date, for further analysis and preparation for the future. You can note something inwardly, making a *mental note* and initiating a state in which you might choose to re-mark at some future moment, and you can out-wardly note by making some record. Tying a string around your finger used to be a clichéd form of noting in order to re-member. The incident recorded becomes an object not only to analyse, but also a component in the building of rich networks of connections and meaning.

Recording definitely requires motivation, for it takes extra energy beyond that required for marking.

Account 5: Write that down!

A colleague was describing an incident from a recent lesson, and I was finding it fascinating, as it spoke to so many incidents in a teacher's day. Eventually I said to her, 'I think you should write all that down'. She looked at me as if to say, 'When would I get the time?'.

Recording does take more time than speaking. Speaking to someone some-times serves to refresh memory and add to the impetus to make a recording immediately; but sometimes speaking to someone seems to use up the energy stored in the account, with the result that there is even less impetus to make a record.

One such energy is found in the grs, the grumbling and griping dissatisfaction which is usually dissipated in those acts, but which can be transformed into desire to achieve something. A written record may serve this purpose. But it is quite different if the initiative comes from outside. If I am required to record observations because of some course I am taking, then a desire to get a grade rather than a desire to record for myself may alter the records and the effects completely.

Here are two examples of noticing becoming marking, one brief and one extended:

Account 6: Why?

In the midst of solving an equation in front of pupils:

TEACHER: You divide by three
STUDENT: Why do you divide by three?
TEACHER: See, it works!

The student did not seem satisfied. Suddenly it came to me (I marked) that what the student wanted to know was 'how do you know what to divide by?' and not 'why do you divide by a number'. I knew in that moment that I must have mis-responded to students countless times. I had noticed but not marked sufficiently to act or question further evident student dissatisfaction. I resolved to watch out for a reactive interpretation of student 'why?' questions, and to work with the students on framing more precise questions!

It is very tempting to assume that when someone asks a question, the question they ask is what they want an answer to. But this is not always a valid conjecture. The effect of 'marking' was to enable me to recognise other situations in which something similar may have happened, and so contribute to my being sensitised to this possibility in the future.

The following account (Christine Shiu, private communication) provides several examples of noticing, marking, and recording:

Account 7: Natasha

I am watching Natasha who is three, and her mother. She wants a cough-sweet though she has no cough. More specifically she wants one of the cough-sweets which her mother is taking – and which are 'unsuitable for children'. Her pleas go as follows:

'Mummy I want a cough sweet.'

'Please may I have a cough sweet?'

'I won't spit it out.'

My first response was a generalised remembrance of similar conversations with my own children at similar ages. The remembrance was of the feelings which welled up in me when engaged in such conversations, rather any specific detail of occasion or topic.

Next I realised I was sufficiently detached from the conversation, unlike those of my earlier experience, to admire her versatility in producing variations in the wording of her requests in order to achieve her ends.

Thirdly I 'noticed' both of the first two responses, becoming aware of the incident in a way which would permit later telling of it to others. (Although my recollection is of these responses succeeding each other in time, the time gaps must have been infinitesimal if they existed at all.)

Later I was telling the story to two friends, who questioned me about my interpretation of the incident. My story was that the girl was completely convinced of her 'need' for the cough-sweet, a need which could not conceivably be denied. Her problem was to frame her request in the right terms to achieve her end. The variations came from her memories of similar experiences – when she failed to say please, when she spat out something she had been given; her persistence from the emotional conviction of the 'right' outcome.

As I told my story I experienced another 'noticing' in the form of a recollection of another recent event which could be described in similar terms. The occasion was a meeting with colleagues. One particular colleague was being (not untypically) persistent in presenting her point of view, endlessly ingenious in bringing back the same point in new guises. In retrospect I ascribed to her the same force of emotional commitment to her ends as I had read into Natasha's behaviour.

Unlike Natasha she achieved her ends.

Here Christine Shiu offers not only a brief account of an incident with a child, but a chain of levels of reflective awareness as the incident first brings to the surface incidents from the past (so shifting from noticed to marked), then abstracts them, and recognises a parallel incident in recent experience. This is typical of the processes of noticing, and of the energies involved, concluding with the transcript as artifact in response to a request to 'record' the first verbal version.

What determines whether we notice rather than not-notice, mark rather than just notice; record rather than just mark? Each level of noticing requires energy, that is, each requires intention and commitment. But as we shall see later, each level also releases energy which *can* be used to support the next phase, although usually it is allowed to dissipate. The Discipline of Noticing is a collection of practices which support the transformation of energy into deeper, stronger, and more robust noticing.

De Bono (1977) offered an image which suggests one way in which noticing can be blocked. Ideas or thoughts are seen as little packages flowing down passages (as in 'train of thought').

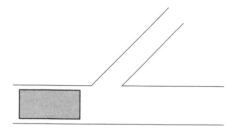

If the packages are too large, then small passageways to either side will simply not be visible. Thus chunking ideas using grandiose or generalised labels to elaborate the simple, may block access to alternatives. For example, labels like 'low attainer', 'high flyer', 'disruptive pupil', and slogans like 'teaching for understanding' or 'whole class interaction' are too broad, too open to multiple interpretation to be useful for precise discussion. They may render invisible details and possibilities in a specific situation, or for a particular person. In his books promoting lateral thinking, de Bono suggests staying away from technical terms and 'big ideas' when looking for alternative possibilities.

Try this soon

Say What You See

With a colleague, take a picture or a scene or an object, and try to draw the other person's attention to some detail by describing it solely in words, without pointing or gesturing. One good way to do this is to use imperative language ('Look at the . . .', 'now look to the . . .').

At first it may be a bit of a struggle, and you may be tempted to point or draw or gesture. It is quite common for people to become aware of detail that they had previously overlooked, because they begin to really look, not simply to see what they have become habituated to see. This exercise is not only a useful way to work on sensitising people to notice detail, but also captures the essence of working on and working with accounts, which is elaborated in a later chapter.

Try these soon

With two or three colleagues, each make a list of things you recall noticing as you entered the premises of the institution this morning. Then compare notes.

Set yourself to become aware of the differences between noticing, marking, and recording.

See if you can become aware of a moment when someone points out something and you can honestly say that you recognise what they say but could not have initiated the discussion.

See if you become aware of initiating a topic of discussion, perhaps through an observation. What prompted you to take that initiative?

Each evening, see if you can recall something from the day that pertains to noticing, marking, and recording.

What sorts of things in your professional activities do you feel moved to record during a day (even if you don't actually get around to it)?

Comment

I suspect that you will find these tasks much more difficult to accomplish in the short-term than the previous ones. If you do indeed find them more difficult, then you have some support for my contention that deliberate noticing is much harder than it seems it 'ought' to be. It is helpful not to be in a rush, to work away at some of the previous tasks for a period of time, to remind yourself regularly of what it is you have set yourself to notice, and to 'grow into' catching yourself having noticed but not marked, or of marking by initiating a topic of discussion or an observation.

The different experiences which ordinary-noticing, marking and recording draw attention to are part of everyday experience. It is precisely because we mostly only notice but do not mark that so much our experience passes us by and fails to be called upon for further development. Noticing can be sharpened, can be developed and refined, as part of personal professional development, even disciplined to form the basis for recognised research. For in the end, all research comes down to noticing. If you are reading analysis and commentary, you can only notice what you are already sensitised to, though this sensitivity may shift over time. If you are observing children or colleagues, then again your observations are theory-laden: you can only see aspects which you are already disposed or primed to see. If you are working on your own practice, then you can only be struck by incidents which you find striking (obviously).

Summary of Chapter 2

Distinctions have been drawn between ordinary-noticing, marking and recording. These are the backbone of noticing, of sensitising oneself to notice, of undertaking systematic professional development, and of converting development into research. The essence of noticing is being awake to situations, being mindful rather than mindless (Bateson 1994).

3 Impartiality

Incidents which stay in memory are usually ones in which we have considerable emotional or intellectual commitment. They are 'important' to us for some reason. For example:

Account 8: Screened

The screen was low to the ground because of the low ceiling in the ballroom, and I had found by experiment that wherever I stood near the projector, I would obstruct the screen. Furthermore the microphones had been placed in front of the screen or a long way away from the audience at a lectern. I had to stand near the audience, leaning against a pillar and peeking out around it at the audience, talking loudly to the succession of slides I had prepared. I found myself shouting to be heard, and out of touch with my audience.

This account has a mixture of description (position of the screen and microphones, talking loudly) and justification ('I had to . . .'). It runs seamlessly from a statement about the microphones to a conclusion I reached. But other conclusions were possible; other arrangements could have been made. It is impossible for you as reader to reach any useful conclusions about the session, because of the interweaving of description and value judgement and justification. Consequently, you cannot evaluate what I say, or indeed make any comments about what I did.

If we want to be in a position to analyse some event, some situation, then we must first be clear on what that event or situation consists of, as impartially as possible. Orage (1930) when he writes: 'The observation of others is coloured by our inability to observe ourselves impartially' suggests that impartiality starts with ourselves, that in order to be impartial in our descriptions of the actions of others, we need to learn to be impartial about ourselves, for otherwise everything we think we are seeing in others may be a reflection of ourselves. Although it is difficult, as the poet Robbie Burns said, 'to see ourselves as others see us', it is all too often the case that what we see in others is what we dislike in ourselves. In order to recognise and identify phenomena worth analysing, we need to learn to give an account of an incident or situation, whether external or internal, as impartially as possible, that is, without explanation, justification, or the use of emotive terms. To this end, it is useful to make a distinction between accounts-of an incident, and accounting-for that incident.

Account-of and accounting-for

If I want to account-for something, and if I expect others to agree with my analysis, then it is helpful first to get agreement about the 'thing' to be analysed, the phenomenon to be explained. If I mix up details of the event with judgements, with explanations and theorising, with value judgements and emotively evaluative terms, then I make it virtually impossible for others to challenge or discuss my analysis and decide whether to agree or disagree. All they can do is be swept along on my sentiments, or react against them. It is ever so easy to slip into accounting–for when 'simply describing', yet if colleagues are not aware of exactly what it is you are explaining, there is unlikely to be much agreement. So it is worthwhile to distinguish between giving an *account-of* a situation or incident, and *accounting-for* it.

An account-of describes as objectively as possible by minimising emotive terms, evaluation, judgements and explanation. It attempts to draw attention to or to resonate with experience of some phenomenon. But a phenomenon is a construction made by a person: as Maturana (1988) famously said, 'everything said is said by an observer'. A 'phenomenon' is a pattern discerned or distinguished by an observer de-sensitised in certain ways, and so from an account we learn about the sensitivities of the observer as well as about the incident. By contrast, an account-for introduces explanation, theorising and perhaps judgement and evaluation.

For example, as a description of an incident observed on a video-tape involving a teacher and two students at a computer, the assertion

'The teacher was brow-beating the pupils'

cannot really be discussed unless there is agreement in advance as to precisely what incident is being accounted-for by these value-laden terms. 'Brow-beating' is an emotive interpretation of some behaviour, and it probably brings to mind some experiences of your own which may or may not be relevant to the particular incident. Furthermore, the description does not refer to a specific episode of the video-tape, but rather to an impression summarised by an emotive term. Contrast that with:

'The teacher approached the pair of pupils and stood close to them looking down at their screen while they sat hunched low, leaning on their elbows on the desk.'

This partial description is less emotive. It tries to recount some of the specific behaviour, and indulges in less summarising and categorising. Of course any word can have emotional content for some people. No description is entirely dispassionate and objective, precisely because it is made by a person who necessarily has personal propensities, sensitivities and concerns. On the other hand, the second description is more likely than is the first to be identifiable by those who were present, and even recognisable by others with experience of classrooms and computer screens.

The behaviour (standing close to pupils sitting hunched low, leaning on their elbows on a desk) can be interpreted in many ways (as brow-beating and as supportive) depending on other features. Until those features are identified, the emotion-laden term 'brow-beating' serves no useful function in the initial description, and possibly even afterwards.

To *account-for* something is to offer interpretation, explanation, value-judgement, justification, or criticism. To give an *account-of* is to describe or define something in terms that others who were present (or who might have been present) can recognise. Thus 'I saw a good move' requires the audience to apply their criteria for good, and to locate a 'move'. 'I saw the leader break into the flow of discussion and hold a silence' is more likely to be recognisable by people who were present or who are watching a video of the incident. 'I saw the leader raise a finger, I heard her say . . .; I saw her sitting quietly staring at the floor' is even easier to recognise, or at least to negotiate as having been seen.

Giving an *account-of* is modelled on the notion of referring back to an incident in a film or video, in which one gives an account-of what was shown, so that others can recognise the film-fragment. An account-of has no particular value unless and until others recognise something similar in their own experience, so that various accounts-of become particular instances of a general phenomenon. So collecting accounts-of is one step towards creating a phenomenon, that is, identifying a type of situation, tension, issue or interaction which is exemplified in several different incidents or experiences. It is helpful, once a sense of a phenomenon emerges, to give it a resonant label which can then serve as the hub for a collection of incidents and associated gambits (more on this later).

Accounting-for through asking why

It is natural to want to ask oneself why incidents occur, and why one has noticed this or that particular aspect. Asking why has several different forms however. Some lead to useful analysis, while others merely dissipate the energy accumulated through noticing. Playfully, I suggest that accounting-for comes in at least three forms: *why-ning* (whining), *whys-acreing* (wise-acreing, meaning talking about things when you know very little about them), and *why-sening* (wisening or 'making wise'). Only the last has real value.

Whining refers to the tendency to explain away or justify acts: explaining why I had no choice or why in this instance it seemed better to act habitually than creatively. It uses up the energy released by noticing and serves no purpose other than self-calming and self-justification. You can recognise when you are whining by the desire to be reassured that what you did was 'ok' if not actually at least good and perhaps the best possible.

Wise-acreing refers to the tendency to theorise about an incident, to classify it prematurely as an example of a general phenomenon before having delved into details and sought resonance with others. Wise-acreing uses up energy and makes it harder to be present in and awake to a similar moment in the future, because it has been classified, sorted, and pigeon-holed.

Wisening (making wise) refers to probing details of a collection of accounts, seeking what underlies apparent similarity, being explicit about positive, negative, and interesting features of specific acts (de Bono 1972) and about different gambits which could be used in such situations in the light of the transformatory actions one hopes will accompany those acts. Through such analysis one may become a bit wiser, a little more likely to choose to act non-habitually in the future. For example, the analysis of *repeating back* (Account 2) as an act exposes positive, negative and interesting features, and thereby helps to inform a choice to be made in the future, instead of just doing it without thinking about it.

Reconnaissance

Of course all description is interpretation, for the act of expressing in words involves stressing some features and therefore ignoring others, which, as Gattegno (1987) points out, is the essence of generalising. There is however, a difference between interpreting intentions, say, from gestures, posture and voice tone, and describing those gestures, posture and voice-tones. Whereas the description makes the behaviour overt, the interpretation is often implicit, and so can hide prejudices and propensities, habits and opinions which could usefully be questioned. Whenever there is any uncertainty as to whether a slide is taking place from account-of to accounting-for, ask yourself whether what is being described is behaviour, whether it is negotiably visible or audible to others who share a similar culture to your own, for the focus of accounts-of is negotiable recognition by participants and by experienced colleagues of some phenomenon, prior to accounting-for it.

Since we are so accustomed to interpreting behavioural manifestations, it is quite difficult at first to reach an account-of an incident. More subtly, every observation is based on a disturbance of some sort, on making some sort of distinction of that incident from the events surrounding it, so there must be some resonance or dissonance with experience. Something energises us to notice, mark and record. Consequently there is always some sort of underlying interpretation. Consider for example the following note used by David Tripp (1993: 18):

> John didn't finish his work today. Must see he learns to complete what he has begun.

This note from a teacher's reflective diary is a starting point. But the notion of finishing may be problematic, especially between teacher and student. More precise descriptions might be

> John finished work on parts 1 through 3 whereas most others worked on parts 1 through 7; John was still working on part 3 when I stopped them working.

or some alternative which enables an observer to judge for themselves what constitutes finishing. As Tripp points out, the fact that it has been recorded makes it available for juxtaposition with further similar observations, and for distanced-reflection later. It may be that by working to achieve an account-of, the notion of 'finishing work' may be brought into question (perhaps the student sees school as a succession of time periods not a succession of tasks to be completed). If the teacher finds on reflection that this incident is typical of many, it might be worth asking questions about how the students see tasks, and this could lead into an investigation centred on the didactic tension and didactic contract and questions about what the students' experience is like, in contrast to the teacher's perceptions. If the teacher finds that this incident is typical of a particular child, then perhaps there are some personal circumstances to find out about. If however, John becomes labelled as a non-finisher, there is a good chance that he will grow to fill that expectation, whereas if the teacher can maintain 'non-finishing' as a description of certain behaviour, it may be possible to work something out with him. Tripp (1993: 19) reports asking the teacher

Why did (does) John not finish his work?
Why should he finish it?
How does he see the tasks demanded of him?
Are the tasks of the right kind, quality, and quantity?

He offers such questions as typical of the 'reconnaissance' that an initial observation can spawn, and which can then develop into a personal research enquiry. One can go further and enquire into ways in which the teacher uses the word 'finishing' and what significances this carries, as compared to the ways in which the students might use that word, and the significances for them. The same applies to any word.

To support 'reconnaissance', colleagues, listening to or reading an account, are encouraged to ask factual questions, but they too must be careful not to imply judgement or evaluation. Brookfield (1990) calls this 'playing detective', one of three roles that help make working on accounts effective. Brookfield calls the roles, *story-teller*, *detective* and *umpire*. When someone is probing a description, others are to moderate by pointing out inappropriate questions. An inappropriate question is one which induces the person rendering the account to justify or explain themselves. The purpose of probing is to develop a more vivid impression of the incident, to reveal an underlying phenomenon, and then to illuminate implicit assumptions and habits, to expose metaphors and to look for implicit metonymic triggers of which the person rendering the account is not strongly aware. It is important to note that the aim is *not* to reach an exact or precise description, but rather to sharpen sensitivity to notice more precise detail in the future.

Collecting and reflecting upon salient incidents is not simply an interest for those trying to develop their practice or conduct personal research. Our entire sense of who we are professionally is based around abstractions derived from our impressions of incidents. In a sense, we all make these collections, but we don't always work to refine and hone the descriptions into accounts that can be used effectively. For example,

> I have a sense of a particular way of being when working with a group of colleagues, but over time I have begun to recognise that I don't actually work that way any more. Where I used to be able to be gentle, and content to stimulate and then listen, to go with the flow, I am now much more driven by what I want to express. I feel much more full of insights, and hence am less able to take time to work with what people have to offer. My cup over-floweth.

None of this report is in the form of specific incidents. It is much more to do with flavours than with details. Yet it is from such generalities that our self image develops. For example, the sentiment:

> 'I find that when I go to certain conferences I come away feeling that I have none of the real qualities that colleagues were talking about, that I am not nearly good enough as a teacher/researcher.'

is far too general. Some colleagues may recognise a flavour, but their experiences may differ enormously in detail. Expressing it in this general way may only depress further or wash away the felt disturbance. If I am constantly feeling that others are much more accomplished than I am then a negative descending spiral is likely to develop. The generality only serves to reinforce the sentiment without being tied to specific experience. I become more and more likely to concentrate on incidents which can be used to support that feeling rather than on incidents which contradict it. I certainly cannot expect to locate alternative actions or responses, because I am caught up in my emotional evaluation of the incidents.

Under suitable reconnaissance, pertinent details of specific instances are sought. Even if it feels somewhat uncomfortable to reveal them, re-entering the moments can be most illuminating. Usually what arises is recognition of missed opportunities to act differently, which can then be transformed into preparation to act differently in the future.

Try these soon

Give a descriptive account of some object which you find interesting in some way. Then review that account to see how you indicated that interest, and what it led you not to describe. Show your account to friends and see if they recognise the object described.

Give a descriptive account of an interchange between two people which you notice. Then review the account to try to see what attracted your attention about it. Show it to people and see if they recognise your account.

Give a descriptive account of something you noticed yourself doing: a sudden feeling, a question asked or a response given. Review that account to try to see what made it stand out for you. Show it to others and see if they recognise the incident you are describing.

Look back over the accounts given so far in the previous chapter, and look for explanations or justifications, implicit judgements or emotive terms which might have been avoided or removed in order to make the accounts more vivid.

Look back over your own accounts of incidents or things noticed, and consider whether you might be able to make them more vivid, more accessible and recognisable by being more descriptive and less judgemental or with less justification.

Try writing two descriptions of the same incident, one with emotively implicit judgements and one without, and then offer them to people to see which one they recognise more readily, and which raises more questions.

People may recognise the emotion rather than the event. But if the emotion you felt is what you are trying to describe, then try to be as impartial as you can about that emotion: what were the physiological components? For example, saying that one is frightened or angry is not very helpful, because there are all sorts of ways to experience these. If you can catch the moment when you suddenly shiver involuntarily, or suddenly become aware of thoughts of what might happen running through your mind; if you can catch a tightening of the chest or perhaps shortening of breath, something rising from your gut to your brain which triggers off a loud or shrill or 'hard' utterance, you are much more likely to find that others recognise what you are referring to.

Most situations involving two people will have at least three readings. In any group of people there are bound to be different ways to account for what is noticed, just as individuals are likely to have a mixture of ways to account for incidents depending on time, place, and mood.

Account 9: Distractions

One lesson, I notice Kelly is trying to distract Sarah, which is not an easy job because Sarah just works. I focus on the techniques she is using to distract Sarah, on her body language, on her gestures. Kelly starts chatting, leaning over to Sarah. Sarah says something back, I think to the extent of 'I am working', because Kelly moves back sitting straight in her chair. She keeps looking at Sarah. She turns her body towards the window, as if something interesting is happening outside. Sarah does not react. Kelly turns back to sit straight. She must be really thinking about this. She has not noticed I have been looking at her the whole time. Some of the girls have noticed it and are looking at Kelly as well. Kelly slowly moves her whole arm, not just her hand, over Sarah's exercise book. Bingo! Sarah looks at her and laughs. They chat together. Then Sarah notices me and other girls watching. Kelly looks up as well. I have to laugh. Kelly turns red in the face and smiles with a grin. And she goes to work.

Since then, when Kelly is not working, which does not happen so often now, I look at her and when she looks at me, I tend to smile and shake my head. In most cases she goes back to work. She also feels more comfortable with me, coming to me and sitting next to me, to discuss her work. Her body language is relaxed. At times, she will even 'lounge' over my desk, body bent over the desk, arms supporting her upper body. (Els de Geest, private communication)

The term 'distract' already contains a judgement and establishes an interpretation. What we could have seen would have been Kelly chatting, leaning over to Sarah, Sarah saying something back, Kelly moving back straight in her chair, etc. Kelly might have been trying to tell Sarah something about the work, or about something else at school. She might have been trying to get some help, or have been making a comment about the work. As an experienced teacher, the person rendering the account here brings much more of her experience to bear than what is reported (including a history of interaction with Kelly). Since these predispositions are below the surface, they represent a strong force influencing interpretation and response. The teacher reads the situation, and that reading carries forward into influencing what is noticed.

One of the virtues of delaying accounting-for (including particularly, analysis and wisening) is that it is often insightful to generate several competing stories for the same incident. Life is complex, and our perceptions, our sense of our experience, is multi-faceted. There is of course a certain force or desire to account-for events with a simple explanation, to label and pigeon-hole, to make sense of things with a simple story. But upon reflection, the most convincing way to account-for some incident is as a fusion of differently weighted story-perspectives.

Maintaining complexity is usually more valuable than achieving simplicity when human interactions are involved, and the same applies to formulating questions or issues to pursue. It is useful to clarify questions, and to consider what an answer might actually look like, but it does not always help to pin things down early on. Again, if the question is focused on a situation or object, then it is important to be clear on what that object or situation is, without immediately being caught up in theorising, explaining or value-judgement. It often takes many attempts to express, refine, and adjust 'the question' before it becomes tractable and resolvable. Indeed a really good question does not have an answer, but provokes all sorts of alterations and modifications in its pursuit.

Brief-but-vivid

It is often difficult to recognise that I am writing or speaking in general terms because the source of my utterances are vivid images, which may be very particular or may be partly abstracted. Even as I write that sentence I recognise that it is self-referently coming from a great deal of experience of having images and of speaking from them yet without referring to them explicitly. The awareness of the self-referential generality of the previous sentences reminds me to look for an example of a mixture of specific and abstracted images.

Account 10: Cinema invitation

I am invited to join someone at a cinema in a city I am visiting. I immediately have a sense of a cinema, a sort of abstract familiarity, in contrast, for example, to being invited to a worm-race, for which I might have little sense of what to expect!

On interrogating my 'sense', I find an image of 'cinema' coming to my mind: tall walls, big white screen perhaps covered with curtains, dark, rows of seats, ... As I examine my image, I see that it is made up of bits and pieces of different cinemas I have been to, and I can soon expand some of those images to more details of the particular place. Other aspects seem unconnected with any particular.

When I go in and find that there are circular tables in some places rather than rows of seats, and that I can see easily, my image is confounded. A pizza arrives, and I am astonished. My previous images did not include these! Then the lights go down and the film begins.

The point is that an initial response of familiarity is based on past experience. There may be specific details or a more abstracted sense, and this is what structures and constitutes expectation, though I may be unaware of the supporting images. When expectation is confounded, the disturbance may bring more vivid images to mind.

Applying the same observations to writing suggests that words are by their very nature general. Even specific nouns like *cup* and *chair* are generalised abstractions. Their use makes sense to us only when they are familiar, when we recognise them from experience. To test this, consider the sentences

The slithy toves did gyre and gimble in the wabe

Pedunking in a himp of grosimony

The first, from Lewis Carroll's *Jabberwocky*, uses obsolete and made-up words some of which can with effort be decoded. The second uses entirely made up words. Making sense of either is at best very difficult until the words touch or resonate with experience. In both there is something about the sounds which make them seem as if they might make sense, prompted by vague images or an inchoate 'sense-of'.

Effective writing does not simply rely on the reader. Writing, such as in a novel or short story, touches us when it vividly resonates with our experience. Where something unusual is being described, I still have to make contact, and I do this through the aptness of the images and metaphors, and through the use of brief-but-vivid descriptions of detail which resonate with my experience.

Compare the following two accounts.

Account 11A: Wrong answer

Sometimes when I ask a child a question and they get the wrong answer I ask them the question that I think they have answered and then they give me the correct answer to the first question.

Account 11B: Wrong answer (again)

I asked my five year old what three times four was, and he replied 'seven'. So I spontaneously asked 'what is three *plus* four? (emphasis on the italicised word)'. After a brief pause he said 'Oh, twelve'.

These are intended to be extreme cases. The first is general. It is an abstraction from experiences. It might remind you of past experiences, it might feel vaguely familiar, and you might be able to work at recalling something similar. Even if recognised, what is being said is hard to develop or work with, and any analysis offered, any explanation or theorising will be built upon sand. The second is more vivid. It comes from a particular incident, some fifteen or more years old, yet it is still vivid for me. I can see my son, the room we were in, his posture, his pause and then excited response.

Recognisability of the second account lies in *describing-from* my own images, rather than processing those images and talking *about* them. By describing-from vivid recall it is much more likely that what I say or write will be vivid for others. In actual fact there were several similar incidents about that time, but I did not mark them until I read a description of a similar incident in a book. The book crystallised what I had noticed, and led me to identify a particular kind of interaction, which I chose at the time to label *jump-response-question* (respond to an answer to a different question with a jump to the question actually answered).

The label *jump-response-question* provided a collection point around which a variety of experiences and strategies could accumulate. When something similar happens in the future, the label helps trigger recollection of possible responses to try out in just such a situation. For that label, or any other, to have significance as a trigger and accumulation point for you, it is essential that you recognise some corresponding incident from your own experience. Otherwise this whole passage is likely to fade from memory!

Account 12A: Getting power

We were working on a case study, and one group had become side-tracked into looking at the language in which the situation was described. At first they were defensive because they weren't doing the task that I'd set them, but once they saw I was happy for them to follow their own interest, they got involved and were eager to talk about what they had discovered. After predictable false starts . . . they got as far as saying:

'It's something to do with power, with the way they think about each other'

The word *power* buzzed inside me. Ah, they've realised that it has something to do with power!

It was almost as if a path opened up, a goal was in sight, I was on familiar territory . . . and off I went.

After three or four questions I noticed their faces, and alarm bells began to ring inside me. They seemed to be following and answering my questions, but the excitement was gone. I was vaguely aware of this, but couldn't stop myself. It was like running in a well worn groove. In the end, all I could do was say to them 'Think about it a bit more', and walk away.

Account 12B: Getting an angle

We were working on a shape investigation, and one group had become side-tracked into looking at tessellation. They had a box of mixed shapes and wanted to know which would tessellate. At first they were defensive because they weren't doing the problem that I'd given them, but once they saw I was happy for them to follow their own interest, they got involved and were eager to talk about what they had discovered. After predictable false starts they got as far as saying:

'It's something to do with angles. If the angle gets too big, the shape won't tessellate.'

The word *angle* buzzed inside me. Ah, they've realised that it something to do with angle!

It was almost as if a path opened up, a goal was in sight, I was on familiar territory . . . and off I went.

After three or four questions I noticed their faces, and alarm bells began to ring inside me. They seemed to be following and answering my questions, but the excitement was gone. I was vaguely aware of this, but couldn't stop myself. It was like running in a well worn groove. In the end, all I could do was say to them 'Think about it a bit more', and walk away.

(Taken from ME234 Unit 5 Anecdote supplement, p. i)

As an account, 12A is rather general and not very vivid. Expressions like 'they were defensive because . . .' and 'they got involved' exemplify accounting-for rather than account-of, for we have no description at all of what behaviour triggered those summary judgements. Consequently it is difficult to recognise the situation, which is a pity because there are important underlying issues, about getting students involved in fruitful tasks, about how to deal with students diverting to something you have not planned, and about catching yourself taking over and inappropriately telling students things based on your own enthusiasms.

The brief dialogue and subsequent report in Account 12B are much more vivid, reporting inner experiences. Of course the experience was not exactly as described, because words at best provide only partial access to experience and often come to define that experience in terms of what can be said. But there is something vibrant and recognisable. I have never worked on power or angle with students in that situation, but I certainly recognise the 'buzz' of a word triggering an irresistible path or stream that swallows me up and triggers me into a for-me rich world of ideas and connections. Mary Boole (Tahta 1972) coined the label *teacher lust* for that almost irrepressible desire to explain something to someone else.

To access the moment of trigger, the first paragraph is at best background. In itself it had the potential of an incident on its own, but the potential is lost in the accounting-for language. It is brief in itself, but not vivid. Omitting it and just using an introduction like

Students in one group were working on a task and one of them said:

would suffice to maintain brevity for the trigger incident. Brevity is valuable for reducing cognitive load. As a device to increase accessibility to the reader, the incident itself is not the major interest, but rather what experiences are triggered or resonated in the reader. A long-winded account may be appropriate in a novel but it does not serve the purpose of personal or collective enquiry because of the attention it absorbs. In professional development it is not the incident itself which is of particular interest, but the incidents which come to mind in the reader, for the reader can only work on their own experiences.

By reading and making accounts of similar incidents I can hope to sensitise myself to see such incidents coming before they happen, and so allow myself the choice of not getting caught up in them, but rather, acting differently in some desired way.

Just as the label *jump-response-question* is a label designed to facilitate triggering me to be aware of similar situations in the future, so the term *brief-but-vivid* is itself intended to become a label, a catch-phrase which summons an image and which is associated with experience of exchanging such descriptions of incidents with colleagues. It may serve as a reminder to go for both brevity and vividness when making a record in a diary or when recounting an incident to colleagues. As such, it illustrates the way of using labels to trigger actions which lies at the heart of all development, and is an explicit component of the Discipline of Noticing.

The idea of a brief-but-vivid account of an incident is not a water-tight well defined notion. Like the qualities and aspects of professional practice which call upon noticing, and like the very notion of noticing itself, the meaning of these terms emerges over time with use, especially within a community of enquirers who focus on re-entering experiences rather than achieving formal definitions. Some of the problematic aspects of brief-but-vivid accounts are discussed in the more theoretical Part V.

The notion of brief-but-vivid has resonance with prompting children to express themselves in writing, music and art. Children are often not aware that the vivid images they have are not common property: young children often speak as if they think that you are present seeing their image. To be expressive they need to become aware of those images, and then to be selective and detailed (brief-but-vivid) in order to be effective communicators. They need to become aware that their vivid images are not shared, and that it is speaking and writing which enables some degree of sharing to take place. Adults too may need to be reminded that vivid images arising from professional practice are personal rather than shared, and that what is needed for effective sharing is the particular detail.

Armstrong (1980) provides a beautiful collection of accounts of incidents with children aged eight to nine, accumulated as he sat in on the class over an entire year. Few people have time to write even a Pepysian-style description of their day, much less to take a whole year off to make lengthy observations. Fortunately it is not necessary to try to be so comprehensive. On the other hand, it is tempting, in the midst of some startling or surprising incident, to think that the incident will remain in memory for a long time ('I will never forget . . .'). Yet it is startling how quickly a vivid moment sinks into the general morass of memory and can be hard to re-contact even a few hours later, unless there is some immediate effort to recall and re-enter it.

What is most helpful is a brief-but-vivid description which enables re-entry into the moment, which enables me to be, as it were, 'back in the situation' at some later time. So all that is needed at first is a few words, literally two or three, enough to enable re-entry, to trigger recollection. Then the incident can described to others *from* that memory, together with any significant further detail that may be needed. Brevity and vividness are what make descriptions of incidents recognisable to others.

Using accounts

Since there is a strong temptation to want to do things with accounts, it is worth mentioning here that as well as allowing yourself to try to account-for situations through asking why in many different ways (as mentioned earlier), you can use them to illustrate phenomena which come to your attention and you can use them to identify recurring situations which may become 'phenomena'. You can describe them to others to see if they recognise them, or as further examples of incidents described to you, and you can search for similarities and differences, for common threads. You can diagnose difficulties, explain experiences, theorise about conditions. You can probe the positive, the negative, and the purely interesting features (de Bono 1972). Working at honing accounts-of rather than accounting-for them focuses on particulars, on details, and so helps in avoiding generalities and labels, which, like the chunks in de Bono's image, can block access to alternative paths, alternative interpretations, and so ultimately, to alternative acts. Every act of theorising, of explaining, of accounting-for is a form of blaming, which pushes the noticing to one side, dilutes your energies, and makes it difficult to learn from the experience.

The teaching device suggested in the next task, of asking people to *say what you see* after encountering something (such as looking at some object, incident, or practice, listening to some sounds, touching some thing, etc.) is designed to develop and make use of the distinction between rendering accounts-of and accounting-for. Participants are asked not to use terms which may be unfamiliar to someone present, not to use similes and 'looks like', but to concentrate on what they see and to use language to focus colleagues' attention to specific details. By reducing the use of technical terms it is easier to get closer to seeing rather than being caught up in what is constructed as being seen. In an extreme form, not only are pencil and paper outlawed, but even the movement of hands. The idea is to strengthen our powers of description using language. But the technique also provides a valuable way of working on practices.

Try this soon

Say What You See

Take a picture or poster or object associated with your practice, and with one or more colleagues, practise giving brief-but-vivid descriptions of details so that others can recognise what you are pointing to.

Real and created accounts

Might it not be possible to create entirely fictional accounts? The answer is that it is certainly possible, but since the accounts are merely to provide entry to experience, it does not really matter whether they are fictional or factual, or some combination. Indeed there is often a fine line between these! What does matter, is whether they trigger recognition of other specific experiences. It turns out to be a great deal harder to write fictional accounts than it is to describe actual observations, and experience is often stranger than fiction in any case. The accounts are not data, and they are not signs of professional development. They are merely entry points to experience. It is experience which is the data. It is richness of recognition which enables choices to be made more sensitively in the future. Montaigne (1588) initiated what we now call reflective journals, suggesting that 'there is no sure witness except each man to himself'.

Summary of Chapter 3

Impartiality is an ideal rather than an achievable goal, since all description involves interpretation. However a useful distinction has been drawn between 'giving an account-of' (a brief-but-vivid description) and 'accounting-for' some incident, which is fundamental to most forms of enquiry, and particularly to effective reflection, whether for professional development or for research. An account-of is a description of what was seen, heard, experienced, described in terms which others can recognise, without elaboration, justification or explanation. Later chapters will go into more detail about using accounts in the context of both professional development (Chapter 5) and research (Chapter 7).

Accounting-for was further dissected into *Whining* (justifying, explaining away, and generally self-calming, throwing away the energy released by noticing), *Wise-acreing* (resorting to theories to explain away, making unsupported conjectures or interpretations) and *Wisening* (probing the sources of the particular acts leading up to the situation, and analysing the positive, negative, and interesting features of an act in order to inform choices to act similarly in the future).

4   Being methodical

Descartes (1637) claimed that each problem he solved became a rule which served afterwards to solve other problems. But there is an easy slide from a method used again insightfully to a method used mechanically. This very brief chapter treads a line between mechanicality and systematic, disciplined behaviour. Being methodical is often associated with being routine and detailed, with acting almost mechanically or clerically rather than creatively. At one extreme, I can rely on spontaneity and serendipity for stimuli in order to respond differently in new situations. At the other extreme I can develop a rigidly methodical pattern of activity which leaves little room for creativity and spontaneity. Somewhere between these extremes, or rather, moving around in the space between these extremes, it is possible to act, to reflect upon, and to sharpen those acts and the way I work on them. I can for example, carry out a sequence of activities of:

> posing a problem;
> seeking data or evidence;
> proposing some action;
> carrying out the action;
> evaluating that action
> re-posing the problem (perhaps making modifications);
> seeking new data;
> modifying the proposed action;
> carrying out that new action;

and so on in an endless cycle. I can follow this cycle step by step, without really thinking or participating deeply, just *working through* the steps one by one. I can also do these sorts of thing with intensity but not necessarily in strict order, referring to the outer scheme or cycle only when I feel I am losing my way or am in need of re-direction. In a similar way, students can *work through* a sequence of exercises or tasks without attending to what is the same and different about them. They can *work through* the process of writing an essay, doing a project or developing a case study concerned with fundamentally endemic tensions and contradictions, but without actually being touched by those contradictions and tensions. Alternatively, they can *work on* the collection of tasks, looking for what is common, trying to generalise a technique and getting a sense of what constitutes a problem or task 'of this type' as reported by Descartes. They can use an essay, project, or case study to confront tensions and to become more aware of the possibilities they afford and the constraints they impose. The distinction being made between *working through* and *working on* is between 'suffering' (in the original sense) a sequence of experiences, and making sense of an experience of succession; between being formatted and being informed; between reacting and taking initiative; between assenting and asserting.

For example, when working on a mathematics problem, I can try to follow Polya's four stages of problem solving referred to earlier (Polya 1945):

pose problem; propose a method; solve; look back;

as a formal sequence. I can stick to the stages and try to proceed from one to another. Unfortunately this is rarely effective. But I can also use Polya's advice to draw me out of being caught up in detail and to help me keep one eye on the greater goal, on the overall process. I can internalise those stages and learn to recognise when a change of activity might be helpful. The four 'stages' can become a reminder, a trigger, to draw my attention out of the doing and to put some of it at least on the overall process, the succession of experiences.

Unfortunately the 'four stages' can also act as a straitjacket. When I get stuck on a problem, I can mechanically write down what I am given and what I want to find, and only then start to think. This is typical of working-through some algorithmic technique. I can also use locating and expressing what I know and what I want to help me re-enter the problem freshly and creatively.

The same applies to the suggestions about noticing which follow. Working through various practices as if they were mechanical sequential stages or phases and using them in an at-arms-length fashion is likely to have no effect at all. They can however be effective if they are entered and worked on, if they are experienced and reflected upon, and then integrated into your way of working so that they are allowed to inform your practice through coming to mind at appropriate moments. But more of that later, as that is the purpose of the Discipline of Noticing itself. The Discipline speaks to its own adoption!

Try these now

Can you think of any activity in which you have developed a fixed or habitual pattern to accomplish some task? Can you recall a situation in which you learned or adopted a sequence of actions which you did not really understand?

What differences (if any) are you aware of between reacting to a situation with a mechanically employed trained sequence of acts, and the use of your professional judgement to respond to some situation?

Training tends to lead to inflexible reactions rather than to flexible and informed responses to problematic situations. But trained habits are often the stepping stone to appreciating and understanding the significance and role of different steps in a procedure. Neither necessarily precedes the other. But trained behaviour is less likely to foster noticing slight aberrations or discrepancies, in contrast to being sensitive to variations and alternative responses.

Summary of Chapter 4

This brief chapter emphasised the importance of combating habitual, mechanical behaviour. No scheme, no sequence of actions will guarantee to generate creative responses. Rather, the distinctions being made which make up the Discipline of Noticing in the next chapter are awarenesses or sensitivities. They are creative responses triggered by intentional preparations.

SUMMARY OF PART II: SOME IMPORTANT DISTINCTIONS

This section revisits and extends some important distinctions which lie at the heart of the practices of noticing.

Not-noticing–(ordinary)–noticing–marking–recording

What we do not notice at all, simply passes us by. What we notice but do not mark we can be re-minded of. What we mark, in the sense of being able to initiate a re-mark, is available at least temporarily, for further analysis. What we record we can re-enter later, and so use both for analysis and for enriching our awareness, thus sensitising ourselves to notice more finely in the future.

Account-of and accounting-for

It is one thing to be aware of various incidents during the day, and to tell stories about them in the staff room or at home. It is quite another to stand outside of the incident and consider it as an object to be analysed, generalised and used to inform future practice. A great deal of energy can be dissipated by simply telling stories, for stories are constructed, among other reasons, as a means for justifying or explaining away something that needs resolving for some reason, perhaps because it was far from ideal.

A fundamentally important distinction can be made between accounts-of incidents, objects, or situations, and accounting-for these phenomena. The act of expressing tempts us into generality, but generality is necessarily ambiguous. Details of particular examples can be negotiated, and thereby offer the possibility to ground discussion in what can be agreed, whereas generalities leave us open to thinking we are talking about the same thing only to discover later that there were significant differences. In order to be able to discuss and debate, to analyse and probe the general, it is necessary to have access to some particulars, so it is essential to agree on the particular phenomenon.

Brief-but-vivid

An account which is brief-but-vivid is one which readers readily find relates to their experience. Brevity is obtained by omitting details which divert attention away from the main issue. The aim is to locate a phenomenon, so the less particular the description, the easier this is, without becoming so general as to be of no value. Vividness is obtained by sticking as much as possible to descriptions of behaviour which others, had they been present, would have readily agreed to having seen, heard or felt. Thus description is as factual as possible. It may describe emotions felt, but where possible these are described in observable terms. Value-laden and judgemental terms are reduced to a minimum. The purpose of a brief-but-vivid account is not to check whether it really did happen, but rather whether it captures or indicates a phenomenon that others can recognise, or come to recognise in the future.

Reflection

Reflection is a much used term covering a wide range of practices and approaches, from 'briefly thinking back' to 'intentionally re-entering specific moments'; from something you do later (*reflection-on-action*) to something you do when you meet an obstacle and so you expose some of your problem-solving processes (*reflection-in-action*), to something you do simultaneously with acting, *reflecting-through-action*. Noticing is about awakening an inner monitor who witnesses and thereby alerts the acting self to choose to act differently. This is non-trivial as it requires energy derived from noticing. Consequently we develop methodical or systematic ways of supporting ourselves in noticing.

Try these soon

Look back over some of your notes and observations, try to re-enter specific moments, and then redraft the descriptions as brief-but-vivid accounts-of.

With two or three colleagues, watch a videotape of someone teaching, or observe a lesson together. Afterwards, each person make a list of the salient moments from their point of view. Compare notes and see just how much disparity there can be between observers. If everyone works at providing brief-but-vivid accounts of what they saw, the task of recognising each other's moments will be much easier.

In your reading, look out for instances of authors launching into accounting-for before you have established what it is that they are explaining or interpreting.

Try mentioning a brief-but-vivid incident to a colleague and see whether they recognise the sort of situation you describe, and whether they are prompted to offer a similar incident of their own.

Part III
The Discipline of Noticing

The Discipline of Noticing is nothing more than an attempt to be systematic and methodical without being mechanical. It is a collection of practices which together can enhance sensitivity to notice opportunities to act freshly in the future. It is however, impossible to see where systematic use of the discipline will take you. As Emerson (1860) put it, 'We are all inventors, each sailing out on a voyage of discovery, guided each by a private chart, of which there is no duplicate.'

5   Disciplined Noticing

This chapter outlines the salient phases of disciplined rather than sporadic and serendipitous noticing. There is nothing particularly demanding about making noticing more systematic, though it is by no means a trivial matter. The idea is simply to work on becoming more sensitive to notice opportunities in the moment; to be methodical without being mechanical. This is the difference between 'finding opportunities' and 'making them'. Instead of being caught up in moment by moment flow of events according to habits and pre-established patterns, the idea is to have the opportunity to respond freshly and creatively yet appropriately, every so often. As Francis Bacon (1605) put it, 'A wise man will make more opportunities than he finds.' Noticing is an act of attention, and as such is not something you can decide to do all of a sudden. It has to happen to you, through the exercise of some internal or external impulse or trigger. The more you notice, the more energy you can accumulate to support noticing in the future. Marking is also an act of attention. It involves attaching connections so that what is marked can come to mind later without the need for outside triggers.

One way to enhance the chances of noticing in the future, to inform (literally, to provide a form for) future practice, is to prepare in advance. Another way is to try to use past experience (particularly recent experience) to assist in that preparation. And it is important not to get caught up in solipsistic activity, spinning fantasies about, for example, how sensitive and decisive I am: I need to be validating my noticing against the experience of colleagues. Each of these elements:

> Keeping accounts;
> Developing sensitivities;
> Recognising choices;
> Preparing and noticing;
> Labelling; and
> Validating with others

is elaborated in its own subsection.

Keeping and using accounts

Describing to myself what I have noticed is not nearly as easy as it sounds. There are two main problems. The first is to avoid as far as possible introducing personal opinion and deduction. The second is working out what sorts of things to recount. When you start to exchange accounts with colleagues, there is the additional problem of what to do with someone else's accounts. This section is extended in Chapter 7, which goes into more detail on constructing and analysing individual and collections of accounts.

Avoiding interpretation and explanation

The labels *account-of, accounting-for,* and *brief-but-vivid* are intended to be of assistance in avoiding unnecessary interpretation, explanation and value-judgements, when identifying and describing incidents, but it is a constant struggle. It is ever so tempting to generalise and theorise before being clear on the incident itself. Recognising that there is something generalisable about the incident, that it has a taste of similarity with other experiences, suggests that it may be representative of a more general phenomenon, but before a phenomenon can usefully be analysed it is essential to gather exemplars, and to share and negotiate these with others. Combing the literature for descriptions that seem to conform with or to contradict your experience is one form of checking against the experience of a wider community; offering descriptions of accounts-of incidents to others, to see if they recognise them and can offer versions of their own, is another. Jumping into interpretation and explanation robs the noticing of its energy and makes it harder to inform future practice.

The practice of keeping accounts is a rather different enterprise to keeping a journal. Although a journal may include accounts, it usually forms a narrative, in the form of fragments of a story, and as such it also includes descriptions of feelings about those accounts, links to other incidents and events, value-judgements, theorising and so on. In telling stories we are committed to putting a particular view. By contrast, brief-but-vivid accounts-of incidents (avoiding interpretation that might be disputed) form the basis for future noticing, as well as for later analysis which may well take the form of a narrative. Furthermore, gripping narrative usually succeeds by being strong on particular details which enable the reader to enter into the situation being described, that is, on brief-but-vivid anecdotes or accounts-of. Writing narratives can be very useful as an aid to making sense, to digesting experience, but in the process the energy for more sensitised noticing in the future may be dissipated. Narratives, by their very nature, are likely to support pigeon-holing, because they smooth out disturbances and provide or imply explanation and justification. The extent to which a collection of accounts leaves open possibilities, does not theorise and account-for, is the extent to which there is potential for influencing and informing the future. Succumbing to the impulse to weave a narrative which explains, links, and organises, may make you feel better, but may lessen the energy available to make changes.

Choosing what to recount

To start with I note down whatever aspect has come to mind. It is useful to do this immediately at the end of a lesson or session, or even during a lull (it does not take long to scribble down a few chosen words which provide access to an incident). Indeed, making a brief note can be incorporated into what students or colleagues are invited to do every so often as part of their working practices too. For one way of thinking about learning is as learning to notice (to make distinctions) the way an expert does. Using one side of the page for 'things that strike me' while I am working on a problem, writing an essay, or making notes in a session can help me to re-enter that moment later.

Some people feel overwhelmed by the mass of incidents they are involved in and feel intimidated by deciding what to record. A useful approach is to note the first few incidents that come to mind as you think back over a part or all of a session. All that is needed is two or three incidents per day, at most. Significance will emerge over time.

It is also useful to find a quiet moment every so often, say once a week, to think back and try to re-enter moments that come spontaneously to mind. Sometimes incidents that seemed unimportant at the time come to the surface. It does require some effort and energy to do this, to push noticing to marking and marking to recording, but it usually pays off very quickly. And brevity is the soul of accounting!

If I have something that is causing me concern, or in which I am particularly interested, or have set myself to notice, then it helps to make brief-but-vivid notes about any incidents which seem to illustrate it. In this way I can accumulate data for future analysis.

Dave Wilson (1994) reported what he found useful as a way of working:

> During much of last year I attempted to reflect on my teaching in a particular way. At the end of each day, or week, I sat quietly and allowed an incident from my teaching to enter my mind. Whatever that was, I tried to recapture the detail of that incident and to set it down in writing as objectively as I could. I then worked upon that fragment. My conjecture was that whatever entered my mind swiftly and easily would have some significance. The fact that they were significant I took for granted. Why, otherwise, would I have remembered them?
>
> . . . I tried to examine myself within these situations, to look at my feelings and actions. I tried to read and reread my stories offering a variety of interpretations of the significance of them for me.
>
> As I proceeded in this way I produced generalities based upon the particularities of my (reflected upon) experience. When my reflection evoked a fragment from my reading I attempted to discuss those readings and to reflect upon their relevance for myself.

Written down it sounds as though impressive self discipline is at work. In fact, self-discipline grows as the process of noticing develops.

Using accounts

It is actually rare to juxtapose strands of experience and learn from them, and as was suggested in the first chapter,

> One thing we seem not to learn from experience,
> is that we rarely learn from experience alone.

George Eliot (1872) observed that although we have numerous strands of experience, many of us never lay those strands alongside each other. Some sort of mental laying of strands alongside each other, weaving them into a tapestry-story even, or using them to sensitise myself for noticing in the future, is usually necessary. Accounts provide access to the data with which to reflect significantly.

The purpose of collecting accounts is several-fold. First, they provide a foundation of identifiable and negotiable incidents. They can be used to re-collect (literally) similar incidents from the past; they can be used to identify what it is that seems 'similar' and hence to identify phenomena and issues, and to locate what I want to work on; they can be used to deepen and strengthen sensitivity to particular kinds of incidents or situations; they can be used to work on seeking several alternative readings of any situation; and they can be shared with colleagues in order to locate alternative responses and to validate my own noticing. Chapter 7 elaborates these much more fully.

Sharing accounts with others involves negotiating in what respect particular incidents are similar and whether there is an underlying commonality that might usefully be labelled and looked out for in the future. Other people's incidents can be used to enrich my own connections and associations with labels, to come to notice and mark freshly, and to locate alternative actions I might take when I notice an opportunity in the future. These actions are all discussed at greater length under subsequent headings.

Account 13: Calling out

> I had barely finished writing a question on the board, when Tanya called out an answer which was completely wrong, indeed, was the sort of answer I was trying to avoid the students encountering. The impossibility-diversion of addressing her response flashed by, and I found myself saying 'don't shout out, think about it', and then asking the question again. Tanya did not offer anything more that lesson. How can I respond to impulsive incorrect proposals? It is so easy to form a low opinion of the student's thinking as a result, and so easy to bruise ego.

Here the report of an incident already contains an issue and a question. It is so natural to criticise the outburst, and at the same time, to dismiss the content of the response, perhaps even to form a poor opinion of the student's understanding. The fact that the incident was recorded suggests some significance for the person involved, so first steps have been taken towards developing sensitivity to act differently in similar situations in the future. Recognition by others indicates that there is a basis in their past experiences for developing a sensitivity to this type of incident, so there may be something worth pursuing for them. If a sense of 'having been there myself' arises, then there may be some experiences upon which to draw, or insights to be gained.

How can this be pursued and worked on? There are unlikely to be definitive answers to the specific question posed, but what is possible is that a collection of different actions could be located, so that there is greater choice if (when) it happens again (and if I notice it in time to choose to respond differently). For example, the enquiry might lead into locating strategies for working on a classroom rubric or set of practices in which students with a propensity to call out answers became habituated to thinking before speaking, perhaps through offering opportunities to try ideas out with colleagues (brief moments of 'talking in pairs' about what has just been said or asked), as well as working explicitly on control over their own behaviour. Over a period of time, students would be given, and would learn to create, opportunities to try out ideas with each other before 'speaking out'. The enquiry might also lead to looking at the form of the question, to see if alternative types of questions or prompts might be more fruitful in generating thoughtful discussion.

Seeking threads and multiple interpretations

Looking back over accounts of a variety of incidents which are not encumbered with interpretation and evaluative judgements makes it much easier to detect themes and similarities which may not have been apparent at the time. Often when I think I am concerned about one issue, I find that what I am actually recording has some other component which I may not be aware of when caught up in the immediate experience. I can then bring a more dispassionate consideration to a collection of incidents, and even choose to use one or another theoretical frame to make sense of them.

Seeking threads is a process of re-entering a succession of moments and allowing a 'flavour' to emerge. It is an act of stressing some aspects (this has already happened to some extent in what you have chosen to record) and consequently ignoring others. The resultant 'feel' constitutes a generality, something similar about a variety of situations, something perhaps characteristic or problematic about your practice.

Detecting themes goes beyond looking for similarities between accounts, whether in the words used, the contexts, or the structure of situations. What is sought is something similar in the feeling of the incidents as you re-enter them, for themes reside in you, not in the accounts. You are actually looking for themes which reflect you, as these are what can inform your future practice.

For example, you may have found that my labels for the various examples of accounts have on the one hand, served to orient you to some aspect of each account, but on the other hand, may have contrasted with an aspect that struck you particularly. This is yet another example of the label-tension (here I have detected and named a theme): labels provide access to links and connections, and hence meaning, but at the same time they stress certain aspects and hence lead to ignoring others (here I have elucidated a principle). When you recognise that sense of 'another' or find yourself thinking 'oh, that again', then you are detecting a theme. You may choose to adopt the practice of labelling your accounts, or not, or to experiment by labelling some but not others, as part of your investigation of the relevance of the practice of labelling to your way of working with accounts.

Elucidating a theme or pattern is worthwhile not only to inform the direction of professional development or 'work', but also to prime you to be on the lookout for informative articles or discussions with colleagues, and for possible alternative practices to modify and try for yourself.

In cases such as Account 13: *Calling out* which involve the actions of someone else, it is tempting to engage in some form of *asking why* (p. 41), to speculate about why the person acted in that way. Here, the question might be *why* the student called out. Such speculation is at best an indulgence and at worse serves to strengthen opinion, habit, and even prejudice. It is unlikely to open up possibilities to respond differently in the future. Rather, it is most likely to reveal pre-judgements and to lead to closure on one in particular. By contrast, several colleagues, having described several incidents which seem to them to be similar, and having negotiated this through discussion, might then speculate together in order to produce a wider range of possibilities without needing to seek closure on any one. Remaining with multiplicity enables greater sensitivity in the future, both in recognising similar incidents, and in appreciating the impulses which lead people to act in this way.

Some things to try now

Can you recall any of the accounts I have offered? What is it about those that you can recall which makes them memorable?

Look back to one of the accounts I have provided, and see if you recognise something in it. Now try to capture in a few words what is general rather than particular about 'such incidents'. Now try to find an alternative 'principle' or 'explanation'.

Think back over a recent day and pick out three or more incidents. Is there anything common to them? What makes them distinctive?

Look back over some accounts you have kept. Try to re-enter each one as vividly as possible.

Developing sensitivities

I can only notice what I am primed or sensitised to notice. At any moment I think I am wide awake to what is happening, but inevitably there are aspects and details which completely escape me. This feature of noticing applies at all levels, from engaging in professional practice (as a mathematician, as a teacher, as a workshop leader, as a colleague in discussions, as an observer of participants in lessons or sessions, as participant in a meeting, as chair of a meeting, and so on). It also applies to ordinary interactions at home, in shops, etc.

Account 14: Irritated

I suddenly noticed my voice becoming harder and my words full of irony as the person I was talking to seemed unable to find a way to do what I wanted. Then a voice spoke in my head saying 'She can only do what she believes she is empowered to do'. At that I was able to soften my voice, thank her, and retreat, in order to look for some other route.

Becoming irritated by people not doing what I think they could do is a common theme for me. But I cannot do anything about it until I become aware in the moment that that is what is happening. I need some part of me to be separate from the immediate involvement. This sensitivity can be developed through disciplined noticing by first recognising the phenomena in retrospect, then accepting that irony and sarcasm are unlikely to be effective, and so beginning to look out for alternative behaviour.

Account 15: In tune

Mrs Jones, the teacher, heard a student thinking out loud. Tracy (7 years old) was not presenting her ideas to another; she was just talking to herself about how she did the problem. Mrs Jones said to me 'Did you hear what Tracy just said? That is the first time Tracy has used ten in such a powerful way.' This teacher was so in tune with the reasoning of her 27 pupils that she noticed that one of them had made a significant construction. She noted this advance in her log for later use. (Wheatley 1992: 531)

Mrs Jones was not 'looking out for' particular use of language, but she was aware of the importance of certain words and phrases. To be sensitive to how students or colleagues are developing is not a matter of keeping extensive records or making a conscious effort to remember. It is about being 'in tune' with them, about listening and trying to be 'with them'. It is about being attuned to underlying ideas and themes, processes and heuristics, to ways of working on content, as much as to the content itself.

Account 16: Catching sight

In a large meeting recently I caught sight of a slight movement of the hand into an upright position by one participant sitting near me, which I read as an indication of wishing to speak. The chair did not appear to have noticed, so when I caught her eye, I indicated my fellow participant.

    In another meeting I noticed someone shift her posture to a more upright position leaning slightly forward. She did not manage to 'get in', and her posture relaxed again. When a moment arose, I invited her to speak. Her posture changed again to a more upright one. What she said changed the direction of the discussion.

It is much harder to notice other people wanting to speak when I too want to speak. Attuning myself to different indicators is important, for different people signal in different ways, especially if they are diffident or unconfident in the group.

I can become attuned to notice through reading something that suddenly strikes a chord with my past experience, either by helping me make sense of something, by fitting with or contradicting something I believe, or by otherwise challenging me. I can notice something that a colleague does, or pick up an idea from something that is said in a discussion. I can stumble on to something through serendipity in a particular situation. What seems to be required is a disturbance or a resonance. Not a tidal wave, but a ripple sufficiently great to be distinguishable on the choppy surface which is my experience.

A simple example of attunement is provided by sensitising oneself to particular words. For example, the word *it* frequently signals ambiguity or lack of clarity. By being attuned to asking pupils to clarify 'what the it is', you can both appreciate what they are trying to say and help them improve the clarity of their descriptions. Similarly the word *just* signals a certain value-laden perspective which can act as a put down for others (as in 'you just add the numbers together'). It can prove fruitful to invite people not to use *just* when working together on mathematics. Another example is the word *should* in relation to teaching, which is sometimes intended as an exclusive imperative, but which can often be fruitfully replaced by the word *could* to open up consideration of alternatives while removing the force of the moral imperative.

It is characteristic of young children learning vocabulary that they often expand a word's meaning to include far more than in adult usage, and then later contract it again to match normal usage. For example, 'cow' may include any animal in a field, before eventually retreating to just cows. Adults often do the same, but adults also tend to reject a word used in a new context because of previous associations and meanings, and only later come round to the new meaning. Even so they may have deep seated objections to particular words. For example, 'forcing awareness' is used technically by Gattegno (1987) to refer to directing and focusing someone's attention in such a way as to awaken a power which is not currently active and so to empower them, but it often generates a strong reaction because of the implications of forcing against someone else's will; the word 'tactic' is useful for referring to acts of teaching, but may be so strongly attached to military contexts as to block acceptance. By thinking back to recent experience I can recall moments when colleagues and I have rejected words used in a new context, as well as times we have reacted to words because of negative personal association. By sensitising myself to these tendencies, I can either try to take avoiding action in advance, or enable myself not to get anxious about temporary misuse or rejection of new words by others.

How can I become more sensitive to noticing things happening in my classroom? One of the common observations of people undertaking personal research is that they find themselves noticing and questioning more. Indeed the principle result of any research is the transformation in perception of the researcher. But it is not necessary to undertake formal research. The tendency for research to be associated with outsiders observing from an outside perspective and so having little to offer to a practising teacher has been transformed into a variety of techniques for individuals and groups of colleagues to undertake. The Discipline of Noticing was developed precisely in order to facilitate practitioners in drawing back from their immediate activity, their practice, to see that practice *as* a practice which can be worked on and developed. There have been many proposals for methods to undertake such standing back, and some are referred to in a later section. They all have at heart the development of sensitivity to notice in the moment and so to make choices previously unavailable. These techniques can be used to develop professionally, and to carry out research.

Primed with questions, however vague and ill-formed, I can be attracted by something that a colleague says or does, I can read about suggestions for alternative behaviour, and I can develop possibilities from my own experience and from reports from colleagues. Being inspired by something that someone else says or does requires very little personal energy, though it does take energy to do something positive about it. Similarly, being struck by something written takes little effort, but transforming that into personal action does. The trouble with reading reports is that it is impossible to describe experience. All you get are general descriptions. From these you have to locate something specific that you can do yourself. Then you have to remember to do it, and to be aware of your evaluation of it as an act. It is very easy to react to writing, and even to colleagues, with something along the lines of 'It's alright for you, but I couldn't do that'.

Instead of allowing yourself to be caught up in judgements, it is more effective to note the fact of internal resistance, and to concentrate on recognising opportunities to try acting differently.

Some things to try now

Look out for people using *it* when describing, and try asking them 'what is the it?'. Look out for times when you use *should* in relation to practice, and see if there is any useful effect achieved by replacing *should* by *could*.

Exchange accounts with some colleagues, or pick out some transcripts or other descriptions from a journal or book. Try to locate some incident or experience of your own that seems to fit with, or to contradict, their analysis. Make a brief note of each so that you can re-enter the state of agreement or disagreement again later.

When you have a collection of accounts, you can work at locating some common threads, some features of sameness, some issues for you that you want to explore.

Sometimes you can be surprised by the themes which emerge, sometimes they are what you expected. It might be, for example, that you want to gain more control over your reactions so that you can respond differently in certain types of situations. By looking back over a collection of accounts you can sometimes see aspects or details which give a direction for further noticing, perhaps in the form of a response to try again or to try to avoid in future.

It may be that you want to know more about how other people have tried to deal with similar situations, and for that you need to read. But your reading is now focused. You know what you are looking for. You can recount particularly poignant moments to colleagues and ask them if they recognise such situations, what they do in similar circumstances, and whether they know of any relevant writing. It may be that working with colleagues proves to be adequate. By recounting incidents to each other, without judgement or justification, but almost clinically, you can recognise different ways of responding that other people do naturally or have worked at developing.

Recognising choices

Although in the moment by moment flow of an event, whether a classroom lesson or lecture, meeting or consultation, there are numerous possibilities for making choices, surprisingly, very few opportunities are recognised as such, precisely because of the presence of professional habits. As Jennifer Nias (1989: 13) observed:

> The minute-by-minute decisions made within the shifting, unpredictable, capricious world of the classroom, and the judgements teachers read when they are reflecting on their work, depend upon how they perceive particular events, behaviours, materials, and persons.

For example:

Account 17: Pausing

In the midst of a lesson in which I am telling them things from the front, I suddenly become aware of a choice: I could pause, I could get them to do some work in pairs or individually, briefly or for an extended period of time, or I could carry on as I am.

What does it mean to become suddenly aware of this choice? More importantly, what does it feel like? In my experience, there can sometimes be a sudden sense of heightened awareness and opportunity, and if a fresh alternative is chosen, a moment of being open to uncertainty as I try something new. There is a fresh energy, a sense of anticipation or expectancy, and a sense of being informed and of pursuing more global and less local goals than in the preceding moments. But most of the time I am really only aware of a choice going by below the surface. By the time the fact of a choice has registered, the choice has usually been made.

I am already in the midst of a pause, and now have to decide what to say or do next; I experience uncertainty, and then find myself embarking on more exposition.

I am aware that people have been working for a time and of wanting to interrupt them to draw threads together yet wanting them to have as long as possible to work together.

When did I actually choose to continue expounding or to interrupt? My experience is that usually I *find myself* speaking, or pausing, and that I am unaware of just when the choice was made. I react rather than respond or choose. I think I am choosing, but in fact I am waiting until an inner dam bursts and I intervene. Being aware of a choice does not make the choice any easier, unless the situation reminds you of some alternative action that you might not otherwise have thought of:

Account 18: Decision point

The class were busy with the task of drawing a quadrilateral and seeing if it would tessellate, then drawing such a tiling. The teacher stopped beside me and said: 'In case I forget to mention it later, I'm at a decision point. I can see that everyone is working happily . . . they're enjoying . . . getting satisfaction from what they're doing . . . cutting and colouring. . . . I've got a strong urge to move them on though. I want to push them on to the next point. . . . I'm not sure that drawing patterns is achieving much.' (Jaworski 1991: 38)

Some decisions seem to involve a conscious weighing up of alternatives, particularly when you are under pressure and aware of not knowing what to do, or when you do not have a strong preference: which dish to select in a restaurant, which type of restaurant to go to, what to do on a Saturday evening, which task to offer to students, which patient to call on first and so on. But by far the majority of choices simply happen. Later, when an observer tries to prompt recall of choices, it is the deliberate ones which the practitioner can recognise and re-enter, while the others are very difficult to remember (Jaworksi 1995).

Many choices have actually been made weeks or years earlier, when fresh responses became reactions to standard situations and were integrated into habitual patterns of behaviour. This is what is meant by a professional having a *practice*. For example, in order to survive in the classroom, it is essential to master the fundamentals of control and inspiration of students. In any professional context, it is essential to develop effective strategies that come to mind without having to be thought about, and part of induction into the profession is helping novices establish necessary reactions. But automatic reactions can also get in the way of development, blocking awareness of alternative ways of acting and perceiving. Whereas certain strategies may be essential in order to cope on first entering a profession, they may eventually stifle professional freshness.

It is essential that automaticities and habits be developed, because otherwise the myriad of choices to be made would be impossible to cope with. But the trouble with habits is that they obscure noticing the possibility of choosing to act differently, precisely because they have become part of habitual practice. My own habits are hard for me to notice, whereas the habits of others stick out prominently. Indeed, where I find myself irritated by someone else's habits, I may be looking at my own: a strong reaction often suggests recognition.

Account 19: Reacting

A teacher of 8-year-olds had a particularly stormy time with one of his students. As he continued to write about him, he began to act differently towards him: 'Whereas I want to kick him across the room, I slowly go over and hug him and say 'Daniel, Daniel, sometimes I don't understand you. Help me to.' And slowly, Daniel did become more understandable. (Holly 1993: 66)

Finding yourself doing something is easy; catching yourself about to do something and choosing to act differently in a more informed manner, is much harder. It requires effort and technique. Choosing in the moment to act in a certain way requires two things:

- noticing a possibility to choose, that is, recognising some typical situation about to unfold; and
- having alternatives from which to choose, that is, being aware of alternative action or behaviour.

Even though you become starkly aware of the unstoppable flow of events in which you are embroiled, this in itself is not an opportunity to do something (awareness alone is not enough); even though you have prepared a dozen different strategies, if none of them occur to you in the midst of an event then no choice is possible (knowing about alternative actions is not sufficient). The two have to come together. The first requires sharpened sensitivity, and the second requires access to an accumulation of possible ways of acting.

Account 20: Quizzical

In a workshop presentation, I caught sight of a quizzical expression on someone's face. Inside me there arose an impulse to get people to talk in pairs about what had just been said.

The arising of this impulse is an example of a possibility being noticed. There is an ever-so-brief moment of choice, between moving to pairs or carrying on, so brief that it is difficult to catch.

Almost immediately I found myself carrying on, but talking directly to that quizzical expression, and I become aware that I am trying to get it to change to a smile of relief, by talking at it. On another occasion I chose to get people to talk in pairs and the point of difficulty soon came to the surface so we could deal with it.

Account 21: Smiling

I noticed one day in a meeting that I smiled at someone who does not normally choose to speak. My smile was part of an expectancy that they would say something, and suddenly they entered the discussion.

There is no guarantee that 'smiling' will always work, or even that the smile had anything to do with what happened, but there is a starting point for further investigation. First it requires becoming aware of what it is like to 'expect' someone to speak, while catching their attention, but without pressure. Then it requires remembering to enter that state rather than be caught up in the flow of events oneself. Even so, 'it' may not always work. Offering someone an entry when you judge from their body posture that they might speak, is better than talking over them and unintentionally blocking them from contributing to the discussion.

The language of *noticing an opportunity*, is misleading because there is an entire spectrum from *being vaguely aware*, through *having a sense*, through *knowing that one could*, to *actually doing something about it*. There are two thresholds of awareness, the first between being subconsciously aware and being consciously aware, and the second between knowing but being unable to act, and being able to act. These thresholds correspond to transitions between noticing–marking and marking–recording. The practices being proposed here are designed to assist with generating enough energy to cross those thresholds.

Some things to try now

Try to notice a habitual reaction and do something about it. For example, try to be aware of your body posture and movement as you enter the room in which some event is to take place. Then try, for example, to take a deep breath just at that moment, or to have an image of what you expect to happen in that event.

You will probably find this much more difficult than you expect. Attention cannot be switched on and off at will, and deeply established reactions and habits are very hard to notice much less to trap and alter.

On some days, set yourself to make a note of some incident at each natural break. On other days, make a note of several incidents at the end of the day, just before going home. You may find yourself in a rush at that time; set aside five minutes nevertheless. You may find that as you go home other incidents come to mind. Try to make notes about them immediately on arriving home. A few moments' writing when you think of it is better than a multitude of thoughts delayed so long that they never get recorded.

Take opportunities to observe colleagues, and select some behaviour which you might try to employ yourself. There will be advice later on how to prepare and carry out such alterations to your behaviour.

Go through your notebook and formulate some labels for different types of incidents.

Some people like to use a special font or different columns, one for incidents recorded when noticed or recalled, and the other for meta-reflections, recording perceived threads and links which emerge later.

Set aside five minutes this weekend to go over the notes made so far, and to record what you consider to have been the ideas and issues of concern to you at the time of writing.

Each day as you go to work, or as you prepare for a meeting, remind yourself of some feature that you want to be on the lookout for, some sensitivity that you want activated. Imagine yourself responding in that chosen manner. These imaginings last only a second; but they require energy to initiate. That energy can come from noticing, and it can come from knowing that you have colleagues with whom you are sharing your investigations.

Many people challenge the use of terms like *mechanical, automated* and *routine,* claiming that they are awake to choices all the time in their professional practice. In the spirit of the discipline being proposed, this conjecture is available to be verified. One way to verify it is to try to make a note of all the conscious decisions of which you are aware during a period of professional activity, and to do this on a regular basis. If a colleague can be induced to observe and make similar notes, then there is the basis for comparison and discussion. It is highly recommended that observations be confined to *accounts-of* salient moments, without attempts to *account-for* them through justification or explanation. The conjecture under investigation concerns whether or not much of practice is mechanical, not whether appropriate and convincing explanations and justifications can be given for actions.

Preparing to notice in the moment

It may appear that excessive attention has been given in previous chapters to reflecting on the past, collecting descriptions of incidents, and sharpening sensitivities. The reason is that it is much harder to be awake to a possibility in the flow of an event than it might seem. It is all too easy to be caught up in the action, whether in the content of a lesson, the argument in a meeting, or even in the boredom of other people dominating an event.

Reflecting on what has happened in the past, and selecting possible actions for the future, are forms of preparation, but do not in themselves guarantee that you will think of them in the heat of the moment. There is more to acting freshly and creatively than merely knowing-that some action can be useful, and knowing-how to carry it out. It requires knowing-to do it in the moment.

Even when a potential action has been found for acting in a fresh way, it is not likely to be used unless I simultaneously notice (through sharpened sensitivity) a moment of choice *and* find that tactic coming to mind. Usually I become aware of an opportunity only in retrospect, after the action has begun to unfold, and it is often too late to do anything about it. The French expression *l'esprit d'escalier*, the thought on the staircase (afterwards) captures the experience of realising later what might have been apposite in the moment.

Systematic preparation is therefore a twofold action:

- continuing to work on sharpening sensitivities; and
- imagining yourself acting in a fresh way in a typical situation.

By mentally entering a typical moment that is likely to occur, and simultaneously reviewing the kind of response one would like to make, it is possible both to perform virtual or *gedanken* experiments to try out the feel of alternative behaviour, and to prepare oneself so that alternative responses become available in the moment while teaching, researching, administering or learning. But being prepared does not mean being pre-determined.

Imagining a putative situation is very much like re-entering a vivid moment, but instead of wishing that you had acted differently, you imagine yourself acting the way you wish. The affective energy of wish is translated into vividness of image. It is essential to enter that action as vividly as possible in your mind, to feel it happening. By becoming aware of muscle tensions, movements and relevant thoughts, you enhance the possibility of remembering in an appropriate moment in the future.

Because preparing involves the future rather than the past, some aspects of your visualisation may be generic rather than particular, fuzzy rather than crisp. You can't predict exactly what others will say and do, but you can vividly imagine yourself embarking on the action. All that matters is getting the action started, because the hard part is remembering to employ a tactic.

Noticing when it is needed

Noticing something significant retrospectively, after the event, is how most sensitivities begin. But recognising after the event is over or after the moment has passed, is of little immediate use. To inform action in the future, it is essential that these moments of noticing move closer to the moment when action is initiated. This requires persistence, which in turn requires commitment. The energy required comes from withdrawing as much as possible from explanation and evaluation, and focusing energy and attention on imagining acting differently in the future.

Account 22: Repeating back (p. 11) again

I suddenly caught myself repeating back to the class what one student had just said. I had resolved not to do this for a while, because it indicated to students that only what I had to say was valuable, but it was too late. I was just finishing my reformulation of what the student said.

When I catch myself in mid-sentence already saying something I meant not to say, it is usually too late. But if I can catch myself about to say it, I might be able to say or do something else. The real work in noticing is to draw the moment of awakening from the retrospective into the present, closer and closer to the point at which a choice can be made.

Account 23: Glancing in rooms

I have noticed that when I walk down the office corridor, I turn my head to look into each office with an open door. I realised one day that very often, when I look in, the person inside is looking at me (if they are sitting facing the door). I was struck by this and decided to stop looking into offices. On my next journey down the corridor, I suddenly realised I was doing it again, and it was only by the last door that I managed to not-turn my head and look. It felt really peculiar. It took many more trips before I recognised the desire to turn my head *just before* reaching a door, and being able to choose not to look. For a period of time I managed to get down the corridor without looking, and I felt much more whole, as if I had been dissipating my attention by looking in doors and catching people's gaze.

After a while this sensitivity was overlaid by other concerns until a chance remark reminded me of the phenomenon, and upon inspection, I found that I was doing it again!

A typical report of this phenomenon of noticing only in retrospect at first was given by a teacher who was working on differences between her responses to girls and to boys through setting herself the task of 'trying to look for the truth in what my pupils were saying so that I could experience a change of state and get something positive from an otherwise unhelpful or uninformative exchange':

'I made several unsuccessful attempts to observe my responses to pupils in general. Despite entering the classroom each day determined to "notice" these responses, this was forgotten in the general activity and business of the first few moments of every lesson.

'I then decided to try to make the task more manageable by simply focusing on one pupil about whom I am particularly concerned. J. tends to be reticent in class. After some time at working on giving a positive and supportive response (e.g. "that's interesting . . . how did you get that?" rather than "that's not quite right . . . have another try").

'To my amazement, after just one positive response to another pupil, J. put her hand up to volunteer to answer the next question!'

The teacher goes on to be sceptical that there was a strong connection between the two incidents (positive response and volunteering), which requires further investigation. 'It has been valuable to try to work against my habitual responses, even though I shall probably never know whether it has been beneficial to my students, because of the many other factors at play.'

Moving noticing from the retrospective into the moment when it can be acted upon usually takes time and energy.

Account 24: Talking in pairs

I was running a session and suddenly became aware that I had just uttered a complex technical sentence, and that most people had not fully understood it. I paused, and invited them to try to say it to their neighbour. There was an immediate buzz which then subsided. Someone reported difficulty so we were able to pause and work on the unclear parts of what I had said.

It was a further two years before I remembered, in the moment, to use the same tactic again, despite attempts before sessions to remind myself to use it. Later I realised that I had come across the idea in another form as part of a research method and had at that time said to myself 'that's a good idea, I'll use that'. So many good ideas fade into the background because they are not energised, not brought to the foreground through preparation and work on noticing.

Imagining yourself acting in some desirable way, and imagining something which will trigger that awareness can be a long, slow process. As noticing becomes less retrospective and increasingly spective, an altered structure of attention is created. Intraspection becomes more frequent and more vivid. This requires continued and disciplined work on observing and activating different selves and on splitting attention.

The energy which comes from noticing is easily dissipated in explanation and judgement, but it can be used productively to set up patterns and positions for the future so that instead of 'finding yourself reacting', you 'find yourself acting in a chosen new way', with a vivid sense of being awake to the situation.

The structure of language can make a significant contribution to preparing for and triggering noticing, based on metaphor, as mentioned in Chapters 1 and 3, and on a second term revived from ancient Greek studies of rhetoric by Roman Jakobson (see Jakobson and Halle 1956) called *metonymy*.

Metonymy

Sometimes something that someone says triggers another thought that to us seems connected but to others seems like a jump. This is an example of metonymy.

Whereas metaphor (literally, carrying meaning across from one domain to another), is structural, deep and meaningful, metonymy is associated with playfulness, tripping along the surface in a trail of puns, homonyms, associations and idiosyncratic emotional triggers.

Sometimes something that someone says resonates with our past experience in some way. What they say has particularly rich meaning for us. It seems to correspond to structures with which we are familiar.

By way of contrast, a rapid train of ideas is characteristic of metonymy. A *metonymy* is literally the use of an attribute to refer to the whole. When we say 'the bench ruled . . .' or 'the crown owns . . .' we do not mean literally that a bench made a ruling or that a crown owns something. The use of bench in this context is a way of referring to the judge sitting on the bench; the crown refers to the whole institution of state and monarch. When an attribute of a current thought triggers a different thought, and then an attribute of that triggers a new thought, we get a sequence of associations. Metonymy is the action in which some aspect of a word triggers, through pun, homonym, or other word play, a 'related' word.

If you listen closely to conversation you can sometimes become aware of a train of metonymic triggers which gives the conversation a jerky, leaping flavour. One person says something, and a word or image triggers an association in someone else who then speaks about that and so on. When someone suddenly asks 'How did we get on to this?', it is likely that a sequence of metonymies is responsible.

Metonymy is usually very rapid and below the surface of consciousness, whereas metaphor tends to be savoured, to mature. Metonymy is experienced as a sequence of associations, as a train of thought, while metaphor is experienced as richness of meaning, as significance. Each may follow the other so quickly that it is hard to separate them. Both are components of meaning: metonymy as in making connections, metaphor as in seeing structure.

Both metaphor and metonymy are useful devices for awakening you in the moment. Something in the structure of the current situation can resonate with a metaphor or some previously experienced structure, bringing associated thoughts and awareness to mind; something in the words or something emotional below the level of awareness can trigger a metonymic connection. Choosing suitable labels for situations or for gambits can exploit the word-playfulness of your mind to trigger metonymic recall of an action or gambit you want to employ (Chapman 1997).

Some things to try now

Set yourself to notice situations in which you make excuses (to yourself or to others) for something. What is the nature of those excuses? One way to try to trap these is to catch yourself saying 'Yes but . . .'. Try imagining yourself as vividly as possible deep in conversation, and substitute 'yes and furthermore . . .' in place of 'yes but'.

Excuses are a form of self-justification and self-calming which is part of the way we deal with personal weaknesses. As with accounting-for, they often leak away the energy which comes from being disturbed by realising our less than ideal behaviour. An alternative way to use the energy is to imagine oneself using some alternative, in this case, changing 'yes but . . .' into 'yes and furthermore . . .'. One can also try turning 'no and . . .' into 'no but . . .'.

Set yourself to catch a moment of playing with words (using a homonym or pun, either explicitly, or finding yourself following a separate train of thought). Watch out for the possibility of chains of metonymic links in conversations or in your own thinking, when thoughts come in quick succession.

A moment of verbal playfulness involves a release of energy (that momentary lightness of spirit), the taste of which might enable you to recognise similar energies arising from noticing.

Set yourself to notice frozen metaphors: words which were originally from one context (such as battle) and are now used implicitly in another context (such as describing or conducting arguments). A rich source is in educational discourse.

Set yourself to attend to the flow of an informal conversation, and be on the lookout for jumps. One way is to record the first few words of what each person says in turn.

The point of these exercises is not to criticise or judge others, but to heighten your awareness of your experience of metaphoric resonance and metonymic triggering.

Labelling

It often helps to have names for complex ideas as Auden and others have noted: if we haven't labelled something, it escapes our notice. As an issue emerges, or a type of situation develops in which you would like to respond differently, then choosing a label for its playfulness to trigger awareness can be very helpful. For example, when I recognise that children (or adults) have forgotten again, I want to be able to respond differently to my automatic complaining–criticising voice. So I choose a label: perhaps *Againing*, or *Forgotten* (in the sense of 'we've forgotten Miss'). The point about a well chosen label is that it has potential for metonymic triggering. For example, perhaps some of the words are quite likely to arise naturally early in the situation as it unfolds. It also needs to become associated with a rich collection of different accounts and alternative strategies which people have employed. Then, in the moment, your mind is able to present you with an alternative *as the situation develops*, and not merely in retrospect.

You may have noticed how odd it is that when you return from holiday there are numerous references in the media to where you have just been, or that when you change your make of car you suddenly notice how many of that make there are on the road, or when you hear a new word you suddenly seem to hear it repeatedly in all sorts of different places. This phenomenon is due to a change in sensitivity. A change in sensitivity often comes about through a particular word having enhanced richness of personal meaning, or because it triggers connections which are particular to you.

For example, I described earlier how you can sensitise yourself to certain words like *it*, *just*, and *should*. Particular words which become sensitised can trigger your attention to shift from the content of what is said, to the way it is said, or to some otherwise hidden aspect. As another example, if you prepare yourself so that when you find someone saying things you don't agree with, the situation triggers the thought 'look for the truth in what they are saying', you can experience a complete change of state, and get something positive from an otherwise apparently useless exchange.

Sometimes labelling is easy but finding alternative strategies is not.

Account 25: Plops

In a session with other teachers concerning the use of computer programs with young children, Rick said: 'I was just thinking how this could work with my class. I don't think I would use the full program, though'. Dead silence. The group sat expressionless.

(Rick Johnson, private communication)

When this account was reported to a group of colleagues, there was also dead silence. Then someone called it a 'plop'. Having just experienced one themselves, they of course all recognised it! There are two aspects: what to do when leading a session and something plops, and avoiding making a contribution to a group which plops. In order to do something about plops in your sessions, it is essential to have something come to mind in the moment, something you can say or do. For example, asking people to discuss in pairs what was just said and what reaction they have to it, what the person who said it could be thinking, what hidden assumptions might lie behind the contribution, or something similar.

However, what is effective may depend on why the contribution plopped, so you need to make further observations.

You need to try to catch what it is about contributions that makes them plop. You do this by thinking back to past plops and trying to see what it was that might have made the contribution plop, and setting yourself to look out for actual or potential plops, perhaps even making a note about them in order to accumulate examples. You can also try to catch yourself about to make a contribution to a group and asking whether it is likely to plop. To guard against instigating a plop yourself, you would act the same way, looking back to past plops, looking out for plops in the future, and trying to catch the moment before you make a contribution.

By describing instances to colleagues, and listening to their descriptions, you can pick up strategies that other people use to avoid or deal with plops, or for whom plops are not an issue, and you can negotiate a range of examples (including deciding that some are non-examples) which illuminate dimensions of the tension you feel about plops. In the process you may begin to distinguish different kinds of plops, factors which contribute to plops, and factors which render plops unlikely or not problematic (for example, the ethos and practices of a group).

I chose the 'plop' example because it relates more generally to picking up ideas, strategies, devices and acts from other people's descriptions and modifying them for your own purposes. There is no need to try to replicate what someone else claims to do, or what you think you see them do. To be effective, you have to modify things to suit you and your own circumstances.

Sensitising yourself to certain key words, such as 'plop', is one form of labelling, in which a few words serve as a focus for a constellation of associations and actions that you might take. For example, in illustrating the difference between accounts-of and accounting-for, and the virtues of brief-but-vivid descriptions, the terms *account-of–account-for* and *brief-but-vivid* were deliberately used as technical terms. They are intended to act as focal points for associations and strategies to use in relevant situations. They can label not just a single instance, but a whole class of incidents and responses, providing access to experience and meaning.

Labels can be single words that describe specific situations, or they can consist of several words which summarise a structure of distinctions. Examples which many teachers have found useful range from

> words for particular strategies like *pausing*, or *talking in pairs*,
> triads like *Manipulating–Getting-a-sense-of–Articulating*, or *Do–Talk–Record*,

which can trigger awareness of students' need for time and support in making sense, and give access to a range of other strategies for use in the moment, to

> phrases such as *Seeing the general in the particular* and *Seeing the particular in the general*, *Only awareness is educable*, and so on, which when triggered provide access to a whole range of attitudes and approaches to teaching.

Of course, if the labels are not familiar and are not meaningfully linked to personal experiences, then they are as liable to alienate as engage.

An incident described earlier in the context of brief-but-vivid accounts also serves as an excellent example of the use of labelling.

Account 26: *Wrong answer (p. 48) (yet again)*

I asked my five year old what three times four was, and he replied 'seven'. So I spontaneously asked 'what is three *plus* four?' (emphasis on the italicised word). He said 'Oh, twelve'.

I reported earlier that it was reading a similar description in a book which crystallized the incident, helped me to mark rather than merely notice it. It helped me to recognise it *as* an incident typical of many. I felt moved to label this type of interaction *jump response*, and to look out for it in future. A more descriptive label might be

answer to a related question I might have asked but did not

but that is rather long and complicated to act as a label. Sometimes it is tempting to use a person's name to label an incident. Such idiosyncratic labels may work well for one person, but are much harder to use with colleagues, for one person's familiar name is not likely to act vibrantly for someone else. Effective labels tend to be succinct, catchy, and to use words which might be expected to arise in a corresponding situation. Over time I discovered that *jump response* triggered a different collection of incidents for people, so I relabeled it *asking the question answered*. Although it is not very catchy, it at least is an accurate description. It is typical of negotiating with colleagues what constitutes an example, and choice of label for a collection of incidents, that labels will change as the instances are collected and further distinctions are made.

Every so often something about a student's response makes me ask the 'other' question which the person may have been answering. I may be reacting, triggered subconsciously to ask the 'other' question. Alternatively, I may become explicitly aware of the situation as an example of *asking the question answered*. In that case, the label serves to help me recall that incident, to distinguish it from the flow of events, to mark it, and so to have access again later. It is difficult to describe precisely how a label functions because it often works below the level of consciousness. It is part of a developing 'common sense' or intuition, the education of awareness.

In one sense, a label brings the phenomenon into existence as a 'thing' which can be recognised in other contexts, or associated with alternative actions. In another sense a label separates or isolates certain features and induces me to ignore others that might also be worth attending to. There is always the possibility that what I think I see, what I bring into existence through naming, is merely a fantasy, a desire for simplicity in a complex situation, which obscures seeing other features. But to be open to everything is to see nothing. Seeing demands selection and distinction making.

Account 12A: *Getting power* (p. 48) provides a good example of how a label can operate, both positively and negatively. The word *power* seems to have triggered access to a number of awarenesses, but with such intensity that the author reports being caught up in the flow of her own enthusiasm. So a label can serve to trigger a response, which may or may not be under direct control. For example, it has been suggested (Cheryl Cox, private communication) that for pharmacists, drug names can become labels for patients, in the sense that patients are recognised as 'the one on such a such of combination of drugs'. This kind of labelling makes it more difficult to be sensitive to the person. Part of the work in the Discipline of Noticing is to develop sensitivity, to gain control so as to participate in choice rather than following whatever impulse arrives.

Prestage and Perks (1992) offer an example of a label arising spontaneously amongst a class of graduate novice teachers. They report the session as starting with a reading from *Paddington Bear* (Bond 1971) in which Paddington correctly answers the question:

> if you cut a piece of wood eight feet long in half, and then cut each piece in half again, and then each in half again, how many pieces will there be?

but when asked how long they will be, answers 'eight feet'. It transpires that he imagined 'cutting them the other way'. When challenged that it was more natural to cut them across than lengthwise, the author has Paddington reply 'not if you're a bear!'.

Prestage and Perks report that a short time later, a heated debate arose in the same class in response to the pupil task

> How many 9s are there in 171? Check by multiplying.

One person wanted to answer 'none' (in the sense that the number uses only 1s and 7s!). The label 'Doing a Paddington' was used, and this in turn suggested a general strategy of taking a question and finding as many different interpretations as possible, leading to creative problem posing and contact with challenging, self-posed questions and generalisations. For members of that class, *Doing-a-Paddington* began to serve as a trigger to action (generating different interpretations) and as a reminder to look behind children's responses when they seem off beam instead of assuming they are either confused, wrong, or stupid.

When a group of colleagues discover (through working on activities, exercises, or anecdotes) that they have similar experiences and problems, the ground is laid for the introduction of a label or labels which remind them of specific experiences and of general principles. The labels become associated with significant moments or perspectives which in turn trigger access to useful strategies and thence a choice of subsequent behaviour. Through resonance with past experience and prepared strategies, labels enrich the meaningfulness of particular noticing.

However, as St Augustine pointed out (in 389 AD), you cannot learn the meaning of a word just from the word itself. You need to hear it used meaningfully (for you) in context. Even if you are given a definition, it helps to have a sample of its use, and bigger dictionaries provide this. St Augustine's point extends to behaviours and incidents as well: you cannot learn the meaning or import of a particular behaviour or of a kind of incident, just from the behaviour or incident itself. Meaning is to do with connection, with relationship, and this requires juxtaposition of the present with the past in some way. How this can be done effectively is part of the issue of validation taken up in the next chapter.

Framework-labels only serve a purpose when they crystallise or store a rich collection of experiences, and are associated with a variety of tried and tested strategies for responding in the moment. Richness arises from working with colleagues, extending and confirming the range of tactics and extending and re-shaping the experiences which the frameworks help you to recall.

> ### Some things to try now
>
> Make a list of key words that come to mind when you are preparing a lesson or in the midst of teaching, and see to what extent they act as labels for you. Try to relate them to specific typical incidents. Do colleagues use the same labels? In the same way?
>
> Choose some typical situation which is emerging for you as something you want to work on or have more choice about, and find a label which you can apply to it. Try using a child's name to label something that you noticed when interacting with them, and compare the effectiveness of that kind of label to one which uses ordinary words (as in account-of–accounting-for).

Towards a summary of noticing: some useful neologisms

The structure of words in English is often useful for making distinctions, even where an English speaker does not immediately recognise the particular form as an English word. For example, *reflection* is a popular word, which can be decomposed as *re* with *flection*, meaning 'bending', but together meaning 'looking back'. This enables us to replace the *re* with other prefixes, such as *preflection* meaning 'to look ahead', and then to use the root *flection* to refer to noticing in the moment (bending in order to look at the immediate).

Similarly, *preparation*, based on the root *paration* or 'readiness', stresses something done in advance, and so could admit *postparation* as something done afterwards, and then *paration* as 'readiness to act in the moment'.

Again, *inspection* is derived from the stem *spective* or *spection*, which appears in words such as *spectacle, introspection, retrospective, spectacular, respect*, and so on. Since *retrospective* means to look back afterwards, and *prospective* means to look forward, *spective* can be taken to mean to look in the moment, neither before nor afterward, which is the core of noticing.

The same root can be used to construct *interspection* (to look between, as in two observers sharing what they see) and *intraspection* (to look within, as in an inner witness). Both are different from *introspection*, in which one person thinks back retrospectively over their own experience, and speculates as to what they might or must have been doing and thinking, and which was found to be an unreliable source of psychological data (see Gardner 1985, chapter 5).

Adding prefixes to *spection* gives:

- *extra-spective* observation (observing from outside, thus emphasising subject-object distinctiveness);
- *intraspective* observation (in which an inner witness observes the self caught up in the action, yielding inner objectivity experienced subjectively); and
- *interspective* observation (in which people share observations as witness to each other, yielding objectivity from negotiated subjective observation).

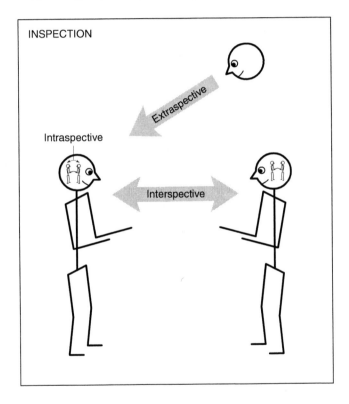

The term *introspection*, while potentially useful to describe self-observation, has too many negative associations and resonances with investigations in the early twentieth century to be useful. People reported on what they experienced in experimental situations (which they themselves had devised), often deciding that they 'must have' experienced or felt something, and this was taken as primary and unchallengeable data. The rigidity of behaviourism arose partly in response to excesses of the introspectionists, and now, in trying to re-achieve balance between the external and the internal observer, the term is too tainted.

Traditional research methodologies are based on *extra-spection*. Studying what students, teachers, and other practitioners do, both inside and outside of institutions, by observing, probing, analysing, making distinctions, and explaining and theorising, is valuable work. Its products can alert practitioners, individually and collectively, to absences of sensitivities, to habits which are getting in the way, and to alternative actions. By contrast, *intraspection* describes the development of an inner observer who watches and witnesses, and when strengthened, can inform practice in the moment by awakening the functioning self to alternative possibilities. *Spection* is being awake in the moment, noticing and responding freshly and creatively in the instant, catching oneself before embarking on habitual behaviour. Developing *spectivity* is the central aim of noticing, enabling *intraspection* to take place.

Interspection describes interactions between colleagues who go beyond extra-spection and begin to form a shared or taken-as-shared (Cobb 1991) world of experience. They develop labels for collections of similar incidents and actions to trigger a rich web of negotiated description and experience. One by-product of sharing descriptions is that strategies and gambits emerge which can turn into possible responses in the future.

These neologistic constructions form useful sloganated summaries of the Discipline of Noticing from slightly different perspectives:

Noticing–Marking–Recording
(as states and as energies)

Preparation–Paration–Postparation
(the essence of noticing based on the root meaning *to get or be ready*)

Extra-spective–Intraspective-&-Interspective
(as forms of research based on what is studied and how)

Prospective–Retrospective–Postspective leading to Spective
(the essence of noticing based on root meaning *to spy, to watch*)

Preflection–Flection–Reflection
(the essence of noticing based on the root meaning *to bend*)

These can be cross-connected as in the following diagram, in which noticing–marking–recording feed awareness of acts, of incidents, and of issues. This awareness, this noticing, tends to be after-the-fact, after the moment has passed, but there are ways in which noticing can become more and more *au point*. In other words, noticing in the moment can be prepared for, enhanced, encouraged, supported, through intentional work, both before and after an event.

Recording what is marked (so as to be able to recall) is the fundamental action which, when used with acts, incidents, and issues to look forward and to look back, contributes to awakening and sensitising an inner witness. The inner witness at first acts *retrospectively* (I am alerted soon after the moment) but gradually the awakening moves into the moment. This movement is the essence of noticing (Bennett 1976). The issue of validity is the subject of the next chapter.

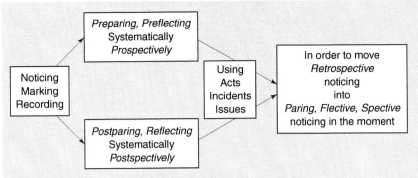

Transforming *Retrospective* into *Spective*

Summary of Chapter 5

The ordinary notion of noticing has been developed into a collection of systematic practices to support and enhance sensitivity to notice, and to make it possible to act upon that noticing, that is, to respond rather than to react as events unfold.

The Discipline of Noticing can be summarised in four interconnected actions (including seeking resonance with an ever expanding community of colleagues which is developed in the next chapter). These actions do not form a sequence to be followed mechanically, nor can any of them be usefully undertaken superficially. They are all aspects of bringing the moment of noticing from the retrospective into the spective, into the moment, so that a choice can be made to respond rather than to react habitually.

- *Systematic reflection*: collecting brief-but-vivid accounts-of salient incidents, working on them so that others recognise something from their own experience; developing sensitivities by seeking threads among those accounts, and preparing oneself to notice more detail in the future.
- *Preparing and noticing*: imagining oneself acting in some desired manner, using the power of mental imagery to direct and harness emotions, and gradually noticing more and more opportunities; reflecting on the past by re-entering situations as vividly as possible and preparing to notice in the future by imagining oneself choosing to act.
- *Recognising choices* by accumulating alternative actions and by working at bringing the moment of noticing into the present; being on the lookout to notice alternative behaviours or acts (in other people's accounts, in texts and articles, while observing others in practice) which you would like to incorporate into your practice;
- *Labelling* salient incidents and alternative acts so that they begin to form a rich web of interconnected experiences associated with particular collections of incidents, and linking these labels with specific incidents so as both to enrich the moments and to empower the labels to act as triggers to notice fresh opportunities to act in the future.
- *Validating*, through a process to be described in the next chapter.

Most of the aspects of noticing described so far fit with any approach to improving practice and carrying out research. Development of the Discipline of Noticing is a personal and collective enquiry into how to sharpen moments of noticing so that they shift

> from retrospective 'I could have . . .' or 'I should have . . .'
> to presently spective 'I could . . .' so that you can participate in making a choice,

by means of

> descriptive but non-judgemental postspective review: 'I did . . .',

and

> prospective preparation of 'I will . . .' using the power of mental imagery.

> ### Try this now
>
> Through recollection of incidents and review of accounts you have made, choose something that you want to work at, and use mental imagery to prepare yourself to notice, not after the event, but while it is happening. This is the most difficult part of the discipline, for it requires effort and commitment. But it is well worth that effort, as the rewards are great. Despite temptations, try not to dissipate energy achieved through noticing in judgements and accounting-for. Wherever possible, use it to imagine acting differently in the future.

6 Validity

How do I know when I 'try something out' in practice that my assessment of its effectiveness is valid? Might I not just be fooling myself, wanting to see some improvement? If there is a group of us, how can we guard against fooling ourselves collectively? Is what I am noticing going to serve in other situations, and if so which ones, or is it entirely situated in the circumstances which gave rise to it? How can I recognise the scope of applicability of an action?

These are not easy questions, for they have triggered generations of thinkers into trying to formulate methods of research which would yield 'true' or 'valid' knowledge. Montaigne claimed that the only sure witness is oneself, but Lytton (1840) noted that the easiest person to deceive is oneself.

Unfortunately, or perhaps fortunately, *no* attempt at delineating a fool-proof method has succeeded. Philosophers like Aristotle, who developed the logic of the syllogism, Leibniz who sought in Chinese hexagrams a basis for a computational logic for philosophy, and Boole who developed the algebra which governs digital computer logic, all failed in their hopes to find secure knowledge through logic. Mystics like Ramus who developed a mechanical device for juxtaposing terms and thus revealing knowledge, and mathematicians like Viète and Cardano, who hoped that algebra would provide the means for resolving all problems, were, in the end, confounded. There is no source of certainty, precisely because any 'truth' has to be asserted in some sort of language, and at the root of all language is generality and ambiguity, and hence interpretation.

There are times when we can be confident that someone is 'making up' their account, for something does not ring true with us, and there are times when what is asserted fits with our experience. On the other hand, sometimes what is asserted so matches our prejudices that we take it as truth because it fits so well, yet later we come to see our prejudice for what it is; sometimes an account seems so outlandish, literally, that we dismiss it, only to find later that we have begun to notice something similar ourselves. If only we could find a means to distinguish between these cases!

Validation

Yet not all is lost. The Discipline of Noticing confronts these issues head on by not trying to locate an absolute truth. It does not recommend making assertions about what is the case for other people at all. Rather, it suggests that the most one can do is to make conjectures about oneself, work on developing sensitivity for oneself to notice and to act, consult with colleagues, and hope that those colleagues also broaden their repertoire of acts, extend their range of sensitivities to notice, and participate in more and more choices. Thus the product of enquiry is not a collection of assertions of uncertain generality, but rather a *way of working* which may enhance sensitivity to notice, or, in other words, educate awareness. The acid test is whether colleagues find that their own noticing is enhanced and their future acts informed.

Personal validation means laying strands of your own experience alongside each other, comparing them, testing whether they do indeed sharpen sensitivities, conform with each other, and inform practice. These strands are themselves the result of selective stressing and ignoring based on personal propensities and sensitivities. For example, someone steeped in ideological conflict is likely to detect strands of ideological significance, while someone steeped in gender issues is likely to detect strands related to gender. Hence Goodman's (1978) wish that our theories be as fact-laden as our facts are theory-laden.

Collective validation means interweaving strands of your own experience with those of others, constantly seeking resonance, negotiating similarities and differences, locating issues, understandings and possible behaviour to employ in the future.

Of course there is no guarantee that colleagues will not be over-awed by a charismatic and forceful presentation. But if the community constantly and continually brings accounts of what is noticed to the surface, and keeps sensitivities to notice in question, then there is at least some hope that prejudice and desire will not dominate.

The heart of all knowing, of personal confidence, is based in a sense of fit and flow with events, and with acceptance in some community. If sessions seem to 'go better', if I am aware of making more choices and of those choices appearing to bear fruit, then my confidence level is maintained. If I find that colleagues also report similar observations, and if those observations are shared, discussed and challenged, then practices are unlikely to stay still and stagnate as unchallenged habit.

Thus it is vital to find some effective and consistent way of exposing one's own noticing to others. Since noticing is experiential, the best way to compare, discuss, and negotiate with others is through taken-as-shared experience.

Products of noticing

The fourth action of the Discipline of Noticing is therefore the construction, refinement, and modification of means to communicate and enrich noticing with others. This takes the form of tasks or exercises, which may provide others with the experience of noticing something . A particular form of task-exercise is proffering brief-but-vivid accounts and negotiating significance as well as similarities and differences between various accounts, and using these to re-call and re-member similar incidents.

More generally,

task-exercises are designed to provide access to something worth noticing, distilled from personal noticing, to produce some moment of awareness for others.

For example, the tasks proposed in previous chapters are of this kind. They have been refined and honed over many years of working with colleagues. The notion arose because I found that in conducting workshops on mathematics education it is essential to engage first in some joint mathematical activity, so that we have immediate access to experiences which resonate with the past, and through which we can try to make sense in new ways, thus informing the future.

As a more immediate example, consider the pictures shown in the panel.

What do you see?

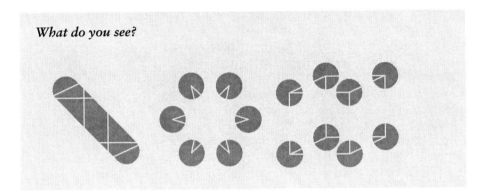

Comment

A careful account of what is seen refers to dark grey spots with light lines, channels, or Vs. Most people see a cube in the third which leads them to see a cube in the first, and either two bent-sided triangles or a six-pointed star in the second. The claim to see an object can be accounted-for by gestalt closure as part of culturally trained functioning of the neural network of the brain. The third figure has been likened to a white wall with eight windows into a darkened room containing a white cube. Careful inspection reveals that the first could be seen as a slanted window onto the same cube. Once it is suggested, it is not too hard to 'see' the missing parts. The second figure remains ambiguous, though people find that one or other reading seems more 'natural'.

This exercise provides a useful metaphor for observation. If you are not culturally sensitised to the standard drawing of a cube, you are unlikely to see a cube. The dark disks are like observations or samples. If you sample at certain 'points' of some situation you may be led to see something, and then to assume that there is a 'thing' to be observed. The second figure is a reminder that there may be considerable ambiguity (two stars or one). In fact there is no actual cube and no actual star(s), just as in other situations there may not be any 'thing' there at all, just an epiphenomenon due to fore-grounding and back-grounding, to cultural or professional assumptions, or to desire to find something.

This is an example of a task-exercise designed to prompt people to recognise the underlying metaphor and what it says about observation and research. The effect is much more powerful than simply making the same remarks without the exercise. Once colleagues have undertaken the task and discussed and negotiated what they have seen with each other, they are prepared to be able to hear and make sense of discussions about how research is also a sampling process and how observation depends on past experience, on what you are sensitised to see.

Just because colleagues also claim to see something does not guarantee that there is something to be seen, and claims not to see do not guarantee there is nothing to be seen. Absence of evidence is not evidence of absence, and evidence of presence may be enculturated or manufactured. But then there is no guarantee, nor can there ever be. As long as there is ongoing questioning there is movement. Francis Bacon (1604: 49) captures this well: 'So knowledge, while it is in Aphorisms and observations, it is in growth; but when it once is comprehended in exact Methods, it may perchance be further polished and illustrated, and accommodated for use and practice, but it increaseth no more in bulk and substance.'

Of course there is never any guarantee that what I notice as a result of a task-exercise is what others will notice. However, experience suggests that it is possible to refine task-exercises so that a few themes usually emerge strongly, and even where people do not spontaneously notice, they usually recognise what others describe. Thus task-exercises are a means to provide 'recent and relevant' experience on which to draw.

When colleagues reflect on their experience and describe briefly-but-vividly what they experienced (both in the present and in the past), there can be discussion about what is being noticed and about what is being illustrated. People can offer alternative ways of acting in such situations in the future, and colleagues can set themselves to look out for similar phenomena in their own practice. These task-exercises are offered to colleagues to see if they also notice what I am noticing; to see if they also find that they can mark incidents and have access to choices not previously available.

Where others report that they too 'have been thinking that but hadn't found a way to say it', or that they too now notice (or have noticed) something similar, there is the basis for shared development. Resonance with past experience, making new sense of that past experience, and informing the future, are the three criteria for validity of noticing.

In mathematics a single counter-example refutes a conjecture, or at least leads to some modification of the conjecture. In education things are very different. Theorising is not invalidated by identification of an awkward case. At best the theory is complexified and at worst it remains untouched. Ideas, observations and acts are neither right nor wrong. Rather they are ramifications of choices and manifestations of theories, however implicit and buried. What matters is to get to the heart of the moment of choosing, and not to be caught in a rut with habits that block us from seeing alternatives.

If a single colleague, or even all of my colleagues, reject an observation, fail to notice what I notice, or have alternative ways of accounting for it, then there are several possibilities:

- I may indeed be mistaken, I may be fooling myself;
- my colleagues may not be in an appropriate state or may not have the requisite experience to recognise what I am pointing to, or what I am pointing to may not connect with their current concerns;
- my task-exercises, or my approach to broaching the issue may not be well designed.

It is unwise therefore to jump to a conclusion that a particular one of these possibilities is operating, however attractive. For example, the second one seems to absolve me of any responsibility. Rather, one keeps all three possibilities open. Validation is a deeply philosophical issue, and some of the difficulties are taken up in Chapter 12 as a research issue.

Summary of Chapter 6

Validation of noticing and acting is based not on convincing others through rational argument or through the weight of statistics or of tradition, but rather through whether the other can recognise what is being described or suggested, usually through resonance with their own experience, and whether they find that their own sensitivities to notice are enhanced, so that their future practice is (literally) in-formed.

Noticing as a discipline can be thought of in terms of the merging of three worlds as shown in diagrammatically (p. 94) (a perspective developed from an idea of my late colleague Christine Shiu):

- the world of personal experience (where professional development takes place);
- the world of one's colleagues' experience, which is where one gets support, strokes, confirmation or challenge, and recognition; and
- the world of observations, accounts, and theories, which informs what might be noticed, structures what is noticed, and which develops with the keeping of accounts and the detection of threads amongst those accounts.

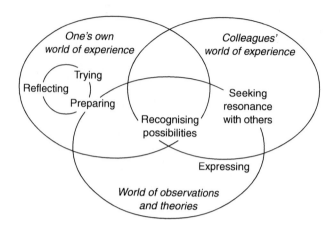

SUMMARY OF THE DISCIPLINE OF NOTICING

When something is noticed, even in retrospect, when a connection is made or an idea suddenly pops up, a little bit of energy is released. This can be released as pleasure, high spirits and self-confidence, and as self-chastisement, judgement and depression, or it can be used to enhance noticing in the future. Energy loss can be reduced by accepting rather than evaluating and judging, by acknowledging that things are not as they could be, and by resolving to be awake to opportunities in th95101).

It is essential to bear in mind that these aspects are merely ways of speaking. As Alfred Korzybski (1933) said, 'the map is not the country', while John Dewey (1929) reminds us, 'the map is not the journey'.

No summary, indeed no words with diagrams can be anything other than indicators. They are merely signs signifying that some traveller has passed this way, and suggesting that there may be something useful to look at or to experience. At best they are idiosyncratic maps sketched with the socio-cultural tools available. To be useful they require re-construction and re-expression by each individual in each generation. A representation only represents something to someone who can see through the presentation. An example only exemplifies to someone who can see through the particular to some generality, and who can see particularity in generality.

My desire to express, manifested in this book, is but one paltry aspect of the embodied action which constitutes my practice. It is my earnest hope that my descriptions 'preach my practice', whereas struggling to 'practise what I or someone else preaches' is liable to divert attention away from experience. Where what is written triggers resonance (whether confirming or conflicting), something valuable may emerge. Where what is written turns into ritualised behaviour, nothing much will happen. Where one is working with others, trying to control or direct what they do and how they do it usually ends in dissatisfaction for at least one party, whether through failing to comprehend generatively through a

Keeping and using accounts, through noticing, marking, and recording brief-but-vivid moments, and considering what might have been done, in retrospect; looking back over a period to find common threads, themes, and issues

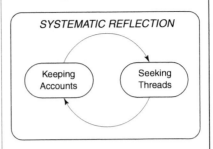

Being alert to the actions of others, as distinct from the effects of those actions, helps extend the range of acts and tactics upon which to draw; picking up ideas of ways to act from other people and from writing and thinking, making a note of these. Identifying and labelling typical situations can help recognition occur in the future.

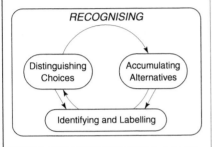

Developing sensitivities through vividly imagining oneself carrying out chosen acts in order to make it more likely that they come to mind in the moment in the future; setting oneself to notice specific events or acts.

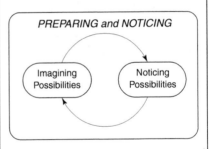

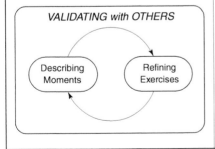

Selecting and honing descriptions which others instantly recognise; refining task-exercises which highlights fruitful issues or sensitivities.

regime of assenting not asserting, or whether through disappointment that proposals seem not to be taken up and activated.

There are dangers in any attempt to express, because expressing necessarily involves over-stressing. Put another way, give a small boy a hammer and everything becomes a nail; introduce someone to a way of perceiving and everything is seen through that perspective. Enthusiasm energises particular sensitivities, particular stressings, and so possibilities are seen everywhere. What has been described here has been reconstructed from many other authors and from personal work. What you as reader make of it will only emerge over time as any immediate inspiration or energisation settles down, and peripheral issues fall away to leave a residual core of awareness and sensitisation. Some aspects may be incorporated (literally, drawn into the body of one's practice). Mixing and matching with other approaches and assigning to a pigeon-hole ('Oh that's just . . .') is not wise, for that is how stimuli are nullified and neutralised. An excess of tools can be just as deadening as an absence.

In a sense one can only develop sensitivity, become adept at stressing some features while consequently ignoring others. In other words, as Gattegno (1987) said so often, one can only educate awareness. But to educate awareness one also needs to train behaviour, and this one does through harnessing emotion, the source of psycho–socio–cultural energy. That is exactly what the Disipline of Noticing is designed to do, and it consistently speaks to its own internalisation. As Maturana (1988) said, 'Reason drives us only through the emotions which arise in us', which is why the practices which make up the Discipline of Noticing depend on accumulating energy which arises from noticing.

Part III is the core of the book. Parts I and II were by way of introduction, and Parts IV, V and VI place noticing in a more general context, showing that it lies at the heart of research while at the same time providing a paradigm for enquiry into one's own practices.

Part IV

Using aspects of the Discipline of Noticing

Part IV is a kind of interlude between professional development and research. It offers opportunities to work on some aspects of the Discipline of Noticing in a disciplined fashion which are useful in different contexts, before going on to the next sections which look at research in general and at noticing in particular as a feature of research, and as a method of research itself. There are far fewer 'tasks' offered, but a great number of techniques for working-on and working-with accounts. As such this section acts as a compendium or handbook of techniques rather than a narrative development of the Discipline of Noticing. If you are interested in aspects of research then it may be sensible to go on to Part V and to return to this part when you are creating and working with some accounts.

Chapter 7 looks again at the distinction between *account-of* and *accounting-for*, since it is of use whenever one is trying to communicate with colleagues about professional matters, whether informally or in a formal setting. It describes different sources of accounts, reviews aspects of working on accounts, and provides some accounts to work on. Chapter 8 looks in more detail at the fundamental action which precipitates enquiry, professional development, and research, namely disturbance, and suggests some useful forms of disturbance-generating activities. Chapter 9 considers briefly the use of aspects of the Discipline of Noticing when leading professional development for others. Throughout, the notion of accounts as 'records of events' corresponds to George Herbert's (1633) glass on which one's eye may stay:

> A man who looks on glass,
>> On it may stay his eye
> Or if he pleaseth, through it pass,
>> And then a heaven espy.

Deeper potential lies in looking through the glass, through the accounts, in order to learn about the world through learning about oneself, reaching a climax in researching from the inside in Chapter 13.

7   Probing accounts

This chapter reviews and extends the use of the distinction between a phenomenon and explaining-theorising about that phenomenon, that is between accounts-of and accounting-for. To begin, you can work on accounts by refining them to make them brief-but-vivid so that they speak to the experience of others as described briefly in Chapter 5 but here considerably extended. This treats each account as an individual entity. Collections of accounts can also be probed and analysed as collectivities. The most important thing to remember is that, although you *can* treat accounts as data, as the things to be analysed, the Discipline of Noticing treats accounts as entries into or pointers to experiences, which constitute the actual data. Probing and analysing accounts is really probing and analysing experience.

Collections of accounts can be used to reveal what individual accounts cannot, by looking for threads or underlying principles such as similarities between accounts (your own, or different people's), by probing what it is that makes an account significant for you, and by using accounts as a kind of currency to exchange with colleagues in order to develop a shared vocabulary for talking about professional tensions and issues. You can also use accounts of one or more particular incidents to locate a more general phenomenon (a sense of the particular as an example of something more common or more general). Other people's accounts, whether verbatim or in the professional and research literature, also provide a source for elements of actions to try out for yourself in the future, while drawing on personal accounts is the most effective way of making sense of reading research literature.

While accounts may provide insight into a particular situation, they may also act as a mirror in which to see yourself through attending to the features which you find striking, and through allowing your own personal experiences to come to mind as additional incidents for yourself, or to share with others. Furthermore, you can look for what you are not seeing by working with others, comparing notes, and seeing what they notice that you do not, and you can enquire into why someone else's account does not mention details which would have been important or informative for you. You can also make use of the literature to connect or distinguish your experiences with those recorded by others. In your own accounts, you can reflect on what in your past disposed you to select those incidents and not others, or to describe those aspects and not others. Thus you can use your own and others' incidents as a mirror in which to learn about yourself.

As suggested earlier, in order to be maximally communicative, and in order to enable others to consider and discuss the effectiveness, appropriateness or insightfulness of some analysis of some phenomenon, it is vital to strive first to locate and agree what that phenomenon is. This applies to any form of qualitative research, and many kinds of quantitative research as well. Thus drawing up accounts-of incidents and situations which describe instances of a proposed phenomenon is a useful skill in and of itself.

The aim is to construct brief-but-vivid accounts with a minimum of accounting-for so that listeners and readers are able to recognise the sort of situation being described. This means concentrating on words which describe behaviours, which describe what could be seen, heard, or otherwise sensed, what could be agreed, or at least, what could have been agreed by participants had they actually been there. It means removing speculation ('I must have . . .', 'probably . . .'). It means removing judgemental and evaluative words, ('unnecessary', 'better', etc.), as well as attempts to justify or explain actions or opinions ('because . . .', 'since . . .', 'therefore . . .'). It means replacing emotion laden terms which are interpretations of behaviour ('angrily', 'condescendingly', 'happily', etc.) with descriptions of that behaviour.

Where the incident involves other people and things, then one can imagine that if a video had been taken, it would be possible to negotiate details such as that 'someone came into the room', which is what is seen (more precisely still, 'the door opened and a person was seen entering the room') whereas 'she angrily threw open the door', or 'he timidly slipped into the room', while evocative, involve unnecessary interpretation, at least in the first instance. They are the stuff of novels, not of enquiry. It may transpire that everyone reads the behaviour in the same way, but assuming this while drawing up the description may not be wise.

Where the incident is a description of oneself, it is hard, but well worth, probing beneath the veneer of emotions, feelings, and thoughts to try to get at sensations, and the triggers and associations which bring thoughts to mind. It is as if there were an inner video-camera, and again, the description sought is what might then be negotiated by viewers of that video. The result will be that colleagues are more likely to be able to recognise what you are describing in their own experience.

To be maximally useful, accounts may need to be created, worked over, and re-worked over. This chapter develops in three phases: creating accounts, working on or working over accounts to hone them, and working with accounts to extract the maximum benefit from them. There is then a section on working on accounts with others, followed by a collection of accounts to serve as stimulus to collect your own and to use as fodder for trying out the various forms of analysis suggested in this chapter.

Creating accounts

At the most basic level, a few brief words scribbled down during a pause or at the end of a session can be used to trigger access back into the moment at a later date. For example,

Account 27A: Two boys

Boy at front, hand up, talking at length; boy at back silent and slouched.

These notes were made immediately after a lesson I observed. They are unlikely to mean much to anyone else, for they are very brief personal memory triggers which enable me, for a time, to re-enter a moment of noticing. Being so succinct, re-entry may become increasingly hazy over time, and the incident may be overlaid with others, so it is worthwhile refining the account as soon as possible. Note that the moment of noticing may appear to concern something external (two boys in a lesson), but in fact what was actually noticed was a shift in my attention, something internal (a change in my state, or attention). That sudden shift may be linked to a mixture of external triggers (contrast between two boys' behaviour) and internal triggers (shift from focusing on the content to focusing on what it is like to be in the lesson).

In order to be useful, accounts need to be brief-but-vivid for other people as well as for yourself. Thus the incident referred to above, when re-entered a week later and expanded, became

Account 27B: Two boys (again)

The teacher asked a question and again, almost immediately, the boy on the teacher's extreme left at the front put up his hand. Again he was called upon, and went on at length, not always articulately, but offering the nub of relevant and important ideas. I was aware at the same time of a boy at the back right slouched in his chair, head down, only occasionally looking at the teacher, saying and offering nothing.

There are some evaluative terms (offering relevant and important ideas), which do not add to the contrast I was experiencing between the two boys' participation, but also some potentially emotive terms (slouched, at length) which could be refined.

In the session I found myself wondering why the teacher kept allowing the boy at the front to speak, and was not calling upon the boy at the back. I noticed that I was assuming the boy at the back was not paying attention and was probably a weak student.

In fact the teacher later told me that the boy at the back was very quick but refused to do homework every night, and hence was getting into trouble with several teachers, even though he would suddenly hand in several nights' work in this class, perfectly done. Thus my initial noticing led to some assumptions which turned out to be wrong, showing the value in marking if not recording so as to enquire later before drawing conclusions. The incident represents for me the value of a having a collection of strategies for calling upon, or not calling upon different students, and the dangers in jumping to conclusions about another teacher's use of such strategies.

Keeping a diary and recounting events is valuable for calming down when there are strong emotions present, or when you are unclear about what action to take in some situation. But usually the strong emotion colours the narrative. Writing affords an opportunity to justify oneself and explain away what has happened. It may *then* be possible, in working through the narrative, to pick out one or more moments of significance, and to give an account with reduced emotive content. But it is also possible that the calming that takes place through the initial writing absorbs all the energy produced by noticing sharply, so that there is nothing left later except the record of once-strong emotions.

The essence of a useful account is a moment of noticing which may be recorded directly, or may be extracted from a more lengthy narrative of an incident, which in turn may have had considerable emotional impact. The moment of noticing may be focused on an incident involving the behaviour of other people, or on some internal incident involving your own psycho-social state of awareness. In the final analysis, noticing begins with a change in your own state, a shift in the locus and focus of your attention.

Describing feelings and emotions in terms of physiological responses is helpful so that others can recognise the state rather than trying to reconstruct it through labels for emotions which are very general and abstract.

For example:

Account 28A: Anger

I overheard a colleague asking for an extension on the deadline, when I had worked hard to meet that same deadline. I was furious.

The first part is readily recognisable, but the 'being furious' does not tell us very much. If the description is probed for physiological and cognitive displays, then we might get closer to recognition of the anger, and perhaps also to what exactly was generating the emotional response. For example:

Account 28B: Anger (again)

I overheard a colleague asking for an extension on the deadline, when I had worked hard to meet that same deadline. I felt my body go tense; images of having stayed up late myself and all the consequences ran through my head; a deep sense of unfairness, of having been short-changed flowed through me.

Now more is recognisable and more is revealed. Here is an account written by someone shortly after meeting the distinction between account-of and accounting-for for the first time.

Account 29: Listening

I have been attending listening courses off and on for the past three years. I notice that although I have improved a lot, I still try to anticipate what somebody is going to say and often prompt them with a word or phrase. And I never stop saying 'mmm, mmm'. Even the other day as I was teaching some Xhosa children and asking for their names – I was sort of impatient to hear them, then tried to pronounce their names correctly, repeated their names more than once, instead of listening the first time and being more patient – sometimes one is worried that the other children will lose attention if one takes too long with an activity in the round on the mat, yet here was I ending up taking time by not listening. (Andrea Henderson, private communication)

Notice how the account begins with a generality. We may feel we recognise the sentiment, but we are not given anything specific to connect with. It feels necessary to 'set the context', and it summarises a personal concern. But it does not actually help the reader. Then there is the incident, and at the end we have a justification for not taking adequate time, despite recognition later that taking that time might have been more efficient in the end. Note the shift in pronoun from *I* to *one*, signalling a shift from specific to general, from account-of to accounting-for. Of course it is important when teaching not to spend too long on an activity, but justification leaks the energy from the awareness of being impatient, leaving only a shell of an incident behind.

The next account is by contrast both very brief and without overt judgement or evaluation:

Account 30: Changing chairs

I suddenly realised that in this second session, most people were sitting in a different place to where they sat in the first session.

Although admirably brief and lacking in overt value judgements, there is not much content either. There could be an implicit judgement (perhaps changing places is desired, or a surprise), but the account offers no indication of anything problematic for the person rendering the account. Because of this, it does not provide access to a situation. At best we learn that the person making the account was sensitive to the issue of where people sit in sessions, and there may be recognition that quite often people tend to sit in the same place. That could serve to raise a question of how to get people to change places, or whether it matters, but there are better ways to do this. For example, an account might report the experience of concern that people were sitting in the same seats session after session.

One lesson from this last example is that there is usually something meaningful, something problematic or surprising which makes an incident memorable and worth recording.

Significance and dredging

Most often, the fact that an incident comes to mind means that it has some personal significance, simply because you have a sensitivity to notice. Thus the two boys incident (Account 27) is a particular instance for me of the issue of working with a group containing those who are insistent and those who are 'desistent', as well as an instance of the wisdom of not jumping to conclusions on the basis of a few interactions. Those who are loudly insistent and talkative may not 'have their brain in gear', while those who are 'desistent' may be taking it all in. By contrast, the 'changing chairs' incident (Account 30) may be relevant to the person recounting, but is not cast in a form which is likely to resonate with readers. It could conceivably catch someone's attention if they had not previously been aware of changing chairs in sessions as an issue, but even so, it is only likely to strike someone who recognises this *as* an issue for them. Thus significance may be very personal.

When you have a sense of meaningfulness associated with an incident, then it is worthwhile trying to locate other incidents which seem similar. This you do by a process of dredging.

You can deliberately dredge accounts by taking one, trying to locate similar instances in your past experience, and then recording these alongside the original. Then you can use an incident to try to locate other experiences at around the same time or in the same place. You don't even need an incident: you can choose a place or person, and try to recall as much detail as you can. For example, you can recall a particular room, or institution, or age, or person, and either consciously seek to add detail, or actively wait for detail to come to mind. People find that having recalled one incident from their past, for instance in a primary classroom, affords them access to other incidents in the same room, with the same teacher, or in the same school. Any one of these can then set off a trigger of associations to other incidents at other times and places.

Another approach to dredging is to take an account and to focus on the taste or flavour, the significance for you, rather than the detail. You then wait for something to come to mind. It is an odd process of relaxing yet remaining focused, remaining steadfast yet not striving. Instead of concentrating, you decentrate, retaining the flavour, the significance, the theme as a touchstone.

Dredging can be exciting and revealing, but most people find it much easier to do when there is some imposed outer discipline such as a leader who directs attention: 'take your chosen incident and try to re-enter it in as much detail as possible. . . . Now recall something else that happened . . .'. A collection of more elaborate methods of dredging can be found in Masters (1972).

Having collected one or more incidents which are personally significant, it is worthwhile working on your accounts so as to make them maximally resonant for colleagues. By exchanging accounts with others not only can you hope for insight from colleagues, but you can check that you are not manufacturing things. If others do not recognise what you are describing then possibly you are over stressing something, though it may also be that they are occupied with other matters and not sensitised in the way you are. By re-entering relevant moments you can try to probe what it is that makes them significant for you, by trying to locate hidden assumptions you might be making, personal investments which are blinding you to alternatives, as well as allowing yet more incidents to come to mind that might shed some light. This process can be allowed to turn into deep introspection if that appeals to you, but you can also direct your attention to actions to use in the future rather than dwelling in the past.

Moments of noticing can be professionally significant even if the initial trigger is not. For example:

Account 31: Is there anyone there?

Walking on a quiet mountain trail I suddenly became aware of the sound of dripping water, not full enough to be called a waterfall. The question popped into my mind: 'when there is no one here, is there still the sound of water dripping?'. I was aware at the same moment of philosophical precedents for this question. Then what popped into my mind was my wife's suggestion: sound requires a means of detecting local variations in the density of air, so for human beings, sound requires a human eardrum. When no human eardrum is present there is no (human) sound, even though there are still vibrations of the air. 'Sound' is thus a label for (human) interaction with vibrating air.

One significance for me is an analogy with noticing. When something is noticed and recounted, words are used (*cf.* sound of water falling) which immediately imply human experience and interpretation through invoking culturally influenced ways of speaking, with both personal and shared associations. The fact that there are words implies a possibility of making distinctions (*cf.* distinguishing air vibrations and recognising them as coming from dripping water). So too, when I notice something in a professional setting, my sensory apparatus and professional experience make distinctions, and some of these are referred to using words. What the words remind me of, like the sound of water falling, does not necessarily exist if there is no observer. However the fact of noticing implies that sensory triggers are present (*cf.* vibrations of the air), and may be detected and discriminated by a person sensitised to make such distinctions.

The purpose of an account is not to capture the totality of an incident (in this case the muscle tensions from climbing, the smell of plants, the warmth of the sun, the pastel colours of flowers, etc.). That is what novelists and poets try to evoke. Rather, the account tries to recreate or re-trigger a shift in awareness, a change in what is being attended to, a noticing.

Significance may appear in the form of familiarity, as in the above account. But it may be that incidents come to mind during reflective re-entry or re-construction without any obvious significance or thematic content. From a collection of incidents, whether thematic or not, patterns and themes may simply emerge, as a result of your dredging in a state of relaxation and openness, without personal judgement or justification.

Working on accounts

Creating accounts involves, as we have seen, more than making a few notes. Those notes have to have sufficient detail to trigger re-entry to the incident at a later date, and to enable others to recognise similar situations. But the core element of re-entry is not to recall the colour of the wallpaper or where you were standing, but rather to afford access to a shift in perception, in the structure of attention, in awareness. To make accounts useful it is necessary to craft them so that they afford access to moments when your attention changed suddenly. In this subsection I stress working-on accounts to refine them, and in the next subsection I stress working-with accounts to exploit and explore them. The difference lies more in your orientation than in what you do specifically.

To work on accounts effectively, it is worthwhile first attending to the description itself. Are there words which require cultural knowledge or experience that others may not share? Are there words which require or imply some conjecture or assumption which is imported by the speaker? Are there words which carry emotional overtones or which imply some sort of value or judgement? Are there hidden assumptions, and are these assumptions shared by the people to whom the account will be offered? Of course these elements can never be eliminated, but the acid test is whether the audience would be able to recognise and point to what is being described had they been present.

Reconnaissance with colleagues

Working on accounts with colleagues is valuable not only because different people can play the different reconnaissance roles (story-teller, detective and umpire) suggested in Chapter 3, but because through such experiences you can sharpen your ability to play all those roles for yourself when working on your own accounts.

As a contribution to professional development, accounts-of incidents provide both access to something to work on for yourself and a means to share experiences with others. The accounts themselves serve as reminders or triggers for colleagues to recall possibly similar experiences of their own. They too can try to describe these, and so a process of negotiation develops in which similarities and differences are located and shared.

Account 32: Evaporation

A colleague reported frustration when, in a chemistry class, the bell rang while the students were fully engaged with trying to carry out and explain a series of experiments; yet in the next lesson it seemed impossible to reconnect with the intensity and interest of the previous session. The energy seemed to evaporate.

A second colleague then recalled an incident in which she took a friend along on a trip which was an annual and personally meaningful one for her. She became frustrated when the friend did not find the trip equally meaningful. Her own sense of meaningfulness seemed to evaporate.

A third colleague reported that in her mathematics lessons evaporation of energy happened all the time, because the outcome-based perspective left children engaging in short unconnected tasks.

A fourth colleague suggested that the leader 'should have given them more time to master the rhythm task [a task that had been set earlier]'. 'The possibilities evaporated before the exercise really got going!'

A fifth colleague wondered how much of the excitement and stimulation of a year's masters course would be squeezed out (evaporated) upon returning to the classroom.

Here we have a mixture of degrees of brief-but-vividness, sparked off by the word *evaporation*. Through negotiation it was decided that the issue for the group was one of re-kindling interest from a previous lesson. The second account highlighted for us a different issue (wanting others to experience an intensity that I have experienced, and associated evaporation of that felt significance). The fourth was seen as tangential, in the sense that for us it highlighted the question of the purpose of tasks, and how to respond to students becoming interested in unintended and peripheral aspects (as seen by the teacher). The fifth was recognised as a concern, but was not pursued.

The first and the third spoke, however incompletely and generally, to the issue of having energy leaked away from having to stop work according to some imposed schedule. Further discussion led to descriptions of similar incidents in which there emerged tactics such as assigning someone to be time-keeper and to signal at a specified time before the bell rings, and ending the lesson with students summarising their current conjectures and concerns orally or in writing before the bell rings. To the extent that colleagues notice these tactics, see them as being relevant and possible to them, the negotiation serves both to highlight an issue, and to provide possible things to try out.

One way to distinguish professional development from research is that in professional development, accounts are used for personal and collective actions, trying out alternative responses in the future, whereas with research the tendency is to use accounts as the basis for theorising, for illustrating and justifying a particular perspective or way of accounting-for. The Discipline of Noticing straddles these two worlds, enabling professional development to become enquiry and hence research while at the same time remaining committed to enhancing one's sensitivity to notice in a more expert fashion, whether as a practitioner, as a researcher 'from the inside', or as a traditional researcher.

By going for details of particular incidents, it is possible to climb out of negative spirals, and to contribute positive pieces to your self image. This is particularly difficult for holists who tend to go for the 'big picture'. Significant personal growth and development only come from working against one's natural propensities, in order to both strengthen and diversify them. For someone who finds detail difficult, collecting specific incidents provides something concrete and specific from which to locate positive contributions. Someone with a propensity for detail may need to work at drawing threads together from many observations, letting go of detail in order to get a sense of significance and patterns.

It is important to observe that it is perfectly possible to over-do stress on creating accounts-of. There is no single account-of an incident which will work for all people at all times. Rather, the distinction between account-of and accounting-for is an awareness which can inform practice. In the midst of discussing some idea, principle, theory, action, or activity, you may notice that some disagreement or distinctive use of language indicates that there may be some ambiguity. Attention can then be shifted to seeking particular examples and checking that there is still agreement on what constitutes the phenomenon.

Grammatical pursuits

As mentioned earlier, the Greek rhetorical constructions of metaphor and metonymy play an important role in description and in the sequence of fragments of experience which William James (1890) called the 'stream of consciousness', and which we call our awareness. Accounts can usefully be probed for the use of metaphors, for although they are the basis for meaningful statements, they are also the source of habitual patterns of thinking and acting which you may wish to question and work on. Using metaphors which you know others will appreciate or subscribe to may achieve resonance, but may also obscure through chunking.

Accounts can be searched for metaphors deeply embedded in the language of the description by asking oneself: what images does this particular word bring to mind, and is that image appropriate, shared, or necessary?

Account 33: Stagnant

> When I was in year 6, there were two mathematics groups: Rushing Blue Water and Stagnant Green Water. After scoring low on a test my name was put into the green chart. When I became a teacher I did *not* use public displays of [evaluations of] students. Rather, I displayed . . . celebrations of success. (Beverly MacInnis, private communication)

Here the use of metaphoric labels for the two groups underpinned the distinction being made, and made a sufficiently emotional impact for Beverly to recall them later in relation to the way she chose to display children's work. Both metonymic trigger (through emotions) and metaphoric resonance (through the structure of displaying children's names as evaluation) are at work here. Note the effect of *my name was* (rather than *I was*) as a separation from the identification–evaluation when a child and not in control, and the repeated use of *I* subsequently, when an adult and in control of the situation. Work on this account might suggest the possibility of looking in accounts for uses of pronouns such as *I*, *me*, and *one* and considering whether they might signal issues of control (Rowland 1999a,b).

Account 34: Reflections

I am walking along a canal, and suddenly I notice that I can see sharp reflections in the water's surface: trees and the way the sun shines through them, weeds and water plants, the bridge, the swans. Yet a moment before I was not aware of seeing these reflections. It was as if I had been looking *in* the water not *at* the water itself.

In trying to make sense of my noticing, I am drawn to generalise: a potential principle emerges in the coming-to-expression of looking-at and looking-in as a summary or label for my noticing. The momentary shift of perception mirrors the momentary shift of attention which lies at the heart of noticing in the moment as a professional. This awareness tempts me to play with other prepositions that go with *looking* to try to find ones that really speak to experience. For the moment I stick with *looking in* and *looking at*. Then I realise that I have seen and used those expressions before. So the moment of noticing acts as a refreshment of previous awareness, even though in the moment, it seemed entirely novel. The noticing juxtaposes itself with a workshop I am to lead soon, and I find myself wondering if I can reproduce for others that moment of shifting from looking in the water to looking at the water. I resolve to take a tray of water and to place it near a window. I put a coin in the tray to attract attention to look in the water, and since, when experimenting, I found a significant difference between reflections in a white tray and a black tray, I make two different ones. A colleague on reading my account mentions Escher etchings, particularly *Three Words*, and I suddenly make a connection which I had not previously made, deepening my appreciation of Escher prints.

Here a single incident has both structural or metaphoric resonance (reflection in water and in mind; noticing being a sudden shift of attention) and a metonymic triggering (reflection as physics and as mental; my need for tasks for a workshop), leading to the identification of an awareness which has more general application.

A complementary use of grammar with accounts is to identify metonymies: gaps and *non-sequiturs* between consecutive sentences or even parts of sentences. While the person rendering the account may experience a rapid sequence of associative connections which gets them across the gap, others may be left mystified. Metonymic trails behind gaps can often be reconstructed by asking yourself what might link the two thoughts, what features of the first might, upon being stressed, make someone think of the second?

Account 35: Changing views

I was chatting to C on the phone about work. I asked her if she had viewed the videos we had scripted together and she said 'Yes . . . the children in

T&G's video were talkative, but the children in J's class were . . .' I interrupted C and completed the sentence: 'controlled?'. I was surprised at the word I used, and aware that I had previously thought that J's lesson on the video was good. (Agatha Lebethe, private communication)

This records a moment of Agatha catching herself having changed her view, through listening to someone else's views. C has drawn attention to a difference, which has in turn triggered the description 'controlled' below the surface of awareness. Here 'controlled' is used partly metaphorically and partly metonymically, since the children were not literally controlled by someone or something, but may have acted as if they were being restricted, confined, controlled. Something in the behaviour triggered that word in Agatha, but only after she was alerted to a difference. But what does 'controlled' mean here? There are many interpretations possible. Probing the account could lead to a more precise description of behaviour, which at the same time might reveal to Agatha what constitutes 'controlled' for her.

In speaking to close colleagues we rarely complete our thoughts, as they can pick up on a few cues and complete the thought for themselves. These sorts of gaps are also reflected in accounts.

Prolepsis and scripts

We make assumptions all the time about what we are seeing, hearing and feeling, so that often we see (hear, sense, feel) only what we expect. For example, when reading long words we tend to assume what the word is, from just part of it, and we even re-arrange letters unconsciously in order to manufacture a familiar word: the proprietary logo FCUK on clothing makes use of that tendency. Musicians see part of a chord structure and can fill in details without thinking, and sounds which are partly familiar are allowed to trigger images which may or may not be appropriate. These assumptions and triggered actions can be accounted for by the notions of scripts (standardised patterns), and prolepsis (speaking in code).

Have you ever overheard two colleagues talking in partial unfinished sentences yet seeming to make sense to each other? When we narrate an incident, we make assumptions about our listener, usually unconsciously. We speak or write in abbreviated form, because we assume that those we are speaking to recognise what we are referring to. For example, 'there should be a balance between different teaching styles' appeals to the commonplace that equity and balance are good, while imbalance and inequity are bad, but it makes this appeal very succinctly, assuming that the audience shares similar values. This aspect of communication is called *prolepsis*. It refers to the way in which our speech implicitly assumes a taken-as-shared collection of triggers to expanded meaning. For example, in this book the terms *account-of* and *accounting-for* are used proleptically to trigger a complex of values associated with distinguishing between a phenomenon and theorising about that phenomenon, with reducing emotive and evaluative aspects of descriptions, and so on.

Prolepsis is successful because we share certain standard cultural scripts (a pre-determined sequence of utterances and actions in the sense of a play or film). As long as reference is made to crucial items, the reader will read within that script. Thus

> John went to Bill's birthday party. Bill opened his presents. John ate the cake and left.

is construable only within familiarity with birthday parties (and the fact that John ate the cake before leaving suggests a North American party rather than an English one in which the piece of cake is often sent home as a present!) (Schank and Abelson 1977: 38). For example, in giving an account of a doctor's waiting room, there is no need to mention the receptionist, the magazines, the studied ignoring of other patients, the adult trying to rein in an active child, or the hopefulness that the waiting will turn into a remedy for our ailment. Similarly, there is no need in describing an incident in a hospital ward to mention the curtains, the tubes hanging from stands, the flowers, the regime of medicines and food brought round. These can all be assumed. And yet, 'the devil is in the detail'. As James Boswell (1791) put it, 'It is by studying little things that we attain the great act of having as little misery and as much happiness as possible.' It may be that prolepsis leads to overlooking crucial differences. In a classroom there are likely to be students and a teacher, but are the students in rows or round tables? Is the teacher in front of a board, walking around, or sitting at a desk dealing with a queue of waiting students?

Unfortunately, assumptions are tentacles that reach deep into our accounts. It is these very assumptions which hide values and interpretations, embedded habits and automatic reactions. One way to work on accounts, to hone them into instruments for useful work, is to locate implicit assumptions in evoked scripts. For example, you can look for stylised or coded ways of speaking which requires contextual experience in order to make sense of it. The best way to find these is to get a friend who does not share your experience to read through the material!

The presence of scripts usually comes to mind when there is a departure from a familiar script. For example, when reading a transcript of a nurse's interrogation of a patient, or of greeting the patient on first encounter that day, it is only when there is a departure from a script that I recognise I was embedded in an expectation. My sensitivities operate when the interaction departs from that expectation, producing a disturbance. When I ask students a question and get a response which is not what I expect, I suddenly become aware of what I did expect, because it becomes present in my thoughts even if I had not been explicitly aware of it before. It is then, and often only then, that I realise that the impulse to ask the question was in order to get the response I turned out to have in mind. So too when reading a transcript which instantiates a script, it is when there is some divergence that I become aware of the fact of a script being involved. This is an example of how disturbance is what provokes, energises, or enables noticing, a point taken up in the next chapter.

Try these now

Work on some of your own accounts to improve their brief-but-vivid qualities. Look for metaphors, for shifts in pronouns, for gaps which might signal a trail of metonymies, for prolepsis, and for fragments of scripts. Check by offering them to colleagues, to see whether they experience a sense of recognition, or even are stimulated to offer some accounts of their own.

Select one or two of the accounts in the section at the end of this chapter. See which ones speak to you and which do not, and consider what qualities of the accounts may be contributing to recognition or lack thereof. For example, are there evaluative or judgemental components? Are there embedded metaphors which do or do not resonate? Are there gaps suggesting trains of metonymies for the author that you do not share? Is use made of standard scripts?

Working with accounts

An account-of an incident is more than an object. It is an expression of sensitivity and of significance. It signals a focus, a perspective, which enables you to identify and elucidate a particular, and through this, to locate a general phenomenon. By focusing on accounts, you can enter a specific state of enquiry, which is among other things a release from the multiple associations and explanations of accounting-for. However, a protracted period of refining accounts to make them brief-but-vivid can make it difficult to stand back and use those accounts to achieve insight.

This subsection is about spontaneous and deliberate methods of working-with accounts in ways which flirt with accounting-for. There is a fine line between explaining away and theorising about, between justifying actions and uncovering justifications which you may wish to question or challenge because they limit your range of options at any moment. Again, describing evaluatively is not useful, but locating implicit values can be very useful in becoming aware of how you think about what you do, and allowing yourself to change.

The distinction between working-on accounts (crafting them) and working-with accounts (exploring and exploiting them) is certainly not a rigid one, for in the process of crafting you are likely to be exposing aspects to explore further, and in exploring you may find yourself re-crafting in order to focus attention even more sharply.

First, here is a quick summary of different uses of accounts, in order to set the scene for the ways of working to follow. There then follow some eleven slightly different but related ways of working with accounts. Trying to read them all one after another may not be the most useful way of drawing upon them as techniques. Rather, skimming to get a sense of what is suggested, then drawing on one or another in detail for use with some accounts of your own may be the most sensible approach.

What can accounts be used for?

Collections of accounts can be used in a wide variety of ways. They can be used:

- as the experiential base from which to draw out some threads or similarities;
- to illustrate issues, tensions, concerns, disturbances . . .;
- to reveal possible ways to respond to situations, and so both sensitise oneself to possible alternative responses in the future, as well as to recognising a possibility to act;
- as a device in professional development, by inviting people to seek similar or related incidents in their own experience; and
- to vivify an analysis based in some theoretical or ideological perspective, or a narrative weaving of various accounts into a story.

Keeping a notebook of incidents noticed is merely collecting; looking back over the accounts and seeking common threads and similarities is beginning to use the accounts to locate personal issues and concerns. Since what we notice is what we are sensitised to notice and what we are disturbed by, looking back over accounts can sometimes reveal things that we had not realised were issues.

Similes and analogues

Metaphor and metonymy are not simply implicit features within accounts. They are also grammatical actions which can be exploited intentionally by orienting oneself to be aware of analogues and similes with situations as they arise. For example, I watch a sheepdog at a dog trial and suddenly I am aware of a similarity with struggles to write a paper. The 'likeness' of simile can be developed into an analogy by recounting the sheepdog trial incidents which struck me and seem pertinent:

> The dog scoots out well to one side and gets in behind the group of sheep. Then it crouches low. At a signal it approaches gently, ever ready to dash to one side or another to direct a sheep back to the rest. Later, the dog has to separate one sheep out from the rest, then return it to the group and pen them all.

Of course what I choose to recount is already influenced by the simile that alerted me. Then I recount incidents, or a flavour of many incidents, when writing a paper.

> I have been trying to get down to writing this paper for some time. I have lots of ideas but I can't seem to pin them down; they flow one into another. I leave it for a time, bringing it back to mind in the shower, on the way to work, as I go to sleep. One morning I wake up and feel ready to write. I pick one idea. As it starts to develop I can sense the other ideas waiting to be picked up. I make a list of them as if they were outline headings. Then when

some detail comes to mind I can put it under the heading. Now as one idea starts to develop away from the main thrust I quickly move to pull it back (I am only allowed a few pages). As the paper grows I recognise that I could actually work on one aspect and simply refer to the others in passing. That way I would have more space to develop what is now falling into place. Eventually I finish and feel pleased that at least one aspect has been addressed.

Note: I mark, and hereby record, that I have intentionally not explored a further analogy with teaching. I *can* be selective!

The analogy between writing and herding is not exact, but it is illuminating for me, in that I see that I could trust ideas to fall into place if I were to exercise my cognitive skills (use examples, edit, select, connect, etc.). It is in-form-ative in that I can see how next time I can be more trusting. I can allow more space for the ideas to tumble around, and I can afford to be selective; I don't need to try to write everything I think of in every paper!

Here a single incident is recounted in retrospect, having been brought to significance by a resonance between structures I perceived between the sheepdog trial and my writing. Later I can hone the descriptions, explore the analogy further and more precisely, even find aspects which are not analogous. The analogy can also be captured as a metaphor: 'writing a paper is herding sheep', at which point I am led by a train of sounds and associations to shepherding, as in shepherding my thoughts, and so recognise through the metonymic word-play that the image of sheep herding has been used before in relation to thinking and writing.

Here is another example of metonymic triggering:

> I am reading a book in a café, when I overhear a conversation in which someone says '. . . red is not strong by itself, but only in contrast to not-red . . .'. But what I hear is '. . . read is not strong by itself, but only in contrast to not-read . . .'. My mind starts buzzing with whether I can make sense of this. Perhaps the suggestion is that where something stands out for me when I am reading, it is only by virtue of a contrast with something not read. Perhaps this means, in contrast with something in my own experience. Later I work out that I heard 'read' instead of 'red'.

The metonymy word-play of the homonym red–read sets me off in a direction based on my own awareness at the time, namely of reading, triggering thoughts about how reading depends on relating to experience. I managed to make some sort of meaning even though it had nothing to do with what was actually being said! These sorts of triggers, tripping lightly along the surface of meaning, happen so quickly that often they are difficult to detect. This time I was brought up short by failure to make much sense, and by the sudden realisation that it was 'red' not 'read'!

Metaphoric resonance and metonymic triggering occur spontaneously, but it is helpful to be able to recognise them as such, and not to mistake them for universal insight into human nature! They can also be used intentionally. I can scan an account for nouns and verbs, inviting my mind to play with them, change them slightly, and see what associations arise. Being deliberate is much less effective than relaxing into playfulness. By keeping part of my mind separate from the effort of making meaning from text or from a situation, I can allow myself to read between the lines, to hear the things unsaid but implied, to locate possible Freudian slips and unconscious resonances.

The actions which are described subsequently are for the most part, mixtures of metonymy and metaphor. Awareness of these forms can support their deliberate use when the spontaneous dries up. It is enormously important to remember however, that associations and resonances are personal. Elucidating them tells us as much about the elucidator as it does about the account.

Assaying assumptions

It is so easy to make inappropriate assumptions. For example, I was listening to the recorded messages on my answer-phone and confused the date on which a message was left, as I just assumed that the time and date preceded the message. I even had a story that the last time and date referred to the moment of listening to the messages! But of course technologically it makes much more sense for the time and date to be added by the machine after the message has been recorded. It took a disturbance to expose this hidden assumption sufficiently to allow me to correct it.

Working with accounts is an excellent way of exposing assumptions which we may be making unwittingly. Working with colleagues can be helpful, as it is often easier to detect other people's assumptions than your own. They can help locate metaphors, metonymies, prolepsis and the use of scripts.

Scanning for scripts

Earlier I drew attention to the way that scripts are implicit in interactions, often proleptically, because a few code words act as triggers to evoke a rich web of taken-as-shared meanings, values and practices. It follows therefore that an important action to perform on accounts is to scan them for scripts. Since normally what alerts us to scripts is disturbance to what we then realise are expectations, some specific and direct action is required to locate scripts which do go according to form.

In their work with scripts, Schank and Abelson (1977) develop a deep structure. They suggest that Scripts sometimes carry out Plans, that Plans are generated from Goals, that Goals arise from Themes, and that Themes are often based on characteristic roles and relationships. Although this structure was developed in the context of trying to teach computers to appreciate and to interpret stories, it can be used to examine transcripts and accounts.

First, you can pull back from the detail and ask yourself if you recognise the type of situation, and whether there are standard patterns of interactions involved. For example, there is a pattern of asking students questions in which it is obvious to students that their task is to 'guess what is in teacher's mind'; an interviewer will adopt a particular stance towards the person being interviewed; a patient will expect to be interrogated in a particular way by a doctor, and differently by a nurse. Elaborating the expected script can reveal aspects of the interaction which have been omitted or passed over and yet are informing or structuring the interaction.

Second, you can use any script you have detected to suggest plans and their associated goals. Alternatively you can look for evidence of what the people involved are trying to achieve through the interaction, and through detecting possible plans, reconstruct or locate scripts. There may be more than one script being activated, for sometimes people operate at cross-purposes. I have for example, noticed numerous times when I have overheard a conversation and been convinced from the responses that the participants are misunderstanding each other. Where two people are employing different scripts, or different variants of the same script, you can get humorous but also tragic consequences.

Third, having detected a script and associated plans and goals, you can see these as instances of more general themes. For example, you may recognise archetypal actions or perspectives. Recasting accounts in the form of fairy stories is a powerful means of achieving resonance with other people, presumably because the fairy story is itself a recognised script, and because if you do succeed in capturing an archetype, it will resonate with most people's experience.

Probing a script for covert or implied plans, then using these to reveal possible goals, and relating these to themes depends on familiarity with the script in particular, and with its use in the culture more generally. Having revealed a possible use of a script, you can try to locate a classic version of the incident, or even construct your own story. You can offer the thematic story to colleagues, and you can also be specific and invite them to see if they agree that the goals and themes are plausible sources for the behaviour. They will relate most effectively to what you offer, whether story or script, by interrogating their own experience for similar incidents.

Interrogating experience

Sometimes something you hear or read or see is accompanied by recall of some specific or generalised incidents from your past. Sometimes it is worth putting yourself in a state which encourages such re-call. *Interrogating experience* means quietly inviting recognition of what has been said, read, or done. One approach is to seek a state of receptive self-opening, in which you relax and, keeping the stimulus in mind, wait for something to come to mind. An active approach is to try deliberately to recall particular times from your past which might then afford access to something related to, connected to, associated with, or similar to, the stimulus.

For example, asked to recount an incident from their school days which was positive, and another which was negative, some people imagined themselves in various years at school: the school, the teacher, the classroom, other children, etc. until they found a possible incident. Others allowed positive or negative feelings to arise, and then waited for something to come to mind.

Interrogating experience is a fundamental tool we all have. It can be recognised as something that happens within any type of enquiry, and it can be used deliberately as part of an enquiry.

Seeking significance

Tripp (1993: 25) suggests that an account such as

> Mary raised her right hand. After about a minute her teacher noticed, and asked what she wanted. Mary asked if she could sharpen her pencil.

is simply description. But being reported, it has also been noticed and marked, so it is likely that the observer has some interpretation which gave the incident some significance. Therefore there may be some assumptions or judgements hiding behind the account. If the observer offers the account to the teacher afterwards to provide entry to that moment of the lesson, then the incident can also play an indexing role. But it indexes something of importance to the observer, and it may be that subsequently the teacher and/or observer find 'hand-raising' as a suitable label for a constellation of observations.

The incident only becomes significant, what many authors call *critical*, if it fits with or contrasts with experience, and if it has a sense of importance or salience for the person rendering the account. An incident is said by some to be critical if it turns out to be a turning point in their awareness, that is, which initiated a re-think about some implicit belief, theory, or practice in teaching. Others refer more generally to an incident being critical if it is salient, that is, if it sticks out or readily comes to mind after an event (is marked). All agree that a useful way of working with incidents, whether through contrasting, confronting or metacognitive theorising, includes:

- recounting the incident as briefly and vividly as possible;
- locating other incidents which seem similar in some way;
- labelling the issue which seems to be at the core;
- collecting alternative responses for similar incidents; and
- re-entering moments associated with the issue to enhance the possibility of noticing an opportunity to respond differently in the future.

For Tripp, it must also lead, through analysis of what makes it salient, to revelation of some otherwise hidden or suppressed assumptions or opinions or ideals. It must become critical either in the sense that it forms a turning point in the teacher's sensitivity to notice, or it provides an item of data for critical analysis. For Brookfield (1995), an incident becoming critical means that hidden assumptions are revealed, and power relationships which distort the educational process come to light. Having been brought to light, these can be explored and investigated through sensitised noticing and further reports of incidents. Tripp goes on to distinguish judgements arising from subsequent analysis of what makes the incident stand out, according to whether they are practical, diagnostic, reflective or critical.

Mason (1986), Jaworski (1988), Mason and Davis (1989), Lerman and Scott-Hodgetts (1991), Tripp (1993), and Lerman (1994) all promote working on, and with, salient or critical incidents. But probing incidents for personal significance, and for the form of that significance is difficult to do alone. It is much easier with colleagues who, through collective *reconnaissance* mentioned earlier, can assist the person rendering the account to probe beneath the surface. What sort of a state do the words used in the description summon up inside you? What significance do individual words and phrases have for you that others might not share?

For example, in the brief note

> John didn't finish his work today. Must see he learns to complete what he has begun. (Tripp 1993: 18)

the word *finish* plays a central role. For some people, finishing is not an issue one way or another. For others, finishing means tying up all loose ends, clearing away and providing a 'clean slate', while for others it is very difficult to achieve closure, indeed closure may be an anathema, so things are often left lying around (literally or metaphorically). Seeking the significance for you is a step towards appreciating that it may not have the same significance for others, which in turn may permit a greater sensitivity to how others 'finish' tasks. Emotional commitment which is not shared is a major source of tension and disagreement.

In seeking significance, it is often useful to try using alternative words to see if they make any difference. In this way you may reveal certain emotional commitment to principles (e.g. children should be . . .) via idioms and phrases constituting 'rules' of behaviour. Locating other ways in which you use the word, rather than dwelling solely on the meaning of the word itself for you, can also be illuminating. You can search for origins of phrases and words, trying to find in what circumstances in the past or present those stock phrases and sentiments are expressed. In short, where might the discourse you employ be found or have been found?

The whole notion of significance is fraught with problems. What makes something significant for you? How did it become a 'something' in the first place? Is it a product of the language being used, or does it touch some personal or collective sensitivity? Does it serve to illustrate or illuminate some theoretical construct, or is it a reminder of past experience? What is gained or lost by having this investment, this significance? These are the sorts of questions which can be probed using the very techniques being described here: seeking further incidents and accounts of them, and probing in various ways to try to locate what makes them meaningful and/or disturbing. Theorising about 'why something is meaningful' which moves into 'it must be . . .' is unhelpful; theorising by suggesting a theme or issue and then interrogating experience and also scanning the literature for similarities can be very helpful. Alternative practices can be located, hidden assumptions which are blocking or obscuring alternatives can be exposed and investments questioned.

As soon as someone feels moved to describe an account to someone else, some significance is implied. Sperber and Wilson (1986) locate the impetus to construe as arising from culturally accepted signals. For example, someone who wants to 'tell me something' adopts certain postures, stances and tones, and their attention is directed and forceful. These signal import, and are what we read as signalling 'time to make sense'. Thus we don't, usually, try to interpret the sound of traffic on a nearby motorway as speech (though we might deduce something about traffic density, air temperature and humidity). But when someone appears to be saying something to us, we work at trying to decode what they are saying, even if at first we catch only snatches through differences in accent, dialect or familiarity with the language.

Having imputed significance, it is very natural to find arising inside us some sense of fit, of affirmation, of agreement, or some sense of contradiction or of doubt. This comes from resonances and associations with past experience. We can be more or less rigorous, more or less systematic in seeking to contradict, or to augment or modify. We can be more or less rigorous in seeking specific incidents or general 'feelings'. We can be more or less rigorous about checking whether the incident that comes to mind is structurally, perhaps metaphorically, similar or whether it is more of a metonymic connection, before deciding whether to contribute an account to the discussion or to keep it to ourselves.

To seek significance, it may also be useful to interrogate your experience for similar or related incidents, and to examine what it is that seems similar or related for you, which I have called threading themes.

Threading themes

Amassing accounts of experiences is one thing, but connecting them together, literally threading accounts like beads on a string of metonymic and metaphoric connections is quite another, almost inescapable activity. A 'thread' in a collection of accounts is a theme, issue, or tension which emerges in the mind of a (th)reader usually by reference to their experience, but possibly augmented or reinforced through structural or other similarities. The tapestry which is our mental lived experience works on several levels simultaneously. At one level, we all have memories of specific incidents in which we have been involved. We may or may not have easy or direct access to individual incidents. Some incidents come in clusters, associated in some way which permits access to their collectivity from a more general trigger than is needed for any one of the specific incidents. At another level there are more generalised incidents which are abstractions from various specific accounts. Interpretation of the individual events is derived from association with a more generic one, and the generic one has meaning in so far as it is linked to the specifics. Themes arise when particular aspects are stressed, and similarities detected, so that clusters are themselves clustered, and again meaning arises mutually from a theme informing an interpretation of clusters, while clusters gain in significance from illustrating or illuminating themes.

A sense of fit between two or more accounts, a sense of recognition, is usually a signal that there are common threads. Interrogating experience for other apparently similar accounts, and adding these to the collection is also likely to provoke an awareness of similarity. The task is then to try to bring this sense of sameness to articulation, often in the form of a label or generalised description.

Often people begin by thinking they are really interested in one question, but when they come to look back at what they have chosen to record, they find that either their accounts are focused on some quite different themes, or that there is little obvious relevance of the accounts to the original question.

Intentional work may be required in order to locate what is the same, and what is different about different accounts. Sameness and difference are a matter of stressing some features and ignoring others, or as Mary Bateson (1992: 89) suggested 'a matter of context and point of view'. It may be necessary to change context or point of view through deliberate acts, or these may occur spontaneously. Caleb Gattegno (1987) emphasised that stressing some features and ignoring others is how we generalise and abstract. Thus changing our point of view (for example the theoretical frame and discourse we adopt, the metaphors we employ) may lead to different generalisations. A sensitivity to noticing certain features is a version of stressing some features and ignoring others, so sensitivity to notice is a state of generalisation or abstraction. This is why we can only observe through our theories and expectations, and why, as mentioned earlier, we hope with Goodman (1978) that our theories are as fact-based as our facts are theory based. Working to remove accounting-for when illustrating or generating theories and principles is one instrument we have for meeting Goodman: basing theories in experience via accounts.

Where no themes readily emerge, it is useful to look for structural similarities and differences in a collection of accounts, because sometimes these reveal scripts or propensities on the part of the person recounting the incidents. Where a single theme emerges, it is useful to consider what may be being overlooked, or what concerns may be predisposing this particular theme to emerge. Where several themes emerge, it is useful to look at how the various themes interact, and whether there really are differences between them or whether they are all manifestations of a yet more general theme.

Another way of threading themes is to select a general theme, such as 'control', 'invariance amidst change', 'attention', or 'sensitivity to client' or a more focused theme such as 'finishing' or 'starting' or 'keeping going', arising from one or more incidents or accounts. Accounts are then searched for relevance to this theme, and experience is interrogated for other incidents which seem to have some bearing.

Sometimes themes emerge from accounts, and sometimes accounts emerge from themes. Sometimes it feels as though the themes are being constructed, and sometimes it feels as though they are lying there waiting to be identified. Constructing, detecting and threading themes is intimately tied up with finding and identifying phenomena as phenomena.

Finding phenomena

Participation in an event, or an account-of an event given by yourself or by someone else, may trigger a sense of familiarity, of re-cognition, that is of having 'been there, seen that, done that'. It may also be the case that a word or phrase comes spontaneously to mind which purports to describe or label that familiarity. Account 32: *Evaporation* (p. 106) illustrates beautifully how the phenomenon being pointed to may not be the phenomenon that people recognise, until there has been some explicit negotiation of what constitutes 'being similar'.

In Account 32, the second colleague's offering was triggered partly by the word *evaporation*, partly by *frustration* and *loss*, and partly by her general sense of the initial description. Further descriptions by others located a difference between the first use of *evaporation* of enthusiasm and engagement and the second. As well as illustrating the need to negotiate meaning, it is also an example of a phenomenon emerging. The label *evaporation* was already part of the first colleague's experience of the incident, and as such points to, or brings into existence, a phenomenon, but not one that she had probed particularly deeply. Others are then looking to exemplify that same phenomenon in their own experience. In other instances, a label may not emerge until several accounts have been offered and perhaps some rejected or sidelined. Labels act as foci, to bring phenomena into existence or to crystallise them. They act as points of coagulation and access for a rich web of experiences. But as this example illustrates, labels and other words in a description can also trigger recall of incidents which have aspects not intended or considered in the initial account.

Another problematic aspect emerges here, however. Incidents are incidents; accounts are accounts. Similarities and differences are aspects of people's sense-making, not of the incidents or even of the accounts themselves. You may be able to point to use of the same (or different) words and so claim a similarity or difference, but this merely pushes the problem further down. Just what constitutes 'similarity' or even (subtle) 'difference' between what is recounted in an account-of? Is there even a 'thing' being recounted? This problem will be addressed more fully in Part VI.

Proposing principles

Sometimes some sort of theme emerges as a commonality to a collection of accounts, or even from a single account. Often this goes hand in hand with a sense of a phenomenon, as something identifiable from the past and in the future. At the same time, or subsequently, some principle can also emerge. For example, in locating and working on *finishing* as an issue of significance (a theme) some principle may be revealed, such as that 'children should be taught to finish one activity before they start another', or that 'reaching some sort of closure is essential in order to avoid evaporation of engagement'.

By allowing the principle to come to the surface, it becomes open to enquiry and to modification. Universality can be tempered by working at becoming aware of circumstances in which it may, or may not, be appropriate. You can seek the significance for yourself, and for others, of such a principle. You can enquire as to the source of the commitment felt, and thence to what serves and is served by such a commitment. You can try to find some things you can do either to test the efficacy of the principle, or to manifest it more effectively by gathering gambits which assist you.

For example, a collection of observations of students or colleagues might lead to awareness that there is a certain passivity or receptiveness which could usefully be turned into more active participation. A label such as *Assent–Assert* might arise as a reminding label for these observations, in which students passively assent to what they are told whereas the teacher wants them to assert what they are thinking for discussion. It then may become a theme. This might lead to formulation or recall of a principle such as 'try to do for students only what they cannot yet do for themselves' as an ideal towards which to strive. Such an ideal is then available for further enquiry, locating instances where the principle might be appropriate, gambits to employ, and instances where the principle seems inappropriate.

Gathering gambits

Gambits–tactics–devices, ways of acting or working, are being manifested around us all the time. These are the fundamental components of practices. There may be associated perspectives and awarenesses which are not visible, but there is always some behavioural component. Where do we acquire gambits? To answer this question would be to choose a particular discourse, a particular theory, a particular way of accounting for what people do. But whatever your favourite way of thinking and speaking about this process, it happens through distinguishing some behaviour from others, and recognising these as something that you could do, which would at least appear to be meaningful, relevant and efficacious.

In the example used above of *Assent–Assert*, sensitivity to the issue of receptive and active student–colleague behaviour, and to an associated principle which places value on getting students asserting as well as just (emotive term) assenting, might provide access to some specific actions which could be taken. For example, every-so-often you could invite people to discuss in pairs or to construct an example of what has just been said. *Talking-in-pairs* might emerge as a general gambit–tactic–device which, among other things, prompts students and/or colleagues to take some initiative. The label *Self-generated-example* can emerge as a collection of gambits–tactics-devices for getting people to engage actively and to participate through constructing their own examples and versions of problems. Furthermore, it is a reasonable conjecture that such students will be in a better position to reconstruct ideas for themselves in the future (even on an examination or under extreme pressure). So the task turns into finding ways to support people in generating examples in different contexts in such a way that they become aware that this is something they can do for themselves at almost any time.

There are plenty of ideas and possibilities for ways of working with students or clients which can be gleaned from accounts provided by others of how they deal with specific instances. Usually what we pick up are fragments of practices, parts of the outer forms. Picking up the inner awareness which drives those is much harder, so we have to re-construct these for ourselves, based on our own perceptions and perspectives, our own ways of theorising about and explaining our actions.

There are other sources, such as observing colleagues either within their practice or at a conference, reading books and articles, and observing people more generally. What is needed is an orientation of enquiry, a sensitivity to a particular issue and personal commitment. The Discipline of Noticing suggests a number of related acts one can undertake to enhance this process. As with everything else, there are mechanical but ineffective ways of gathering gambits, and there are effective but uncontrolled ways of proceeding.

You could scour the internet or the literature for descriptions of elements of people's practice which might help. You could ask colleagues. You could try to analyse the situation and work something out logically, based on experience. Alternatively you can re-affirm your commitment, for example by imagining yourself in some situation and suddenly realising that there is something about the situation you could do or use. You can try to catch yourself doing whatever it is you want to alter, so as to increase your sensitivity. You can 'let go' of intense desire or commitment and try to open yourself to possibilities, acting as if you were inviting possibilities to come to you while you wait as if 'on a park bench'. You can even act as if you had an alternative behaviour and see if something happens in mid moment.

The two approaches, the active and the receptive, correspond quite closely to a distinction made by Polanyi and Prosch (1975) between *focused* and *subsidiary* awareness. In the active, deliberately seeking mode, attention is focused and effort is made to focus and concentrate. The subsidiary mode is more like peripheral vision: we have certain receptors which are trained to catch movement to the side, and we are conditioned to turn our heads to look more closely when that happens. Thus you can be focused in seeking gambit fragments, and you can use practices in the Discipline of Noticing to attune yourself to notice a practice that might be useful through subsidiary awareness. Sometimes it will 'appear' through a surprise or disturbance; sometimes there will be a structural resonance between the current and some previous situation; sometimes there is a metonymic trigger. Whatever the mechanism, a distinction is made (a gambit–tactic–device–practice) is brought into existence, identified, and perhaps labelled.

For example, Jaworski and Watson (1994b) show how an incident can become a seed-crystal for a rich web of related incidents and strategies. The expression 'taking on the mantle of expert' was encountered when reading a book on drama education (Johnson and O'Neill 1984). It is a particular example of William James' notion of 'acting-as-if' (James 1890). It became a possibility to use in their own lesson by asking a pupil to act-as-if they were expert in reporting on some topic.

This [reading] triggered a reaction of 'yes, I could use that' and subsequently, of 'I do use that'. It created an awareness of situations in the classroom where it is valuable for pupils to 'take on the mantle of expert', for example, when a pupil has worked on some mathematical idea and is asked to express this to someone else. In this situation the pupil is the expert [locally]. No-one else can express that idea, or explain that thinking. If the teacher says 'you're the expert', this at once values the pupil's thinking, and provides a confidence boost. On the other hand, a pupil could be asked to be the expert – to act 'as if' they had expertise in some situation – perhaps to come up to the front of the classroom and explain the theorem of Pythagoras 'as if you were Pythagoras' – be the expert. Pretending you're an expert can be an act which encourages you to be more actively and confidently involved in the thinking. It is likely now that some situation will arise, when we are in the classroom, in which we find it quite natural to ask a pupil to 'be an expert'. (pp. 135–6)

Jaworski and Watson go on to suggest that if there is some sense of potential then you can investigate variations and how they might be used in different contexts. Perhaps it becomes part of classroom practice, perhaps it falls into disuse; perhaps pupils take the initiative to refer to this role, perhaps they begin to find it tedious. Above all, trying to find ways to suggest the tactic to colleagues, through accounts of incidents and through other task exercises, further refines and hones awareness of possibilities and constraints. This is how an inner mentor develops, which awakens one to possibilities, and it is entirely consonant with the Discipline of Noticing.

It may be worth noting that *acting-as-if* is one of the chief ways we have of developing or changing. We cannot be sure until we have tried something, but we cannot have really tried it until we have acted-as-if we believed it will work. If you suspect or believe something will not work, then you are likely to get only confirming evidence. On the other hand, if you believe that something will work, you may delude yourself. So you undertake some sort of external validation of the form suggested by the Discipline of Noticing.

Mirroring myself

As has already been suggested, gathering accounts and seeing what it is about them that occasions a reaction, whether antipathy or empathy, coolness or warmth, reveals aspects of yourself as much as of the incidents. Particularly, whenever something about someone else produces irritation, it is worth examining whether that irritation is perhaps a resonance with something that you do or say or think which you wish were otherwise. For example, I become aware of middle-age bulge partly through finding myself sensitised to notice and dislike it in others. I recognise my own use of a cliché through noticing irritation when others use it. I discover a weakness in my practice through being annoyed by some aspect of someone else's. Become aware of something in others may produce enough energy to enable me to notice something in me, which in turn may produce sufficient energy to enable me to do something about it.

Other people's accounts can serve the same role as any other external stimulus, as something to respond to, and in responding, to discover what it is I am sensitive to. Thus what I observe about a situation tells me as much about my sensitivity to notice as it does about whatever was being observed. It reveals issues and concerns, likes and dislikes of myself. As such they are useful mirrors in which to see ourselves as others see us, at least to some extent (and in any case they see us through similarly half-mirrored perception, for what they 'see' is also partly themselves!).

Linking to literature

While it is perfectly possible for a group of people to work together with and on the accounts which they generate and develop, it is sensible to guard against solipsism and against believing through habit. That is why noticing includes creating task-exercises for use with colleagues in order to check whether what you are noticing makes sense to and informs others. Another way to link to the wide world of experience is to look for related experiences in the professional and research literature.

Reading articles for the sake of it is not usually very thrilling, but reading articles when you have some concerns and issues, some tensions and uncertainties, can be most informing. Encountering accounts can inform interpretation of your own experiences, as well as adding to the rich web of connections you are developing. Encountering theories can provide threads to connect together incidents you already have, as well as stimulating further observation in order to find out whether you can find resonance in your own experience, or whether the theorising really does help you to notice more acutely. At the very least it can inform you as to the issues and concerns of a wider community, thus enabling you to relate your concerns to theirs, and to draw upon the work of others to inform your own enquiry.

Working with accounts arising from other sources

What do you do, what can you do, with other people's accounts that you meet? This is what you have had to do throughout this book, as I offered my own and other people's accounts. I hope that you naturally juxtaposed your own experiences with those described. But suppose you are reading an article in which some incidents are described or some phenomena referred to but with account-of and accounting-for intertwined? What can you do with them if they are not brief-but-vivid or do not speak to your experience? What can you do with transcripts of interviews if the person interviewed is intertwining accounts-of and accounting-for?

The answer is that there is not a great deal you can do except take them as stimuli for interrogating your own experience. If the person giving the accounts is present, then you can probe, perhaps by direct questioning, perhaps by undertaking reconnaissance of the incidents being described, as mentioned earlier. If you are interviewing, you can probe what is being said by asking for specific examples, and you can keep probing until the account-of can be distinguished from the accounting-for.

The same principle applies to interviewing candidates for a job. Asking them to say what they would do in some hypothetical situation which you think may arise in the job simply invites speculation on their part. You can have no confidence that what they say will have any bearing on what they would actually do. They are looking for your response to what they say so that they can 'press your triggers', 'say what you seem to want to hear'. This is a perfectly natural response to being interviewed, and applies not just to job interviews, but to any research which probes other people's responses.

However, if you describe briefly-but-vividly some situation, and then ask the interviewee to describe some similar situation in their own experience and how they responded to it (e.g. facing a problem concerning people, making a decision, finding something out, etc.) then you will quickly find out the sorts of situations to which they are sensitive (how well does their account correspond to yours?), how perceptive they are (how they claim to have dealt with the problem), and how attentive they are to your question (do they have access to reasonably brief-but-vivid accounts of incidents?). Probing, either by asking for particular examples, for brief-but-vivid accounts of incidents and situations, or by offering your own and asking whether they are similar, is usually the best way to check whether you comprehend what someone else is saying in any context.

If you have no access to the sources, then you have to disentangle the phenomenon as best you can. If you need more detail, then you are stuck. Attempting to read negotiable detail in an accounting-for can at best reveal what features you associate with the theorising–explaining–justifying– generalising that makes up the accounting-for. You are better off interrogating your own experience for something which resonates, and proceeding from there.

Broekman (2000) develops the image of a hologram, an image stored on film created by the superposition of direct and reflected coherent light, which can be seen as a metaphor for qualitative enquiry. Shining light through the film creates an image in depth, but the record on the film does not have a one-to-one connection with the original image. In a standard image, if one loses part of the picture, then it is irretrievable, whereas in a hologram, the whole can be reconstructed from a fragment. Broekman suggests that 'by looking at the individual in the intersection of past and future, one can reconstruct a broader picture'. I would go further and suggest that stories (accounts) represent the interference patterns of personal propensities and desire for objectivity, and that when considered-viewed by someone else, a whole can be reconstructed. It depends on the coherence of the viewer as to whether further interference and hence image degeneration takes place.

Using accounts with others

Ways in which accounts can be used are drawn from the previous sections in this chapter to form yet another way of looking at the use of accounts and of account-like stimuli. Accounts form the basis for accessing other people's experiences, and for seeking resonance with others.

In this section, the term *stimulus* will be used to mean any source of stimulation for generating accounts, such as

- a live session observed by participants;
- a segment of video or audio recording, for example of a session or from an interview (with or without transcript);
- a segment of some teaching material (animation, presentation, poster, work of art . . .);
- a task of some sort; or
- a written description of one or more incidents.

Any stimulus can be used with and for oneself, as suggested in the previous section. They can also be used with others in three basic ways: as attempts to focus participants' attention, to attract them or even enable them to notice something they may not have been aware of previously; as a source of illustrations and examples when describing or theorising; or as fishing expeditions (what will they notice? What will strike them?).

Fishing expeditions

The point of a fishing expedition is to see what colleagues make of a stimulus, perhaps to check against your own perceptions, perhaps to add depth and richness to your own analysis. Instead of having previously identified themes and issues, tensions and phenomena, you can invite colleagues to work from scratch on some stimulus such as a videotape of a lesson, or a transcript, in the expectation that it is rich enough to prompt one or more issues to arise for the participants without knowing in advance what these are likely to be. The idea is to see what they notice, what strikes them. Participants are invited to locate something that stands out for them, something striking, and to describe or otherwise locate the incident in the source, so that others can locate it. They are asked to give an account of the fragment. Sometimes it helps to give an account of the selection process as well, but it is important not to account for why the selection was made. What is important is *that* it sticks out, not theorising about why this might be.

If it seems sensible or necessary, the group can then negotiate the identification of a specific fragment in the source by finding details that everyone recognises. Sometimes one person notices something that others do not recall, or recall differently. Negotiation is then required, either to locate the incident so that people know what to look for upon re-viewing (where that is possible), or to locate surrounding details which may give participants access to re-entering that incident mentally. Negotiation may also be needed to identify what it was that seemed striking about the incident.

Here are two minor things that stuck out during a 'fishing expedition' using a videotape of a science lesson.

Account 36: White pens

While viewing a video-tape of a science lesson, I was struck by a period when one person on the video was tapping the table with a white pen. Everyone recognised the incident, and how irritating it was for the viewer. That raised a question about whether it might be irritating for other students, which developed into a discussion about the ways in which tension, excitement and boredom are revealed in similar body movements.

Someone else was struck by one person on the video having what she thought was a sucker hanging from his mouth as he talked. By concentrating discussion first on what we could all agree we could see (a white cylinder sticking out of his mouth) it was possible through discussion to agree that it was more likely to be another (the same?) white pen.

The 'tapping pen' provided a gateway into discussion of how attention can be distracted and diverted from what the teacher or leader believes is the main point, and how difficult it can be to read behaviour. The 'sucker' reinforced this, by showing how easy it is to become transfixed by some minor feature, whether as teacher, carer or researcher, and how it can suddenly become necessary to clarify the matter in hand before returning to the main point. By sticking to accounts of what we recalled, we were able to reach agreement, which might have been more difficult if people had been allowed to stick to unsubstantiated impressions.

Once the fragment is located and the striking feature identified, people can be invited to offer accounts of incidents that come to mind resonated by the chosen fragment, and the group can negotiate similarities and differences between the various accounts. The object of the activity is to seek a collection of apparently related incidents which seem to be 'about the same thing', whatever that emerges as being, as the accounts accumulate. The collection of different accounts provide significance for each individual, and richness of breadth for the other participants. During this process it is likely that some sort of label will emerge which provides a way to refer to the constellation of accounts. Labels which use words that can serve as triggers in some future situation are more useful than idiosyncratic or situationally specific ones. Thus people's names are not very good as triggers in the future, whereas words that might actually be used in such situations are preferable, as they are more likely to bring possibilities to mind. In the course of collecting related accounts, it is likely that alternative responses to the situation will be described. Whether this happens or not, people can set themselves to look out for other ways of responding to such situations, for example by describing accounts to colleagues and getting them to describe something they think is similar from their own experience.

As a fishing expedition, I am offering the initial stimulus to find out what strikes others. This provides me with access to a variety of readings of the proffered accounts that I might not have achieved by myself, and so enriches any subsequent analysis that may be undertaken. I may also be wanting to see if others are struck by something which struck me, as a step towards honing a task-exercise. There are of course questions of fidelity and validity, but these are more properly discussed in a later section.

Dredging

Engaging colleagues in dredging for accounts concerned with specific themes, or for issues is a very productive way to use the notion of accounts-of with colleagues. Details of dredging techniques were described earlier in this chapter. Dredging is a form of task-exercise, in which you try to prompt colleagues to experience a shift in their perception, in their attention, which corresponds or is similar to a shift you have experienced.

Using as task-exercises

Working in much the same way as in a fishing expedition or dredging, I can offer an account as a stimulus to colleagues in the form of a task-exercise, in the sense that I find it highlights some feature(s) or aspect(s) of professionality that I think is important, and I am testing whether others recognise what I am referring to. Thus they may spontaneously identify the same features which struck me (so we can work from there), or I may offer my own location of a fragment and then see whether others see it in the stimulus, and recognise it in their own experience.

What makes a task-exercise different from a fishing expedition is that the purpose of offering the task-exercise is to work on something specific, whereas in the fishing expedition I am trying to broaden my awareness of what might strike others. Dredging can be used both to help locate an issue supported by relevant accounts and to test the recognisability of a theme or account.

When colleagues offer their own incidents, we can negotiate (as described above) issues that are raised. If colleagues fasten on to other aspects, other interpretations, other (th)readings, other fragments, other significances, then I can work at locating a more focused account, and at honing my description, or at enriching my interpretation.

Illustrating with accounts

Throughout this book I have been using accounts of various forms to illustrate points being made. When working with colleagues, my preference is to work the other way, offering task-exercises, and then drawing out from the reported experience of working on them, whatever themes, tensions, concerns and issues of interest may arise. Here is an example of an author using an account to make some points. It is taken from a project 'Talking Mathematics' (Corwin and Storeygard 1995), aimed at supporting teachers in listening to children and generating meaningful classroom discussion in kindergartens. It begins and ends with commentary from the researchers:

Account 37: Attendance

This is a sample of discussion in a kindergarten classroom. The students have developed the habit of looking at attendance numbers each day. Today the teacher probes their understanding further by posing new questions. At this point all but three children have put their name tags under the labels 'boy' or 'girl' [and there have been equal numbers of boys and girls].

TEACHER: Right, now, look at the chart; we've got the same number of boys and girls. Do you think that by the time all the kids put their tags down there are going to be the same number of boys and girls? Bobby?

BOBBY: I think no, 'cuz if just one more girl puts hers down and then two more boys put their's down, then the boys will be much longer.

TEACHER: . . . So you think if one more girl puts hers down, then two more boys, the boys put theirs down, the boys will be longer. Who else thinks something? Jennifer?

JENNIFER: I think there's going to be ten boys.

TEACHER: How come you think that?

JENNIFER: Because I counted in my head!

TEACHER: Can you tell us in words?

JENNIFER: I counted all the boys in the line. And then I imagined that two more boys put their cards down. And I counted that!

. . . later in the same discussion

REBECCA: I knew that Bobby was right. Because there's eleven boys, and ten girls! But if there was eleven boys, I mean eleven girls and ten boys, then, then, and they changed their line, then our line would be longer!

Here the teacher combines careful reflection of the children's language back to them with probing questions. She repeats, and does not change, the children's language. When a child seems unclear she asks questions to clarify the thinking underlying the words. The children are listening to one another, as Rebecca's comments indicate. They are making mathematical meaning through talking together.

You may wish to pause at this point and consider the interaction between the transcript as an account-of, and the commentary surrounding it, as an example of how an account can be used both to generate and to illustrate themes and issues.

Comment

In text, it seems perfectly natural to make a remark about what in the transcript the writers marked, and what therefore they think we should see in it. But are we being misled? The words 'careful reflection . . .' suggest action by the teacher which is not available in the transcript, for all we can see is that just once the teacher more or less repeats back what the previous child said (as in Account 2, 'repeating back'). We cannot impute a general practice from one instance, and we have to trust the accuracy of the transcript, knowing that they are notoriously difficult to make. From Rebecca's utterance we can assume that she listened to Bobby, so some listening is going on.

What struck me was the authors' apparent urge to digest transcripts for the reader. Why do they feel the need to make assertions about the transcript? Can I catch that impulse in myself? Am I fearful that the reader will miss something? If so, perhaps the transcript is ambiguous and can be interpreted differently.

On reading other people's analysis, I find an urge to locate alternative stories: Can we really conclude that mathematical meaning is made through talking together, or is this an instance of children talking and discussing, with mathematical meaning perhaps being made before, during, and after the talk?

Generating theories and issues from accounts

It is very difficult to refrain from accounting for incidents for very long. The reason for holding off at all is, as has been said before, to distinguish between the phenomenon and the explanation or theorising. There are significant philosophical problems here, because the act of noticing, observing, perceiving requires past experience and perhaps even a language in which to make the distinction, which means a prior theory. Again, I can only notice what I am attuned to notice. But trying to leave that aside for the moment, in order to retain the pragmatic features of this part of the book, it is worth looking at how issues and conjectures arise from working on accounts.

Once accounting-for is opened up as part of the group activity, theories are likely to come thick and fast. The process of accumulating a number of related incidents usually provides sufficient foundation for discussions of similarities and differences, and since the question 'why?' is never far away, generalisation and theorising soon follow. Furthermore, the process of stressing some features and ignoring others is itself an act of generalisation.

Now one of the virtues of trying to separate accounts-of from accounting-for is that the process of locating or becoming aware of issues, and of reaching towards generalisations and theories, can be clarified and attended to because there is less confusion between phenomenon and accounting-for that phenomenon. Furthermore, the process can be supported through establishing an ethos of conjecturing and enquiry. Instead of announcing that such and such is happening because . . ., participants can phrase their proposals in terms of conjectures. Conjectures can be tested against experience through looking both for confirmatory incidents and for incidents which call the conjecture into question; they can be modified through negotiation of further related incidents; and they can be tested against experience in the future.

Sources of accounts

For professional development, the best source of accounts is your own experience. For research into your own practice, or in supporting similar research in others, accounts are most useful when they afford access to your own experience. Other people's accounts are useful when they trigger corresponding incidents from your own experience, so that you can re-enter your moments, and consequently, as it where, re-enter the issue being discussed.

One way of working is to have a notebook handy and to pause briefly immediately something strikes you, and make a very brief note. If you are the teacher or leader of professional development, you can use such moments to suggest that participants make a note of something that has struck them. By seeing you record they are more likely to feel like recording something themselves. Returning to the brief note at the end of the lesson or of the day, and elaborating details so that the moment can more readily be recalled is important, because brief notes can turn into impenetrable code within hours or at best, days.

Another source of incidents is of course actually taping (audio or even video) incidents and interviews. At first it seems that taping provides much more reliable data than mere accounts, for they are 'true recordings'. But experience with them shows that the data they produce is actually just as problematic as personal accounts: choices of when to record and whom, and which fragments to use, mean that they are also selective; gestures and postures remain invisible in audio, and for video the single camera has a single focus of attention whereas people are able to attend to multiple aspects of a complex setting (Pimm 1993).

Transcripts

Transcripts are always problematic no matter how much care is taken. Natural speech consists of fragments of utterances which are rarely if ever complete sentences, often overlapping, which makes them very hard to discern. There are hesitations, stutterings, repetitions, umms and aahs, and so on. There are pauses whose import is usually construed from gesture and posture, from tones and undertones, and from being present in the moment oneself. These are very hard to denote on a transcript, even if you have access to some of them from videotape.

Interviews

Interviews can be placed on a spectrum from minimal contact, as in a questionnaire filled in by the responder alone, to a colleagueal discussion amongst two or more participants. The more pre-constructed and pre-formatted the interview, the less likely it is that the responder will enter a state of insight, but if many people are to be interviewed, comparisons are difficult unless not only questions, but their interpretation by the responders, is similar.

Sometimes interviews are undertaken as fishing expeditions, looking for something striking to emerge, and sometimes interviews are undertaken in order to illustrate or justify theoretical positions (perhaps derived from other enquiries). An intermediate position is using interviews as a search for theories-in-action, in which the person interviewed displays behaviours which suggest or are consistent with recognisable theories known to the interviewer. For example, interviews might be employed in order to understand how junior members of staff see and relate to senior management. If the enquiry is in response to some perceived difficulties, then the interview questions are likely to be slanted in that direction; if it is routine practice then there are probably some established or habitual questions being asked. Those being interviewed are very likely, like students, to try to work out what it is that the interviewer wants to hear. For example, the game of 'getting the interviewer to write on their pad' is a version of games that children and patients both fall into in their respective settings.

As Kvale (1996) has so eloquently pointed out, interviews are very curious interactions. The interviewer may see themselves as a miner trying to dig something out that is buried in the person being interviewed, or perhaps as a traveller, visiting the interviewee's world. The person being interviewed may see them as threat or opportunity, as a chance to learn about themselves, to be helpful, or to be heard. These metaphors have implications for the assumptions being made about what constitutes data and knowledge, and what subsequently can reasonably be done with what is rcorded. With his title, Kvale suggests that an inter-view involves the collision of two different views (no matter how alike they may feel their views are). The very fact of an interview may bring to expression what has previously not been expressed, with the concomitant but tenuous assumption that what is said 'is the case'. Where an interview involves a developing relationship, one can be more confident that views expressed are at least representative of the current state of the person interviewed in a way that questionnaire data cannot, but even then opinions and articulations of beliefs may be situation and context specific, and in flux. Questionnaire data assumes that the responder is as taken with each question as is the person who posed it, and that they make similar interpretations, yet experience of responding to questionnaires challenges this assumption.

Furthermore, as Wittgenstein (Glock 1996: 324) pointed out in the context of grammar, but was almost certainly not the first to do so, the rules of grammar are not how we speak; they are our expression of standards, of perceived invariants; they are not consulted in order to generate speech. The same applies to behaviour generally. Our beliefs do not usually generate behaviour. Indeed observed behaviour often bears little relationship to espoused and avowed beliefs.

Summary of Chapter 7

This chapter describes a large number of techniques for creating and crafting accounts, and for both working-on and working-with them. As such it augments the Discipline of Noticing by suggesting ways of working when you are creating or refining accounts, or wanting to do something with them. The Discipline itself applies not only to the accounts you work on but to the process of working on and with them: significance and meaning are examples of the effects of noticing.

The important thing to remember is that from the perspective of noticing, the objects of study are experiences, not accounts-of experiences. Accounts only provide access to experience. However the techniques in this chapter are useful in other approaches to qualitative enquiry which analyse accounts, including transcripts, audio and video tapes, and field notes.

Attention was drawn to different ways of describing what is essentially the same process, but with different wrinkles or emphases: grammatical actions, assaying assumptions, scanning for scripts, interrogating experience, seeking significance, threading themes, finding phenomena, proposing principles, gathering gambits and mirroring myself. Whatever insights emerge, whatever is found as a result of these cogitations, comes about because of your participation in an action, and as such, are at least as much a reflection of you as they are of the situations and incidents which give rise to the accounts. Collections of accounts can be used as a source of experience for spawning and generating phenomena, themes, issues, and principles, for locating possible gambits, for offering to others as a source of inspiration and provocation, and for learning about oneself.

Fenstermacher (1997) proposes that accounts go through three phases of use: telling and construction; re-telling and re-construction; and deconstruction and critique. The process of re-telling may anaesthetise the incident so that it becomes amusing but loses its bite, or it may revivify intentions and desires that have faded from memory. Each re-telling produces a reconstruction pertinent to current perspectives and significances. If your focus is on your current sensitivity to notice, then retelling can feed as well as starve. Deconstruction is a process which can be invoked by using the various processes described in this chapter, with the aim of revealing what it is about the person rendering the account which leads to the account being constructed and offered to others. This includes seeking significations of apparently trivial details which are present, and of those which are absent, and their significance to the person rendering the account.

In the next chapter I turn to the action which initiates the kind of work summarised in this chapter, in the context of professional (and by implication, personal) development.

Sample accounts to work on

Here are some sample accounts to consider. I offer them because, as a namesake John Mason said in 1810, 'Examples not only move, but teach and direct, much more effectively than precepts.' Alfred North Whitehead (1933) put it succinctly as, 'We think in generalities, but we live in details.' Instead of simply reading through them, it is worthwhile examining each to see to whether you recognise what is being described, and then to consider what elements of a description make it relatively easy to enter into, and what aspects make it hard. You may wish to look for similar incidents in your own experience and to see if this raises any issues or concerns about your own practice. You can also use them to practice looking for working on accounts by pretending that these form a collection made by one person over a period of time.

Account 38: Typical

I gave the class a problem involving the composition of a typical group of 100 people, in a population with known proportions of people categorised by three types of hair colour. I expected to have some discussion work about the meaning of the word typical, but I had not expected this: one pupil, Penny, insisted that it depended on who misbehaved in the village. It took me a few moments confusion before I suddenly pictured one of Penny's elders, upon seeing her do something naughty, saying 'That's typical' (adapted from Lerman and Scott-Hodgetts 1991: 295–296)

Account 39: Dividing coins

I asked a boy to divide eight coins (four of 2p and four of 1p) between three people equally, but it took me some time to realise that the reason he couldn't was because he was trying to share the coins as objects without attention to their value, whereas I expected him to share them as money!

Account 40: Revisions

I was testing a 14 year old yr. 9 boy at the reading and language clinic. Once his writing was complete, I asked if he wanted to go over it, edit, make revisions. 'No' he replied. I asked him to please read out loud so that it would be recorded on tape and that way if I had any difficulty reading his text later, I could consult the tape recorded version. There were many parts of his writing that were confusing even to him but he glossed over them and didn't ask to make revisions even then. I asked him what happened in class, did he read over his writings – act as first audience of his own writing – to see if he had said what he wanted to. His response was 'No, that's the teacher's job'. (Beverly MacInnis private communication)

Account 41: Pressing buttons

L. was having problems identifying the correct operation to use on a particular set of questions. She had done the first couple and in fact they were all multiplication questions. So we talked through the first one and, after a long piece of teaching, we came to the conclusion that it was multiplication and the second was multiplication, and so the rest must be multiplication. So she was quite happy then pressing buttons on the calculator and doing multiplication sums. But I knew really that I had done nothing, that I hadn't really taught her that that particular set of situations were to be interpreted as multiplication sums. All I helped to do was get those sums right on that particular page. She was quite happy with that (adapted from Brown and Dobson 1996).

Account 42: Piloting

TEACHER: Right. I think people are getting there, aren't they?
PUPIL (*quietly*): No.
TEACHER: You're doing alright (soothingly).
PUPIL: I can't do it.
TEACHER: You look like you are doing alright. You do really.
PUPIL: I don't understand . . . Do you have to like put . . .
TEACHER: I'm going to show you now. Yeah?
PUPIL: That's what Miss Black says. (Edwards 1995)

Account 43: Panic

I've never taught this topic before, and I'm not very confident about it. I prepared myself thoroughly by reading a number of books, but I couldn't bring myself to make it as open-ended as I usually do. I taught it very straight from the blackboard and didn't really invite questions. When E. asked a question that I didn't know the answer to I nearly panicked. But I was able to invite the rest of the class to comment on the question, and N. said something that I realised was right and I took it from there. (PME234 Unit 5: 16)

Account 44: Struggling

I found myself with students just two years behind me, and I was supposed to show them how to do the assignments, even though I had no idea what some of the questions were about! I found myself asking them what each of the technical terms meant (they would look in their notes), then I would ask them for theorems or techniques connecting these together and they would always find something in their notes. As soon as I had enough information to see how to do the question, I would then embark on 'doing it' on the board 'for them'. I decided that what was most valuable for them was to see me struggle, and what was most valuable for me was to become aware of how I operated when I did not know the content.

Account 45: Decision point

A first-year geometry teacher was discussing the proof of a theorem with the class. In the back of the room a student who was the band's drum major was twirling her baton. After a minute or so, the young teacher noticed her behaviour. The teacher's confusion about alternatives was mirrored on his face. Apparently alternatives did not exist since the teacher avoided the situation. But the impact on the class of the indecisiveness could not be discounted. (Cooney 1988: 284)

Account 46: Hanging high

A coach told a basketball player who was practising shooting to 'jump high, hang there, make your shot and then come down'.

Hanging there can be seen as analogous to inserting a gap, to the creation of distance. Caught up in the momentum of my experience it is impossible to notice and choose, in the same way as a shooter, caught up in the momentum of jumping up and down, does not have the space to aim and shoot. (Hanley *et al.* 1995: 30)

Account 47: Catching myself in the moment

A primary teacher reported the following interchanges:

P1: I have only ten parcels, there should be eleven. I must have missed one.
T1: Why don't you [pause – I was going to say . . . 'go through them and check each one'. Instead I said] . . . you need eleven to do the investigation. [At this point I walked away but continued to observe.]
P2: Have you got the same as me?
P1: No, we had better match them.

[They then started to place the parcels on the sheet of A4. How I wanted to intervene! I made the decision (almost too late!) to leave them with the problem. Even now when I re-read the extract I can recall the feeling of being awake to the moment of decision and being able to choose an alternative to what may have been an automatic response]. (Hanley *et al.* 1995: 31–32)

Account 48: Not seeing

A 12 year old girl was asked to talk about the expression $3x + 6$. She said

'3 is an odd number, and I don't like odd numbers. 6 is ok, 'cos it's even.'

No reference was made to the x or to the +.

Account 49: Imagining

T: Now boys and girls, shut your eyes and imagine a large fish tank half-filled with water. Drop in five marbles: plop, plop, plop, plop, plop. Alright, the marbles are now at the bottom of the tank.

S: But my marbles are in the middle!

T: [rather impatiently, eager to get on with lesson] What do you mean by 'in the middle'?

I then realised that his marbles were somehow suspended in the water. I asked him whether he could try to push his marbles down. He said he would try as he flashed his unmistakably winsome smile and shut his eyes as if nothing had happened.

The astute reader will have noticed that a majority of the accounts I have used have come from women. This too provides something to work on: if gender-specific conjectures come immediately to mind, is there any basis in experience for those conjectures?

8 Noticing and professional development

This chapter considers the role of disturbance in prompting and sustaining professional development, and at ways in which the noticing can be used explicitly to foster and sustain professional development in others. Francis Bacon (1609) captured the spirit of this beautifully: 'So knowledge, while it is in Aphorisms and observations, it is in growth; but when it once is comprehended in exact Methods, it may perchance be further polished and illustrated, and accommodated for use and practice, but it increaseth no more in bulk and substance.'

Responding professionally to disturbance

The term disturbance is intended to be neutral with respect to response. It is intended to signal simply that some action is initiated, something happens. I can be surprised by something that happens, concerned by what I see or hear, struck by a thought, or irritated by something said or done. I can find myself thinking about something, suddenly attending to something different, or find myself doing something without recalling quite how it got started. All of these are referred to as disturbances.

In this chapter two useful types of disturbance generators are described in addition to a reminder that sharing accounts of critical incidents, which forms the backbone of the Discipline of Noticing, is an important source of disturbance.

Organisms are in dynamic equilibrium with their environment, whether we are thinking on the scale of cells, humans, groups of humans or planet earth. But nothing is static, and as the environment alters, disturbances are created and removed. Furthermore, response by an organism to disturbance is yet further disturbance to the environment and in this way there proceeds an endless process of adjustment and change: the dynamic of life. Disturbance is neither positive or negative, simply part of constant adjustment, just as when riding a bicycle there is constant adjustment of weight and handle-bars, just as when looking at something there is constant adjustment of eye direction and focus, and just as when sitting or standing there is constant adjustment of muscle tension.

Response to disturbance, whether through assimilation or accommodation, through rejection or adjustment, constitute the organism learning, which may be unsophisticated through being particular to the current disturbance, or which may be sophisticated through being recognised as a particular case of a more general disturbance and of a possible general response. In this perspective, learning in general, and professional development and enquiry in particular, can be seen as activities in which the scope of generality of some sensitivity, action or interpretation is extended.

Locating disturbances in professional and research literature

The classic source for disturbances to professional practice is in watching colleagues at work. Something that someone does, the way they interact, a phrase or two that they use, strikes a chord, and this leads to asking questions and trying things out. A less immediate source of disturbance is in reading professional journals, and in following up research articles. While any encounter can prove disturbing, especially if the other person is being more successful under some criteria, encountering stimuli which lead to enquiry through reading requires a certain degree of sensitivity and concern to begin with. The cycle of Grrs described in the opening chapter capture some of the different forms of disturbance which motivate people to look outside of their own practice for ideas. Often people are looking initially for ways to augment what they currently do, and for some this remains a career-long stance. But for many, encountering the odd clever idea to include is insufficient. They find themselves wanting to locate a deeper or more secure basis from which to make choices. Having recognised an itch, noticing offers a way of scratching that itch, and as the Zen saying 'If everything is going well, get a goat' suggests, insightful professional development invites people to 'scratch first, itch later' (Shigematsu 1981).

Locating disturbances in striking accounts

Collecting and exchanging accounts can be a form of disturbance, for it often happens that what we notice and what we think we are concerned about do not align precisely. By collecting accounts and then seeking common threads you may find that what you think is an issue does not actually come through very clearly, while some other issue does. By sharing accounts with others you may find that someone else's accounts are initially shocking or unusual, yet still trigger memories of forgotten events of your own.

The most useful accounts are ones which are striking in some way, which set up at least a frison of disturbance. If a collection of accounts seems merely to confirm what you 'have always thought', then there will be no stimulus to action.

Protases

Protasis is a noun meaning *premise* or *assertion*, derived from the Greek word *tasis* meaning tension. It refers specifically to the first statement of a syllogism (as in 'all men are mortal'), which is general, and which in the classic Aristotelian syllogism is usually followed by a particular ('Socrates is a man') leading to a conclusion linking the particular to the general. In the context of professional development, a protasis is a general aphorism or arresting statement which when juxtaposed with one's own particular experience produces a tension. This tension may lead to an action of questioning and challenging current practices, and ultimately, to greater clarity or even change (a form of conclusion).

Strictly speaking any assertion could be a protasis for someone, if it happens to set up a tension for them. In practice there are various statements which catch most people:

To be alive, every teacher must be a researcher

Only awareness is educable;
Only behaviour is trainable;
Only emotion is harnessable.

I cannot change others; I can only work at changing myself

Teaching takes place in time; learning takes place over time

If you want sense you have to make it yourself

Habit forming can be habit forming

Sleep is to the hunter as excitement is to students

Wounds are to the patient as assessment is to students

One thing we do not seem to learn from experience is that we do not often learn from experience alone.

Try to do for students only what they cannot yet do for themselves

Scratch first; itch later

Presence always contains absence

Discussing responses to a protasis may be stimulating, but is not always maximally fruitful. Using the protasis to select specific illustrative or challenging incidents and giving brief-but-vivid accounts of these to others can lead to a more systematic and robust form of analysis. For when a protasis 'works', it is not resolved and then put away. Rather it hangs around, irritatingly coming to mind over a period of time, just like the grit in an oyster. Juxtaposing it with incidents which come to mind is then a good way to use the energy of irritation.

Some things to try now

Take one of the protases listed above, make a poster out of it, and place it somewhere prominent, where you and others cannot help noticing it. For example, I used to have one on the back of my office door so that as people were leaving, they would catch sight of it.

Wait until someone asks about it, then invite them to locate examples which illustrate or contradict it. Try to find more than one interpretation.

Surprises

One of the tacit assumptions about education is that it is a process which happens to students, and the aim of educators is to make this 'happen' smoothly and effectively. I take quite a different view. I see learning as the response of an organism to disturbance, and education as the intentional creation of conditions to promote learning. This view is implied in the clichés: 'I won't do that again', 'Live and learn' and 'You learn something new everyday', all of which are said after a disturbance has raised the possibility of responding differently next time. But as has already been suggested, we do not often learn from mere experience.

From this perspective, the role of a teacher is not to ease students through an ordeal, but rather to stimulate them to using their powers to make sense, to see things freshly, to make the obvious problematic, to challenge and be challenged, to alter the locus and focus of their attention. The real issue for teaching is then to judge the appropriate degree of challenge, for too great or too small a challenge may induce some people give up.

An example of a surprise which arose as a defensive measure is the following:

Account 50: 'Good'

When a participant in a session raises a challenge to something proposed, I find myself responding with 'Good!'. My tone of voice is chosen to suggest that I do indeed mean it, and my posture is 'full square' and not defensive.

The utterance 'good' has a number of features. First, it surprises people, catching them off guard because they are expecting either justification or counter-attack. Consequently there is almost always a definite pause, a holding of breath as people consider what I might see as good. Second, it provides me with time to think during the inevitable pause. It is not a matter of running through twenty-three options, but rather of allowing time for a suitable possibility to come to mind. A standard development is to ask for elaboration of the point, and to get others to give their own versions, and even their responses. By deflecting attention in this way I support participants both in listening to each other and in thinking about the issue, as well as giving myself space to choose my moment to take further initiative if that turns out to be necessary or desirable.

The point of significance is that 'Good!' is provocative (as long as it is not used too often!). It sets up a disturbance in participants and so has the possibility of provoking them into participating actively. If I always have a pat answer to student questions and challenges, then students will quickly get the message that they have only to wait until the lesson gets back on track before paying attention again.

Great care is needed with provocation however. Deliberate intention to provoke, to shock, often has the opposite effect. The reason seems to be that in deliberately trying to shock one is led to be too extreme. As with any disturbance, if the tension is too extreme, either too great or too small, people are liable to turn away and reject the input altogether. Instead of focusing on provoking others, it is most effective in my experience to be on the lookout for what challenges me and then to offer that to others.

Although there is rarely any need to go looking for disturbances, it is possible to insulate yourself from their effects, so that they do not serve to challenge, just as it is possible to be on the lookout for surprises as a source of stimulation. This is illustrated by comments made by two different teachers early in a school year:

Account 51: Surprises

A: 'I know the pupils; let's put it this way – there won't be any surprises.'
B: 'I've got to know the pupils – I am now ready for surprises.'

On the one hand, deciding there will not be any surprises is likely to make any surprises that do come quite disturbing, while at the same time many possible surprises will be overlooked or masked, and so opportunities lost. On the other hand, expecting surprises may escalate what counts as a surprise, making it more difficult to recognise, or it may make it easier to use any small disturbance that is detected.

Some things to try now

Consider some of your habitual expressions to see if any might have the effect of provoking students into thinking about the situation (as with 'good!'). If necessary tape a session so as to provide some data. Ask a colleague if you can observe a session of theirs, and look out for provocations.

Select some situation in which you wish you could deflect attention or gain time in some way, and construct a provocative response to use. Before each session, form as strong an image as possible of yourself using that response.

Using noticing for leading professional development

The previous chapters have elucidated principles behind a disciplined form of noticing, lying at the heart of development as a professional. It has also been suggested that professional development is a process of sensitising oneself to notice opportunities to act freshly and of seeking alternative ways of acting using new gambit-tactics. But these principles apply equally well to the situation in which one is trying to support others in their professional development.

Change may be response to disturbance, but my basic principle is that: I cannot change others, though I can work at changing myself. Change is problematic when someone intentionally tries to disturb others. Intentionally disturbing others is at best, likely to be steadfastly resisted and at worst, to backfire. No one likes to be told to change. Effective change is something that people do to themselves; more radically, but more aptly when investigated closely, change is something that happens to people who adopt an enquiring stance towards their experience. You may be able to force changes in behaviour in the short term, but forcing changes in awareness and perspective is almost impossible. Eventually the dam will break and what changes there appeared to be will be nullified, unless the individuals have participated fully and found it self-confirming.

Mary Bateson (1994) observes that

> change and constancy [are] often two sides of the same coin. We can only makes sense of the relationship between constancy and change by thinking of them in layers flowing under or over or within each other, at different levels of abstraction.

The notion of invariance only makes sense when there is change, and change only makes sense when there is relative invariance. Thus we are all hurtling through space around the sun at around 26 km per second, but since we are all moving at the same speed in the same direction, we cannot detect it. We experience it as invariance. If cars are driving along a motorway all at the same speed then there is no relative speed, and it is as if they are standing still with respect to each other, until you juxtapose them with the sides of the road and so experience movement. Similar things happen with social and psychological awareness. I may feel I am changing as I notice more, but outwardly others may see no difference; pre-adolescents are constantly being told 'my how you have changed' but since their awareness is based in their body, they are much less aware of those changes than of other invisible inner changes.

Real change is not simply a matter of psychology, of convincing yourself and then acting differently. Real change is based on becoming aware of possibilities which were not previously available. Sometimes people are attracted to new ways of describing practice, and over time begin to change the practice itself as well; sometimes people adopt and adapt new practices and only later begin to describe it in new ways. But at the heart of change is the recognition of new possibilities for acting. That is why the very heart and essence of noticing is being awake in the moment to possibilities. The discipline comes in working to open oneself to new possibilities, having become aware of them from watching others, from reading literature, from discussion or from exchanging accounts of incidents, so as to harness the requisite energies to make those possibilities come to mind at the relevant moment. Indeed, one could go so far as to say that any intentional professional development has the aim of enhancing noticing, and any practices employed are contributions to the Discipline of Noticing.

Real change also requires the support of a compatible group of people whose presence can sustain individuals through difficult patches, and who provide both a sounding board and a source of challenge for observations, conjectures and theories. That is why the Discipline of Noticing is aimed at individuals working within a group. It is essentially about psychological transformation, but this is almost impossible without a supportive community which develops a shared language, helps.maintain focus and enables individuals to compare and share experiences, hopes and struggles, so that there is transformation of the social as well.

To support other people effectively in their professional development (including everything from supervising higher degrees to 'managing change') is not to offer solutions, not to suggest what they 'should' do. At best one can offer some things they *could* do, to put them in the way of some literature or of a colleague with relevant experience, but even that is fraught unless the person is in a position to hear what is suggested and sees the suggestion as a resolution of a felt problem or tension. When someone is up against a significant difficulty in their practice, they may need reassurance that it is indeed a difficult problem, otherwise they may feel they are inadequate. If the reassurance is not forthcoming, they may be inclined to conclude that other people do not understand. While it is reassuring to hear that others have similar problems, it does not always help to hear that someone else 'has a solution'. The reason is that 'the solution' is an alternative practice, a different way of acting. But this usually involves a different way of perceiving, and so may depend on different beliefs and assumptions, on a different world view.

What one person can do for another, or for others, is to guide them in a way of working which enables the individuals to work their way through states of rejection and 'my situation is worse than you imagine', into a frame of mind where they can hear and consider alternatives. Have you ever suggested a course of action to a colleague who was complaining about some aspect of their professional practice, but been mystified as to why they did not simply adopt your practice? It is the same reason that students do not seem to internalise what they 'learn' so as to be able to act upon it later. There is a difference between 'being told' and 'hearing'.

For example, if someone has begun to realise that they find it really hard to get one task finished before embarking on several more, it is not sufficient to tell them to make a list and to prioritise. There may be deeply personal and social forces acting which make self-organisation problematic for them. The person has to recognise list-making or prioritising as a possible action for them to carry through. On the other hand, someone in a break in a session who is unhappy with 'how it has gone so far' may be in a perfect position to hear a suggestion which comes from a respected colleague, not in the form of 'why don't you try', but in the form of 'I've tried . . .'.

One way to try to expose people to alternative practices is to write about those practices, to employ them with the people concerned (to 'model' them), and to provide case-studies in the form of video-tapes, audio-tapes and written descriptions. This is where exposure to professional and research literature can be powerful, but it is only likely to be effective if the person is disposed to enquire, to reach out to a wider world. If they persist in seeing their own situation as different to those described, then they are not in a position to benefit.

Where attention is directed to new practices specifically, there will often be reaction. This happens particularly when people are shown video-tapes of supposedly expert or good practice. Because behaviour is multiply interpreted, viewers often stress different features from those stressed by the proponents of 'the practice'. Indeed, it is often difficult to be specific about exactly what constitutes the new practice. And as with any professional development, the issue is not so much what is displayed, given, or demonstrated, but what the participants are sensitised to notice. Thus if I am concerned about some aspect of a video-tape I may not even see other aspects I am intended to see; if I am unfamiliar or unconfident about overt content, I may not even notice how the leader is modelling certain practices.

A good way to expose people to alternative practices without pressuring them to suddenly adopt one and to act differently, is to arrange that one person gives a brief-but-vivid account of some problematic situation, and then others recount situations which they think have some similarities. In the process, different practices will be revealed, but in a non-threatening manner. It is not a matter of 'oh, I do this, so I'll tell her by describing an instance of me doing what I do'. It is a matter of offering a brief-but-vivid account without the intention of 'offering a solution'.

Of course you do not know what different people are attending to as they hear the accounts and negotiate what seems to be similar and what different. If people get caught into a pattern of 'yes but', in which they continually find some reason why their situation is tougher or more demanding than anything offered by others, then it is necessary to do more work on the rendering of accounts and what one does with them, for the purpose of the accounts is to ground generalities, to provide contact with experience. They are used to try to locate in more detail what the issues, tensions, struggles and problematicities are for participants. A sequence of 'yes but . . .' is a form of justification and simply acts as an energy leak to avoid facing the issue.

Once some specific practices emerge, it is not helpful to shove any of them down someone's throat by saying 'why not try . . .?'. On the contrary, the best approach is again to use the discipline of noticing: after several different accounts have been given, with some negotiation of what is similar and what is different, participants can be invited to think back over the various accounts and to select one or two features that have struck them, and perhaps even to imagine themselves in a similar situation in the future, making use of a new possibility. For in the end, it is only what strikes someone, what they mark, that has a chance of influencing their practice.

Jaworski (1998) reports on a two-year project involving six teachers and two academics in which the issues for enquiry and development came from the teachers in response to probing from 'respected others'.

Account 52: Seeking answers

> Teachers acknowledged that what *they* referred to as *hard* questions from the researcher were instrumental in enabling them to delve deeply into their own purposes and become more overtly aware of personal theories motivating their practice. (Jaworski 1998: 4)

The Discipline of Noticing in general, and working with accounts in particular, provides a useful structure for supporting and provoking professionals to question judgements and to ask 'hard' questions, for this works best when there is an agreed phenomenon to be questioned, which means some brief-but-vivid accounts. Trying alternative actions is enhanced by preparing oneself in the manner described in Chapter 3, because the whole point about a habit is that the action is invoked long before the incident happens, so you have to work at recognising the early signals and you have to have some alternatives to put into place.

Some things to try now

Say What You See (again)

Take a picture or poster or object associated with your practice, and, with one or more colleagues, practise giving brief-but-vivid descriptions of details so that others can recognise what you are referring to (without pointing or touching). Then extend the task to describing how some item is used in practice, again without touching or pointing. Use imperative language: 'pick up the . . ., turn it . . .' in order to enhance the connection between your mental image of what you do, and your description. Have colleagues give different descriptions (again using imperatives) and then discuss differences and similarities.

Describe, using imperatives, how to make use of a case study in training or teaching someone a new procedure.

All professional development could be described as changes in sensitivity to notice and accumulation of alternative actions to initiate. *Say what you see* can be a useful label to remind yourself to work on brief-but-vivid accounts-of before launching into accounting-for.

Working with colleagues informally

Try asking colleagues informally to describe some incident from their recent practice. Then see if that triggers an incident of your own, and if so, offer a brief-but-vivid account of yours. Ask them whether they recognise yours as similar in some way to their own. As others begin to join in, you can suggest reducing the emotive and explanatory features of accounts, concentrating instead on entering other people's situations as trigger to re-entering one's own. Doing this a few times is likely to prompt others to join in, and thus to begin to establish a practice of sharing experience without moaning or seeking sympathy.

If you find yourself with a group of colleagues, perhaps leading a professional development session, you do not need to know a great deal about the details of their particular practices. You can use the notion of brief-but-vivid accounts of incidents to enable colleagues to share practices as well as issues and tensions, without the suggestions coming from you.

> ### *Working with colleagues formally*
>
> Ask participants to recall some incident which was in some way problematic or of concern to them (which is presumably why they have come to the session). Get them to describe it to a colleague, briefly-but-vividly, with as little emotion, as little justification or explanation as possible. The colleague is permitted to ask questions of detail, but only where they are needed in order to enter the specific incident. No commenting is permitted. Then get them to write down a honed version of their incident. These can either be collected and re-distributed so that someone else reads it out, or read out to the whole group by the author. After each incident, each person is invited to see if they recognise something of the incident, and to make a quick note of any incident of their own which comes to mind. After three or four, or perhaps more accounts have been offered to the whole group, people are very likely to start noticing commonalities and contrasts. Once discussion starts, your task as leader is to keep discussion away from explanations, theories and solutions. The intention is that in describing 'similar' incidents, people also describe their own practice, and this can inspire the author of an incident to try a different approach to their problem.

Summary of Chapter 8

Noticing is triggered by a disturbance. It is marked by a sudden shift in what is at the centre of attention. It involves making a distinction between foreground and background, stressing some features and consequently ignoring others. Working on accounts can produce relevant disturbances, as can working on other stimuli such as catchy slogans and other surprises.

The principles elaborated in Chapter 8 for using accounts, and more generally in the Discipline of Noticing, provide a way for supporting colleagues in their professional development as well as ways to work on one's own development. Experience suggests that where I am working on my own practices, others are likely to find it more attractive, more appealing, and more supportive to work on themselves than when I am simply acting as a facilitator, conduit or agent.

SUMMARY OF PART IV

Part IV completes the description of the Discipline of Noticing in relation to professional development. The claim has been that professional development, seen as a process of pragmatic enquiry, is enhanced and sharpened by carrying out practices associated with the Discipline of Noticing. Suggestions have been made for ways to use accounts of incidents (and other stimuli such as video or audio recordings etc.) to provide a focus for employing the Discipline of Noticing. This can lead to changing one's own practice, as well as supporting others in doing the same.

Moving from there to research is actually in many ways a very small step. Indeed, systematic and disciplined professional development is itself a form of action-oriented enquiry, if not research, but it lacks overt discussion of problematic aspects of data collection, interpretation and analysis, and the products of enquiry are usually changes to practice, whereas the products of research are usually descriptions of the studies, presented to colleagues for their critique. The next section explores these differences, and shows how the Discipline of Noticing can straddle the two worlds of professional development and research.

Part V

From enquiry to research

Here in Part V we cross a divide between enquiry and research. Enquiry is the response we make to a desire to find something out. It can be more or less systematic, more or less methodical, and there can be greater or lesser effects as a result. There may be no need to convince others as long as one is personally satisfied. Academic research also involves systematic enquiry but it requires explicit attention to context (including what other authors have said about the particular question or related questions), method employed, some form of validation or cross-checking, and some form of reporting of the results of that enquiry to other people so that it can be criticised, debated, challenged, and perhaps taken up by others. For research to be seen as convincing, the questions have to be clearly formulated, the observations and experiments appropriately probing, the analysis relevant, and the research methods have to conform to accepted standards, the elucidation of which is known as methodology.

As with any practice, research has Dos and Don'ts which vary over time, from community to community, from place to place, and from individual to individual. The particular practices which are followed in a project constitute the research method. These become a research paradigm when a community of practitioners repeatedly use a similar approach.

Chapter 9 addresses the general question of what constitutes research, suggesting various essential aspects and using the notions of different worlds (as in world-views) to make rough distinctions between different forms of enquiry.

Chapters 10, 11, and 12 apply the ideas of Chapter 9 to noticing. What emerges is a four-fold structure:

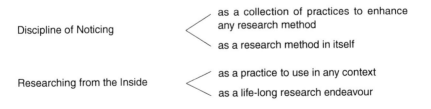

Chapter 10 proposes that all research depends upon noticing, because to develop as a researcher following any method requires developing sensitivity to notice, to choose to act in certain ways as part of the method being followed. It further suggests that despite attempts to delineate formal methods for locating or approaching 'truth', there remains a natural way in which ordinary people come to know things which affect their practice. The case is made that the Discipline of Noticing systematises what is largely natural, and supplies practices which enable it to become a research paradigm itself.

Chapter 11 proposes that the Discipline of Noticing itself constitutes a research method, ideally suited for improving and researching both content and form of professional development, and hence improvements of professional practice.

Chapter 12 uses the Discipline of Noticing to develop a particular form of practitioner research called *researching from the inside*. At a superficial level, all questions and assertions can be worked on through contacting relevant personal experience, but the methods can also be used by practitioners to research their own experience of, for, and with themselves. As the Zen proverb has it, 'We do not need more knowledge, but more wisdom; wisdom is found in our attention.'

9 What *IS* research?

Ordinary seeing is based on making distinctions (light–dark, edges between regions of differing brightness, colour or texture). The distinctions you make both imply and are implied by a theory about what is worth attending to and what there is to be seen. In the case of ordinary seeing, these theories are built into the neuron structure of the brain so that neural connections and seeing co-emerge through early encounters with sight. For example, perceiving depth perception in photographs is trained, not natural. The same applies analogously to the more general notion of perceiving or noticing. Noticing means making distinctions, constructing and distinguishing foreground and background. What we notice is what we are prepared to notice, both literally and figuratively, and depends on what distinctions we are prepared to make, on what we are attuned to notice. It is structured by what our theories expect, and by the language we have available (not necessarily just verbal language). This is why philosophical issues intrude on any discussion of research. Any rigorous enquiry must concern itself with what is perceived and by whom under what conditions. We cannot escape questions of epistemology (the study of knowing and how it comes about), or ontology (the study of how ideas come into existence) even though they may at first seem abstract and unrelated to professional practice. They turn out to be critical if the enquiry is to be shared with colleagues.

There is an apparent circularity in the argument that what we perceive is what we are prepared to perceive, and what we are prepared to perceive is what we have perceived in the past. How does one ever come to perceive anything new?

Research, as systematic enquiry, is the modern response to these perplexing questions. You enquire systematically, you subject that enquiry to criticism, and you try to persuade others that the findings are valid. But this apparently simple formulation is highly problematic.

To address this question in a scholarly manner, it is necessary to read what the experts have written across the ages, to find out what they said, and to locate what rings true to us today. To address this question in an enquiring manner, you interrogate closely your own experience, and you juxtapose that with what others have said. In a later chapter I report briefly on the results of such approaches, as an outline guide for others who wish to do likewise. For now I wish to maintain the pragmatic theme of the book by turning to descriptions of traditional forms and formats for research.

In order to crack the mysteries of 'research', I shall first look at various components found in virtually all research to do with people. Then I will describe types of research according to different worlds and world-views which they embody.

Components of research

In order to make sense of someone else's research, or to build a research project, it is helpful to break research up into a number of components, many of which appear as chapters in theses or as sections in papers. This brief summary is elaborated in what follows.

Questions asked	What questions drive the enquiry; sometimes it helps to outline what an answer would look like or what you would do with an answer if one were found
Objects of study	Who or what is studied and in what context or setting?
Methods	What is actually done? Often there is a specific chapter of a thesis which outlines the methods used and justifies their choice by appeal to previous researchers and established paradigms, and by indicating why other approaches were rejected
Purpose of study	Who gains what from such a study? What is it trying to achieve? Who is the audience and what are they intended to do with or because of it?
Data	Facts and observations are gathered in order to make conjectures and to abstract generalities, and are put forward as evidence to justify, validate, or illustrate a conjecture or thesis
Analysis	To make sense of data, to draw and justify conclusions, data has to be selected, organised, grouped and linked. Connections are imposed between constructions and it is those constructions or interpretations which have to be justified to others. How this is done is part of the method, the theory of which is methodology; analysis includes discussion of the robustness of the analysis if the situation data were to vary somewhat
Claims	Assertions are made as a result of the research, whether as explanations or as predictions, and they include a description of the range and scope of generality or applicability to other situations. They constitute a thesis, which is then presented in some form, often as a Thesis or published paper or book

Products	How claims are expressed, how they are offered to the community for others to criticise, check, confirm or contradict, build on or reject, employ or ignore
Validation	How the researcher expects to convince others; how conditions can be replicated, repeated or otherwise interpreted in other situations.

It is typical of research to make new distinctions and to break complexity into simpler components, just as has been done by producing these headings. The effect is often to make things seem more complex than before. Unfortunately this also has the effect of implying that the separate entities can indeed be separated. My list implies that you can isolate those various components, whereas they are in fact intricately interwoven and overlapping. For example, a research question is asked from a particular viewpoint, and often this includes a propensity for certain methods. Any collection of methods has a concomitant justification or methodology (which strictly means the 'study of method') that is itself an integral part of the philosophical stance adopted, the way of viewing the world. These include overt and covert purposes and aims of the researcher, not to say personal goals such as status and attention from colleagues.

Someone who has had little contact with a sophisticated tool is unlikely to use that tool to resolve some problematic situation. So too a researcher unfamiliar with factor analysis or phenomenography is unlikely to use these methods unless prompted to learn them. So question and methods are inter-related, and these are bound up with purposes and world-view.

When a question is asked, it already contains an implicit expectation of the form an answer might take, which is why the cliché 'If I were going there I wouldn't start from here' is so apt: it is often the case that to address what someone wants to know you do not start with the question as they are posing it! For example, you do not get far asking a physicist about divining, nor asking a historian about why power corrupts. Each discipline, each methodical approach within a discipline is designed to address only certain types of questions. In mathematics, the methods used to obtain an answer can be apparently unrelated to the domain of the original question, but the actual method does not matter as long as the transformation between domains can be justified. By contrast, in mathematics education in particular, and in education more generally, questions and resolutions are intimately bound together.

Take for example a question to do with children's errors. It could take many different forms:

How prevalent is this error? (quantitative–statistical);
What is it like to make this error? (qualitative, phenomenological);
What features do people who make this error share? (anthropological, qualitative or quantitative);
What might be the cause or origin of this error? (psychological, social, cultural, historical, political, discipline specific);

What experiences would lead to someone making this error? (phenomenological, cultural, historical, pedagogical);
What analogous errors have made in the past? (historical, cultural, psychological, social).

The practical things one does as a researcher are based on an underlying philosophical, psychological, social and ideological stance. Often these are implicit, and part of the research process is to bring them to the surface. For some researchers this is a matter of declaring assumptions at the beginning of their investigations and of their report, while for others the process of making them explicit and charting their changes can become the topic of research itself. The very language used to express, conduct, and report research are manifestations of a philosophy, which includes:

- a view of epistemology, that is, of what it means to know, and to come to know), within that paradigm, and a self-consistent view of the role of theory and its interaction with practice (e.g. by cause-and-effect argument, by sampling, by correlation, by personal experience);
- ontological commitment, that is, what distinctions or phenomena are brought into existence through being named or labelled, and how strongly are we committed to them being attributes or just handy ways of describing;
- a value system indicating what types of questions are researchable, worth asking, and resolvable within that paradigm;
- a view of the psychology both of being a researcher and of being the subject of research;
- a view of the socio-cultural forces which both support and delimit enquiry; and
- an ethics, which is a view of how the individual (researcher and subject) is influenced by the environment (including people), how the environment is influenced by individuals, and how the fact of participating in research as researcher or subject, together with the effects of the relationships between researcher and researched, influence the enquiry; and
- a validation system for convincing others that there is substance to the assertions and claims made.

The nature of knowledge sought, and how such knowledge is justified, depends on the standpoint from which questions are asked, what sorts of answers are deemed researchable, and the audience to whom results are to be addressed. The researcher has a complex perspective for viewing the world, and for trying to convince others that their stance is sensible, productive, and effective.

Questions

Formulating a question is not as easy as it sounds. Merely asking questions is not the same as formulating questions which are meaningful rather than rhetorical, fruitful to pursue, and likely to be tractable. Questions like

'Why don't they remember what I told or taught them?'

suggest personal frustration and expectation, and need considerable refinement before they become fruitful (e.g. what makes something memorable? How can people's evident power to remember be activated with a minimum of effort?). It may be necessary to probe personal expectations and assumptions about what constitutes professional practice, or more abstract actions such as learning and teaching, before finding something sufficiently precise and detailed to investigate.

Once begun, posing questions is relatively easy. However, posing probing questions requires personal commitment to really want to find out. Such a question identifies something which is truly problematic and disturbing. The presence of a colleague can be most helpful in drawing forth what is problematic in professional practice, but even with supportive colleagues, it can take some time for a recognisable question to emerge. That is why the discipline of keeping a record of your current questions (and of salient incidents) and periodically reviewing them can be so helpful. Asking yourself what you would do with an answer were someone to walk in with one often shows up that the question as posed either has no answer, or that an answer would not serve any useful purpose. Trying to outline the form or shape of a possible answer, to describe how you would recognise an answer, can also assist in reformulating questions into a useful form.

Formulating a researchable question often takes considerable effort and time. To be researchable, a question has to admit some method of enquiry and report, usually involving the collection of observations which confirm or contradict conjectures, or which contribute to illustrating claims. The very formulation of a question involves language, which requires externalising, precising and articulating notions that may in fact be very fuzzy and inchoate. Furthermore, the words chosen carry with them a perspective and assumptions about the profession and about your practices. One outcome of research is to make the familiar strange, to bring into question what previously was not even noticed, to bring to the surface implicit assumptions or perspectives.

Objects

Things studied by researchers vary across a broad spectrum,

from the structure of ideas or topics and pedagogic implications of these,

through pupil-client behaviour (in a classroom, on assessment, in an interview etc.) and attitudes,

to behaviour and attitudes, acts and frameworks (as espoused, or observed),

to the forms of technical discourse employed as part of the practices,

to the role of media in instruction and learning (texts, own materials, apparatus, calculators, software, etc.),

to institutional influence (school, community, government),

to methodology and epistemology,

to name just a few. The very act of identifying some 'thing' as what you are studying is an ontological act, that is, an act of bringing into existence. Whatever feature you think you are studying becomes an object once you label it with a noun, thus making it into an 'it'. Once you commit yourself to study some thing, it begins to be noticed everywhere, and to take on a life of its own. Once brought into existence, it is likely to remain there! It is very hard to conclude that the phenomenon you thought you identified does not actually exist. What you can conclude is that a distinction you thought you could make is too fuzzy to sustain, is not recognised by others, or is not fruitful.

In parallel with Chevallard's *transposition didactique*, in which expert awareness is transposed into instruction for novices, there is a *transposition recherche*, in which what is originally questioned is changed into something more tractable, but which becomes the sole focus of further enquiry. For example, an initial question about human learning is transformed into a specific question about certain rats in certain mazes, or a question about student experience is turned into questions about their responses on a questionnaire. In each case the original phenomenon (memory, recognition, skills, attitude etc.) is replaced by an indicator which, it is hoped, permits comparison, measurement or classification.

Methods

Methods encompass two aspects of research: finding out and convincing others. It is possible to learn a great deal about any practice by noticing and thinking about little incidents. Professionals do this as part of their daily activity. But it is very easy to think that you are making great changes or being very sensitive, when it is mostly in your imagination. And it is difficult to sustain energy and not develop habits, simply in order to reduce tension and strain. So it helps personal development to externalise your thoughts in some form, in discussion with colleagues, through personal or shared writing, and by attending conferences and workshops where you encounter other styles and other stories.

Trying to convince others about what you are noticing provides a force to clarify and précis, and an opportunity to check alternatives, because once you become convinced of something yourself, it is much harder to recognise a counter-example to, or a contradiction with, your favourite assumptions. Language enables us to shift and slide in meaning so as to justify ourselves. Convincing others that you have observed something which generalises to their situation involves even more effort, because you have to be able to describe the relevant phenomena, the action taken, and the expected outcome in ways which the other person recognises and is inspired by. You also have to establish that these really are linked, whether by cause-and-effect or through association and mutual co-development.

Purposes

One useful perspective when reading any research is to ask whose purposes the research serves. Who benefits from making the question problematic? Who would benefit from a resolution or from making the question more complex rather than resolving it? Is it pragmatic, investigating some technical matter in the practice, and if so, does it truly serve the purposes of professionals or the people with whom they work (students, patients, clients)? Does it address general issues or questions about details of practices? Does it serve wider political or institutional interests to concentrate attention as it does and to make that aspect problematic? Is it more general, leading to critique of institutional or societal assumptions and structures? Does it offer practical advice or provide a particular way of seeing which will enable me to act differently in the future?

The intended audience is an important aspect of any enquiry or research endeavour. If what you want to do is to develop and improve your children's experience of your discipline, such as mathematics, then there is no immediate reason why you need to consider any audience beyond yourself. Reflective practice is precisely that, but offers little in the way of confirmation or validation; professional development involves interaction with a community, but again does not demand any product beyond behaviour with pupils or students and perhaps colleagues, and offers confirmation and validation only to you; research requires some sort of identifiable product which can be examined and criticised independently of your own behaviour and practice. Philosophers have thought and written at length about methodology and validation, robustness and validity, precisely in order to guard against solipsism and self-delusion, in order to turn practice and personal development into research which has implications beyond the individual and which is open to challenge by colleagues.

Data

Measurements of time taken on tasks, opinions and responses to questions, homework and test results, video-tapes and audio-tapes of incidents and interviews, and personal accounts, all become data *only* when they are constructed as such by someone taking a research stance, with the intention to analyse it in relation to other data. Thus data occupy a space between observation and analysis. Data might include:

- descriptions of experiments, and publication of their outcomes, as in the natural science paradigm;
- descriptions of surveys and presentation of responses and their analysis, as in a social sciences paradigm;
- descriptions of discoveries, and interpretations of how these might be located in an historical record, as in geography, science, anthropology, paleontology, etc.;
- descriptions of relationships between people, and between people and institutions, characterised or classified, or descriptions of discourses employed by different people at different times, as in a sociological paradigm;
- descriptions of events and experiences, and comments on those, by the researcher and others, as in a ethnographic paradigm;
- descriptions of significant incidents and constructed exercises which highlight informative distinctions and alternative actions, as in the noticing paradigm.

Descriptions are more useful if they include indications of how and why the data were collected: for example, instructions (of how to carry out experiments), instruments (for conducting surveys or interviews) and orienting frameworks (background theories).

The data then take the form of measurements, photographs, counts, quotations, transcripts, recordings, notes-in-the-moment and reconstructions of events. In experiments the scientist takes the initiative and constructs the situation for their own purposes; in surveys and interviews the researcher takes initiative to probe an existing situation but does not construct the situation itself (in one sense, the researcher always *constructs* the situation, through their description, but *construct* here is used in the sense of the event not the construal of the event). In describing events and experiences the ethnographer influences the situation by their presence, but their presence is not the primary focus. In describing incidents and constructing exercises for colleagues the researcher seeks recognition from others that current sensitivities are or can be shared.

The method of biography, in which subjects are asked to write an account of salient incidents relevant to their current concerns which are then interrogated, probed and analysed by the researcher, is a response to the observation that:

> every text that is created is a self-statement, a bit of autobiography, a statement that carries an individual signature (Smith 1994: 286)

Pushing this notion a little further, whatever a researcher reports observing or detecting, tell us as much about what the researcher is sensitive to as it does about what was observed. How do we know that another observer differently attuned might not observe something entirely different? And how do we know that what was claimed to be observed was actually observable and not a figment of the researchers expectations? Data are supposed to reassure readers, by enabling them to try test the method of analysis for themselves.

Field notes, audio-tape, videotape and transcripts are media in which people accumulate data. Each provides a slice of an event, but each has its own problems. As well as providing data to analyse in order to shed light on the event from which they were derived, their very form, not to say their analysis, reveals as much about the researcher as the researched.

A video-tape of a lesson is a statement of what seemed to be important to the editor or camera-person at the time, not to say the producer in selecting that classroom at that time. The transcript of an interview already makes choices about pauses and voice tones, as well as about which incidents are selected for analysis. Finally, and most fully, analysis of video-tape, audio-tape, and transcript reveals sensitivities in the way that the analyser speaks about what they see.

One approach to achieving objectivity is to form a panel of people not previously involved in the research, and to train them in the use of a derived framework, measurement or classification system. If the panel has a good measure of agreement in classifying transcripts or video sequences, then there is some evidence that those sensitivities and structures can be trained. It does not however prove that the categories are actually 'there'. Nor can it ever.

The methods of biography and autobiography grasp this nettle and refine methods so as to achieve systematicity and discipline. The method of biography is clearly one person researching another (what in Chapter 5 was called *extraspective*) to the extent that it purports to be an account of the person whose biography is recounted. Biography seen as a mirror in which authors reveal themselves, and autobiography, are introspective to varying degrees, but while they may lead a reader to new perceptions or ways of seeing or construing situations, they are not aimed at informing future action. Biography does not usually aim at a generality, and validation is particularly problematic unless the reader is in a position to check assertions out in their own experience.

Data can be used to generate hypotheses, by standing back and detecting patterns or common threads or similar aspects in several situations. Data can also be used to illustrate general or abstract constructions and to validate predictions derived from theory. Records of events can be used as a source of insight into possible patterns, thus moving from the particular to the general, and as illustration of theories, as a means for the reader to move from the general to the particular.

Data can be used to illustrate a principle or generality, or observation. Thus an account of an incident can be offered as an example of a particular tactic or technique just as an account of an experiment can illustrate what may be possible in other situations.

Data are often used to provide evidence for or against some conjecture. When logic and cause-and-effect are central, a single counter-example disproves an assertion, and indicates that as a conjecture it needs modifying. But in educational research a single counter-example does not often disprove an assertion, because it is so difficult to state all of the necessary conditions which an example would need to meet in order to qualify. Where assertions are made about what people did, data untainted with judgements and explanations (e.g. accounts-of rather than accounting-for) can usually be checked. Once data are interpreted and theorised, analysed and generalised, it is a matter of judging the plausibility of interpretations (which in the end comes down to resonance with your own experience).

Conjectures arising from disciplined noticing are not about what is the case in a particular situation, but about what may prove to be a fruitful perspective or way of thinking, a fruitful distinction which enables noticing to take place in the future. Evidence therefore has to do with whether a person, and a wider community, are able to develop sensitivities which enable them to act freshly in the future.

Sometimes people find themselves caught up in collecting, whether interviews, children's work, case study data, or personal accounts, to the extent that they lose sight of the purpose of collection. Then they are faced with a massive amount of transcript or video, stacks of children's work or notebooks full of accounts, and wonder what to do with it all. Collecting data without prior prediction of how the data will be analysed, or without adumbration of relevant theories which inform the observations and analysis, does not in itself constitute systematic research. It may possibly suggest some conjectures, but to test those conjectures usually requires going back to the sources for more focused probing from heightened sensitivities. Data collection in anything approaching an action-research mode normally goes hand in hand with elucidating and reflecting upon recently collected data in order to inform future action and collection. It is a continuous and integral process, and does not fall neatly into separate stages.

Marton (1981) developed a particular approach to educational research called phenomenography, in response to dissatisfaction with the problematic nature of transcripts and interviews as a means of finding out what people think, feel and believe. The aim is to describe and characterise different ways of experiencing (Marton and Booth 1997: 111). While maintaining that language is the principal means for communication, phenomenography shifts focus from the content of what people say, to the way in which they express what they say, both in language and in action. It charts. Thus the objects researched are variations and changes in capabilities for experiencing the world, and the method is to examine differences and changes in forms of expression and behaviour.

One of the features of collecting data is that the data either become increasingly attractive, seducing the researcher in trying to make sense of, to say something insightful about, the data, or else become deadening and depressing because they are so massive and impenetrable. It is worth remembering that data collection is for a purpose. At best it is an indicator of something else. Measurements, and patterns among them, are only indicators; interviews and transcripts of events are only indicators of aspects of some behaviours. In the case of accounts, these are only useful for enriching one's connections and sensitising triggers to action in the future. There is no point in analysing accounts of incidents themselves, except in so far as to reveal possible sensitivities or actions.

The hardest thing to do with data is to analyse them, to draw out of them some essence, so as to abstract and generalise from them.

Analysis

Data once collected and selected as relevant to a research question has to be analysed in order to turn it into evidence. The wise researcher predicts how she is going to analyse the data before it is collected, not to make a rigorous straitjacket, but to avoid collecting far more than can be dealt with, and to avoid having the data turn into the subject of the research. Usually data have been collected as evidence for or against some hypothesis. Even where the researcher thinks they are observing in order to find out what they notice, it is useful to have considered whether the noticing will be taken primarily as evidence for the researcher's particular sensitivities, whether what is noticed will be the subject of further focused observation, and how the data will be dealt with. Will they be searched looking for themes and issues to emerge? Will some techniques of discourse analysis be used to locate patterns in word use, primitive (in the sense of unanalysed and unprobed) jargon terms, or to isolate particular behaviour patterns or habituated 'scripts'?

Responses can be categorised, grouped, or otherwise assembled as being similar or dissimilar. A quantitative approach seeks to convince the reader through credible interpretation of ratios, percentages and statistical significance, and through locating patterns and clusters; a qualitative approach seeks to convince through detailed description, comparison with other research writing, and resonance with readers' experience.

Claims

Claims or assertions form the backbone of any research programme, whether it is attempting to classify, to explain, to predict or to locate in historical context. Sometimes the researcher sets out to prove that something is the case; sometimes to try to find out what is the case; sometimes to provide the foundation for making predictions. But claims have to be justified. This may happen through statistical data analysis, through reasoning and appeal to the reader's experience or through providing data as evidence.

Reporting findings to colleagues (locally and globally), whether in the form of descriptions of significant moments, descriptions of things worth attending to, exercises to give others a taste of what you think you are noticing, gambits that you have found effective, analyses of accounts of incidents, tables of successes or of qualities of response to probes and test items, are not just about contributing to knowledge, nor merely adding to the overload of paper to be read. It is part of externalising inner thoughts and perceptions so that they can be looked at critically. It is part of a conjecturing atmosphere in which public exposition is undertaken in order to generate response in others, to test for resonance, to trigger other perspectives. It is actually to the researcher's advantage to contribute to the world of research reporting

Products

What is research supposed to produce? Usually one thinks of *knowledge*, probably in the form of answers to questions which initiated the research enquiry in the first place. But knowledge is tricky stuff. There is factual knowledge, often memorised or otherwise internalised. There is knowing-how to do something (usually techniques), like how to organise and run a meeting, or plan a lesson or workshop, and in more detail, how to attract the attention of a chair-person, or how to regain the attention of an inattentive student. There is knowing-about a topic, which probably includes facts and how-to, but also includes connections to related topics, as well as historical, pedagogic and philosophical dimensions. Then there is knowing-what-it-is-like to be doing something, or experiencing something. Finally, there is knowing-to act: knowing it is appropriate to use some know-how and facts, apply some knowing-about, in a particular situation. One of the weaknesses of educational rhetoric is to conflate knowing-how and knowing-to. I can know how to bandage a leg, give an injection, comfort someone, control emotional outbursts, write an essay or perform some specific technique, yet fail to realise that that know-how would be useful in a particular context. A good deal of educational and professional energy has gone into why it is that students who have shown that they can carry out a technique fail to do so on a test, when the teacher sees that it is appropriate.

Research can reveal factual knowledge, techniques, enriching connections and unsuspected complexities. Novels can enable emotions to be experienced vicariously, and hence to appreciate a little of what-it-is-like to be or to act. Both novels and research reports can be a source of knowledge about actions that one might take in certain situations. But there is a huge and endemic difference between knowing-about actions, knowing-how to do something through having done it in the past, and knowing-to act in the moment when it might be appropriate. Educators and trainers in every generation have railed against the failure of students and clients to 'use what they know' in some new or slightly new situation.

Research is not very good at producing knowing-to, except in the researcher. Yet equipping others to know-to act in the moment is the central reason for much research. Since knowing-to-act in the moment involves having a possibility come to mind at an appropriate moment, it requires sensitivities to trigger or activate know-how. The principal effect of research is to develop and enhance the sensitivity of the researcher, with the hope that the reader will be sufficiently convinced (whether through logic, through quantitative reasoning, or through resonance with their own experience) to be sensitised sufficiently to act. The researcher may write a report, but the report becomes at best knowledge-about the findings, not the knowing-to acquired by the researcher.

The most common form of research products are research reports which summarise what was done and why, to whom and with what results. But reports can vary from the apparently scientific, written in a passively detached and objective voice and reporting behaviours, through the production of transcripts with theory-based explanations, to diary-like accounts of daily or weekly striking features of professional life.

The overt product of research is some assertion(s). A covert product of research is a transformation in the perspective and thinking of the researcher. Undoubtedly the most significant effect of any research in education is the change that takes place in the researcher. The more you probe, the more that becomes problematic; the more you explain, the more there is to explain. The effect on the researcher of collecting data varies according to the paradigm being used, but the most common experience of researching in any paradigm is that the researcher asks more and more questions and becomes more sensitive to subtleties than previously. Paradigms differ in the extent to which such changes are even recorded, much less offered in some practical way to others.

Although it is tempting to try to state research results in writing, and to try to communicate results to others through description and summary, such direct transmission can at best be a rough approximation, and at worst can turn insights into trivialities, awareness-of into apparent knowledge-about, and frameworks for seeing into proforma for mechanical action. No matter how precise or fuzzy the assertions arising from research, if they are to be of benefit to others then they are likely to consist of, or to lead directly to, some or all of the following aspects, drawn from the Discipline of Noticing:

- changes in awareness and sensitivity to noticing, alteration in the structure of attention while engaged in professional practice or in research;
- frameworks (succinct labels) which resonate with typical events to remind people of things worth noticing, of their intentions to act in certain ways and of possibilities for alternative responses;
- activities and exercises which highlight or facilitate noticing significant aspects of practice, which may usefully be summarised by a framework and thereby serve to strengthen or sharpen noticing in the future;
- collections of strategies for responding freshly and productively in typical situations; and
- collections of strategies for studying incidents (whether in the classroom, during preparation or marking, or in organisational meetings).

The discourse of knowledge as some 'thing' developed or revealed through research and stored in books in libraries, is very strong. Researchers and policy makers behave as if there is some disembodied collection of theoretical knowledge which is re-organised, augmented, and modified through research. Consequently, in order to participate in this culture it is necessary and worthwhile to contribute products which other members of the community recognise. The Discipline of Noticing is directed towards the growth of wisdom through knowing-to act in the moment.

Validation

Conjectures and generalities have of course to be justified, by a combination of logical argument in the analysis of data and theory-spinning or conjecture formulating. A significant investigation will help to make the familiar strange and/or the strange familiar, to provide a fresh way of seeing, just as a lens might enhance the visibility of previously unrecognised features of a physical object.

Offering a conjectured generality requires clarity in delineating the scope of the domain in which some things are changeable while others remain invariant. If conjectures are too highly situationally specific, then the scope is necessarily very narrow and they are unlikely to be informative for others. If conjectures are too general and too vague, if the scope is too broad, then they are unlikely to offer any new insight or possibility for action, nor any useful distinctions.

Any proposed method of research seeks to develop standards of rigour and robustness, so that the scope of generality allows conjectures to be informative, to make useful distinctions and to inform future actions in different situations. Seeking excessive robustness forces attempts to delineate and control all relevant forces and conditions so that others can replicate the actions; inadequate robustness means that the situation is too specific to the point of being unique, and so findings cannot be applied elsewhere. Demanding excessive rigour in methodical and systematic use of specified methods limits the possibility of serendipity, while insufficient rigour leaves findings open to question because they may be built on sand.

To count as research, there has to be some form of submitting claims to criticism and discussion in a wider community of researchers and practitioners. The most common method is through publication. Not all enquiry has to produce writing, but enquiry without some form of validation is vulnerable to self-delusion, idiosyncrasy, and solipsism. In order to convince others something has to be put forward, whether it is tables of statistics showing success, transcripts demonstrating success, or task-exercises to heighten and sharpen noticing.

The history of Western philosophy can be read as a search for objective truth which will stand up against personal predilection and commitment. But that history is also a record of failure, because theories are always able to be refined, and shifts in paradigms can bring about a re-formulation of even apparently certain knowledge (Kuhn 1970). The sort of truth which is accessed through the discipline of noticing is in one sense subjectively-personal, since it resides in the individual, yet in another sense it is objectively-impersonal in that fruitful action can be recognised, studied and developed by a community.

It is not surprising that despite an enormous amount of research in education in general, and mathematics education in particular, very little has had significant influence on a majority of teachers: the challenge to describe phenomena, actions and predicted outcome to a large and varied audience is at best daunting and perhaps impossible. Unlike scientific research which concerns repeatable experiments on inanimate objects which have a constancy over time and place, education is of course about people, who constantly change over time and place, and who furthermore have to interpret in their own terms what is asserted and suggested.

Worlds

The questions asked and the things examined or observed are constituents of a world in which the researcher moves, and this in turn determines what methods are philosophically appropriate:

- a world of external facts supports repeatable experiments, and is typical of research in the natural sciences;
- a world of attention to language supports grammatical, etymological and interpretative analysis, and is typical of socio-linguistic research;
- a world of opinion and belief supports surveys of representative population samples, and is typical of social-science research;
- a world of others' experience supports vivid description based on interactions, and is typical of phenomenographic and ethnographic research;
- a world of involvement in action and decision making supports description, prediction, and evaluation, and is typical of action research;
- a world of self supports sense making through story telling, and is typical of narrative enquiry and creative writing; and
- a world of reflective practice supports sensitising, noticing and resonance seeking, and is typical of noticing-based research.

Integral to research is the placing of current concerns in historical and cultural context, through locating sources of similar ideas in the past, as expressed by current and earlier authors. In a thesis this is often presented as a 'review of the literature' or, less commonly, an extensively annotated bibliography highlighting the most significant influences in the researcher's development.

A world is brought into existence, or occasioned (Maturana 1988) whenever questions are asked or something is noticed, for the disturbance which triggers a noticing triggers a collection of associated sensitivities, and hence also triggers a perspective, a way of seeing and of thinking about what is noticed. The worlds as summarised here are not disjoint. They are overlapping and mutually interacting. The following exercise may give a little taste of the occasioning of worlds.

Present?

Cover up the figure on the right. Examine the figure on the left. Then cover it up and reveal the figure on the right. Is the left figure present in the right figure?

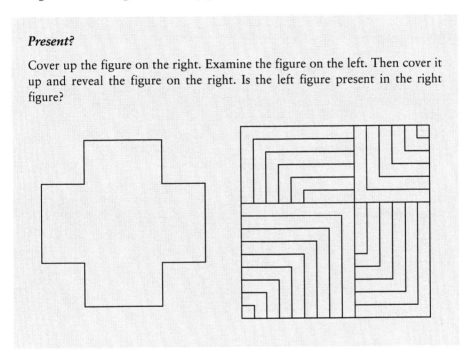

Comment

The interesting question is how you go about the task. Some people assume it is present and try to find it; others suspect it is not present and try to see why it cannot be present. The former experience is like research in which one is looking for something; the latter is like research in which one sets out to contradict or challenge someone else's assertion. Both are limited. A more flexible and fruitful approach is to alternate between the two stances. It is impossible simply to 'look at what is there', since the sensitivities we have to notice are what determine what we see; or put another way, 'observation is theory-laden' (Hanson 1958) and 'a name or label immediately shapes what is seen and what is recalled' (Bartlett 1932).

External facts

- A world of external facts supports repeatable experiments, and is typical of research in the natural sciences.

This type of world includes much of both mathematics and the natural sciences. The researcher is interested in verifiable truth concerning facts, usually to do with measurements of some sort in science, and logical deductions in mathematics, and it is possible to describe a typical situation in such a way that others are able to reproduce the situation for themselves.

For example, in mathematics, you always get the same result when you add two given numbers, and the order in which you add is irrelevant; the perpendicular bisectors of the sides of a triangle all meet at one point which is the centre of the circumcircle of the triangle. These facts are independent of the particular context, and can be justified by recourse to logic, not to specific instances. Similarly, sodium added to water produces heat and vigorous action, again, independent of context. It can be predicted from theory and verified in practice. Photosynthesis has many variants, but works the same way in a given plant in different parts of the world. Mathematical models are proposed and checked against experiments which others can repeat for themselves because the important conditions are specifiable and reconstructible.

In this sense, a world of facts supports repeatable experiments, and validity is based on inference and significance in experiments and effective repetition by colleagues in other contexts. Mathematics calls upon the repeatability of logical reasoning, going through the proof and accepting it step by step as well as globally. Science calls upon mathematics and upon reproducible experimentation.

In a world of facts, the methods of locating facts involve observation and detection of patterns (in mathematics, looking for patterns and structure), the formulation of a conjectured generalisation or theory that encompasses the observations, and the development of a theory which accounts for what has been observed. Observation, pattern seeing and generalisation or theory speculating often happen together, and in no particular order. In mathematics, such accounts-for are arguments starting from already accepted facts. Often in mathematics, as in science, observations arise which challenge accepted facts and lead to further deeper questions and an alteration of theory. Kuhn (1970) proposed that major shifts in fundamental theories are more like complete changes in perspective, and only come to fruition and broad acceptance through a change in generation of researcher.

Education also has a world of facts, encompassing among other things, population figures: numbers of students of a given age, number of teachers, performance on tests, etc. Confusion arises when matters of opinion and belief are presented as factual ('teachers should . . .'), when sampled statistics are presented as facts and used to make generalisations about all members of the population, or when the 'fact' presented has to do with observations made by inspectors or other researchers, and which are therefore necessarily made from a theoretical or value-laden stance.

Questions addressed are about facts and relationships concerning an external world, often assumed implicitly to be unchanging. The aim is to make more accurate predictions and to manipulate the external world to one's advantage. Data tends to be some form of measurement, for this is what can be reproduced and replicated by others. There is a premium on being able to specify what conditions must be held constant and what is permitted to change. Validation is through replicability and relation to current or evolving theory.

Language

- A world of attention to language supports grammatical, etymological and interpretative analysis, and is typical of socio-linguistic research.

In a world focused on language, the objects of study are utterances, or 'text', in the broadest of senses. Arising from interpretative studies of religious texts, the hermeneutic tradition encounters and raises difficult questions concerning whether a text can be said to contain a meaning or whether meaning resides in the reader, and whether what a reader makes of the text is what the author intended, and whether that matters or not. A text triggers interpretations in the reader which are then brought to bear on the text, producing a 'hermeneutic circle' which is ever-present and either has to be broken, or incorporated.

Instead of seeking meaning within the text, you can look at how the text appears to operate, at its structure and at the devices used within it. For example, you can look for embedded and frozen metaphors and images, for hidden meanings based in etymology, for how the language used reflects or stems from historical–cultural–social usage, and for what is not-expressed as well as for what is. The purpose is to situate what is said in a broader context, thereby enriching our reading of the text. Analysis can extend to include explanation (through exposing possible influences) from a wide range of different ideologies, such as psycho-analytic interpretation or social-critique. Assertions are judged by the coherence of the analysis, and the extent to which others find it convincing.

Opinion and belief

- A world of opinion and belief supports surveys of representative population samples, and is typical of social-science research.

People's likes and dislikes, preferences and opinions, beliefs and attitudes, belong to a separate world. Short of asking everyone, it is necessary to take representative samples of the population, to ask them to fill in questionnaires (which can vary from selecting preassigned answers to making open ended responses) and to undertake interviews. Interviews can be done in a relevant context (during a lesson, for example, or in school time), or in a different context (in a laboratory, at home, on the street). Interviews can be pre-structured (as in opinion survey research) or unstructured, following the interests and responses of the people interviewed. In clinical-interviews, researchers sit with an individual while they work on a task, and interact to a greater or lesser extent according to the design and purpose of the project.

The purpose of research of this type is to find out what people think about issues. Often researchers start with something of this form (pre-test) to gather information which can be used to justify or theorise about some proposed intervention, and as a base line from which to measure changes over time after some program of intervention (teaching, changes in setting or environment, contact with an expert, etc). In education, it is rare to obtain significant alteration on both a post-test and a delayed post-test as a result of a specific intervention. One notable exception is Alan Bell's research on diagnostic teaching (Bell and Purdy 1986).

While large scale surveys are best treated statistically, there is increasing interest in professional development and especially in education, in the use of in-depth case study, in which a few (perhaps even just one) student, teacher or administrator is followed closely and interviewed many times over a long period.

Analysis of surveys and interviews varies from the statistical to the summative, based on significance and correlation in survey data. But correlation need not be statistical. In an excellent study, Perry (1968) interviewed students each term during their time as undergraduates at Harvard, and from their comments, distilled a number of 'positions' which they seemed to hold about their responsibilities as students, and the responsibilities of their lecturers. Perry then trained a panel of independent judges in classifying accounts according to these positions, and submitted his data to them. He got very good agreement amongst the panel, thereby simultaneously demonstrating the effectiveness of his training and the consistency or robustness of his delineated positions.

Methodological difficulties with research in this world are bound up with the whole notion of asking questions. If I ask you a question, it is difficult for me to know whether you take the question seriously and engage with it in the way that I am hoping or intend. Indeed it is difficult when designing questions to notice alternative interpretations, which is why researchers use a pilot version to check for ambiguity and other weaknesses before expending effort on a large survey. Questionnaire design requires sophisticated inter-related questions which can be used to check for consistency by the responder, and well thought-out forms of analysis *before* the questionnaire is administered.

Interviews are similarly fraught. What someone says at one time and in one context can be completely at odds with what they say at other times, and claims made about how they do things are often at odds with what is observed in practice.

Getting people to respond to a stimulus is at best an indirect form of measurement of probe. For example, setting tests for children only really shows their response to the particular questions at the particular time, yet we take those responses to be indicative of their competence and understanding in a range of topics and techniques. So any responses are at best indicators. Just as physicists cannot observe a molecule directly so they invent indirect measures using electron-microscopes and magnetic fields, so educational researchers have to be content with indirect observation of behaviour related to the topic of interest. The design of experiments to provoke people into revealing themselves is not nearly as easy as it first seems.

In psychological and sociological research it is common to use or to develop an *instrument* (by analogy with a physical measuring device) which is usually a questionnaire that has been statistically shown to give answers which correlate well with some less easily probed but more fundamental feature. For example, instruments have been devised to elicit aspects of motivation, creativity, anxiety, social status and self-concept, school organisation, etc. In each case the developer has attempted to show that the quality being measured is the one intended, that there is some consistency with other instruments, and that the distinctions made fit with expectation. (See Cohen 1976 for a summary of a wide variety of instruments in education.) Whether there really is 'something there' which is being measured is of course open to question, as are the assumptions behind any method of enquiry.

Even if the responder is sincere, they have to interpret the questions and make a response, and the researcher has to interpret those responses and analyse them. The topic of interpretation is a major concern of almost all educational research and is explored in the final chapter.

Other's experience

- A world of others' experience supports vivid description based on interactions, and is typical of phenomenographic and ethnographic research.

The object of study is the culture of others, what it is like to inhabit their world, to live as they do. Dissatisfaction with surveys, questionnaires and interviews led people interested in what it is like to operate in a different culture to become involved in those cultures themselves (Mead 1928). Through extensive fieldnotes of observations, one hopes to build up a picture of what it is like to live in the culture.

Such a report is a case study. The data consist of reports of incidents and events, interactions and observations. Analysis tends to be incorporated in the editorial selection process and the organisation of the field notes. Validity often depends upon triangulation through recording the views of different participants and observers in different roles. Assertions do not claim to be generalisable beyond the particular context, and as such are a record of what struck the researcher at the boundaries between their own culture and the new. Generalisation lies with the reader, who may or may not recognise similarity with or applicability to other contexts. As researchers become integrated to a greater and greater extent, their sensitivities and access grow but their contact with their past culture begin to dissolve. If they become fully integrated, then they have crossed the boundary and are no longer considered to be researching ethnographically. For example, Carlos Castaneda (1968) purports to be engaged in ethnographic–anthropological study, but the boundary between fact and fiction is completely uncertain in his accounts, and the focus of his study turns into his own experiences rather than the life of a Shaman. In education, researchers have joined classrooms (Armstrong 1980 Jackson 1992), departments and work-shadowed heads, teachers and children.

To undertake an ethnographic investigation it is useful to choose a culture which is in some way unusual or likely to prove insightful. The validity of an ethnographic study cannot be based on whether members of the culture recognise themselves, since they may not be able to see what the researcher sees, and they (usually) lack the researcher's perspective. Validity is based more on internal consistency, on adherence to disciplined separation of accounts-of and accounting-for.

Phenomenography (Marton 1981; Marton and Booth 1997) is a slightly different approach in which one still wants to learn about the experiences of others but not through living the culture oneself. It uses the methods of interviews, questionnaires and observation, but its analysis is more linguistic, placing emphasis on the language people use to express their experiences with the meaning and import of what they say taken as secondary.

Action and decision-making

- A world of involvement in action and decision making supports description, prediction and evaluation, and is typical of action research.

Administrators are involved in planning and decision making about the way others will conduct and structure their work, but most professionals have some degree of managerial or administrative function. But what constitutes a good decision? Which decisions have positive effects, and which have no effect or even negative influences? To research the world of actions and research, the notion of action research was formalised by Stenhouse (1984) who defined research as 'systematic enquiry made public' and then taken further by Kemmis (1985). Kemmis recast action research as a form of reflection:

> reflection is action oriented, social and political. It's product is praxis (informed, committed action) the most eloquent and socially significant form of human action.

Stenhouse's form of practitioner-research blossomed into a variety of practices under the general heading of action research. It is based on the idea that a practitioner is involved in analysing a situation, planning an alternative action, carrying out that action, and then evaluating the effects of what they have done. Rice (1993) quoted Henry and Kemmis (1985) describing it as:

> a form of self-reflective enquiry undertaken by participants in social situations in order to improve the rationality and justice of their own social or educational practices, as well as their understanding of these practices and situations in which these practices are carried out.
>
> (Henry and Kemmis, 1985: 1)

McNiff (1988), McNiff *et al.* (1996), and Carson and Sumara (1997) present action research as a living practice, trying to counter act the forces to automate and tabulate a sequence of specified actions.

In some cases, the researcher is the actor-practitioner making changes. In other cases the researcher supports, observes and studies the effects of other people going through the cycle. By addressing questions such as 'What can I do to improve my practice?' in a systematic manner, participants are led to explore:

- their goals and aims as practitioners;
- what their practice consists of as opposed to their ideals and wishes;
- what they mean by effectiveness and improvement;
- how they can recognise effectiveness and improvement; and
- what actions they can take and what the effects are of taking those actions.

In attempting to pin down these issues they find themselves led into wider issues of the social role and structures of education on the one hand, and into personal issues of their own responses to situations, attitudes to students and colleagues and subject-discipline, etc. This in turn brings them into contact with other practitioners and authors and a wide literature on philosophy, sociology, psychology, education, subject-discipline and even as far afield as religion and personal development, depending on their interests and emerging concerns.

The main disadvantage of routinised action research is that what was intended as a fluid and flexible responsiveness to conditions employing four interactive phases, has become, in the hands of many supervisors and project directors, a rigid cyclic sequence of analyse, plan, act, evaluate, analyse, plan, ... The pressures to achieve a systematic, and hence a recognisable, replicable, and robust methodology, have become ossified and contrary to the experience of people involved in day-to-day emergent management, whether in teaching, caring, or business.

Some forms of action research have directed attention to the forces which appear to block people from making change, and so have become socio-politically oriented. They analyse the conditions which make global and local action difficult or impossible, on the grounds that such local action as is possible is too feeble to make any significant changes.

The objects researched are actions, and the purpose of research is to improve and validate actions which others might then choose to adapt and employ. Action research cannot prove that an action is effective even within stated parameters of applicability. The most it can do is report evidence for effectiveness against stated criteria while the action was undertaken in one or more situations. Thus validity lies with the beholder who can recognise similarities with, and hence possibilities in, their own situation. To make assertions convincing, it is common to employ *triangulation*, which means reporting observations or comments from several people with different perspectives on the same situation, in analogy with geometrical triangulation as a means of checking accuracy in surveying land. If there is agreement between students, teachers, other observers, then there is a stronger sense of confidence in the observations made.

Often the researcher is drawn into using methods of research from the outside (observations of self by others, or of others by self) to demonstrate effectiveness of their action and achieve a form of generalisability. In so doing, the very character of action-research is lost, since to remain true to form, the beholder has to undertake their own action research in their new situation.

Action research straddles the border between the researcher researching other people, and the practitioner researching their own actions. Some forms of action research involve a researcher suggesting changes to practitioners who then undertake those actions. The effects are then observed or measured in various ways by the researcher, a colleague, the practitioner themself, or by probing the people being acted upon (students, teachers, other administrators etc.). Some forms of action research take the form of a researcher supporting practitioners (teachers and administrators) in studying their own decision making.

Self

- A world of self supports sense making through story telling, and is typical of narrative enquiry and creative writing.

A world of interest in myself, in my own experience, is like ethnographic, anthropological, and psycho-analytical study of 'me' (rather than of others). The objects of study are my own feelings, the connections and associations I have between the personal-past and the personal-present, and the purpose is to discover who I really am, and explanations for why I feel and act as I do. Questions tend to be centred on 'why', trying to find historical–cultural– ideological–psychological roots and antecedents which 'explain' or connect to present experience. Data consist of remembered incidents, and analysis consists of narrative links between the past and the present (van Manen 1990). Underlying this approach is a form of cause-and-effect, in which past experiences are sought which dispose me to act and react in certain characteristic ways. Only then, the theory goes, can I hope to change, to develop. Fenstermacher (1997) suggests that in order to be useful, narratives go through a sequence of transformations: of telling and construction; retelling and reconstruction; and deconstruction and critique. These phases parallel the sorts of thing one does with accounts in the Discipline of Noticing, but whereas noticing is centred on accounts-of, narratives are all encompassing, merging and interweaving factual accounts-of with explanations, justifications and theorising, because these constitute the narrative, and provide substance for further story-spinning during deconstruction and critique.

Studying oneself can become solipsistic and even narcissistic, if gaze is always inward. If gaze is only sometimes inward, studying oneself can provide the basis for communicating with and developing sensitivity to others. If gaze is always outward, then the most valuable resource one has as a researcher, namely oneself as instrument, is denied.

Because it is ultimately concerned with the self, the only person who can judge validity is the narrator, and since self-delusion is always a possibility, validity is of concern. There may be considerable therapeutic benefit for the narrator–researcher, but even this is a matter of assertion and difficult to validate. In order to escape solipsism, one looks for resonance and recognition in others reading the narrative, whether the form it takes is a novel or other creative writing, or whether it is some form of task-exercise. Validity depends on the narrative speaking to the experience of others.

Reflective practice

- A world of reflective practice supports sensitising, noticing, and resonance seeking, and is typical of noticing-based research.

The world of reflective practice is based on personal sensitivities and propensities, on noticing and marking. It is most relevant to practitioners wishing to develop themselves, or who want to study their own decision and choice making in the moment-by-moment flow of events, in order to inform their practice in the future.

In the context of education, the principal object of study is the classroom incident, the critical moment when something changes, or a decision is made, whether by teacher or by student. Attention can be focused on the teacher, the students, or the structure of the ideas, on tensions that exist between pairs of these, on interactions between all three, on the influence of environment, and on activities in which some or all are engaged.

Since making observations is always problematic, making them in the world of personal experience is doubly difficult. Data is of three types:

- records in diary-form of brief-but-vivid accounts-of incidents;
- transcripts and tapes of incidents; and
- task-exercises designed to highlight noticing for colleagues.

Incidents may involve other people (colleagues, students etc.), but they may also be accounts of your own work on mathematics, on preparing for teaching, as well as carrying out some action in the classroom or in a meeting.

The purpose of research in this world is to develop personally and professionally in a way which makes you more sensitive to others, and of more use to them in their own (re)search. By becoming better at being aware of your own experience, you have more to draw upon when you try to enter the experience of others. If you set out to try to change others, you encounter resistance and reaction, and for good reason. If you work on yourself, you are likely to influence many around you, and thereby contribute to an atmosphere of development which benefits everyone.

Since it is all too easy to become locked up in a solipsistic world in which you imagine that you are making great changes and achieving great insights, it is essential to remain grounded in a wider world. To this end you can seek to validate observations by audio and video taping of events, and by asking colleagues and students to discuss their observations. You can offer transcripts and accounts-of to colleagues to see if they recognise in their own experience what you are noticing. You can develop and refine task-exercises for colleagues to undertake themselves which are likely to highlight noticing that you have found pertinent. These two components, accounts-of and task-exercises, constitute the source of validation for noticing and are the basis for effective professional development courses, for they are the principal ways in which to contact and resonate colleague's experience. Generalisation is evidenced when colleagues report that their noticing has been sharpened and their actions informed, and are able to offer similar brief-but-vivid accounts-of incidents and choices of their own.

The products of research in this world can be reports to colleagues of brief-but-vivid accounts-of incidents, transcripts etc., and task-exercises. The most significant product is of course the change in sensitivity, the choices available in the future in the midst of action. Such changes are visible in the being of the researcher–teacher, the confidence they display, the sensitivity they exhibit, the possibilities they notice in the moment. Presentation of and writing about task-exercises designed to stimulate or highlight noticing form an important, but secondary contribution.

Summary of Chapter 9

In order to turn from personal professional development to research, you have to address the question of convincing others of what you claim to have found out. This in turn leads to being explicit about questions, about the objects which one studies, the methods used, the purposes of the enquiry, the nature of data and how they are analysed, the form of claims or assertions or conclusions made, the products of research and the ways in which those claims are validated.

While the notion of enquiry, of asking questions and seeking answers, seems unproblematic, it becomes very complex as soon as you realise that the very act of asking questions assumes some sort of perspective, and some anticipation of what an answer might look like. Further analysis reveals that every moment of noticing, every question asked, arises from a disturbance, which brings into play a world of past experience, or ways to account for that experience, and ways of convincing others.

The chapter attempted a rough summary of some of the variety of worlds occasioned by enquiry, and descriptions of the nature of the components of the different forms which enquiry takes.

10 Noticing *IN* research

In this chapter I suggest that noticing lies at the heart of most research. Various aspects of the Discipline of Noticing, particularly the techniques for preparing and pro-flecting, are pertinent to researchers in any domain or discipline, as Pasteur (1854) implied when he suggested that where observation is concerned, chance favours the prepared mind. As James Middleton (1998: 63) put it:

> in order to display intelligent behaviour, a person must first be sensitized to the potentialities of information (attentive or alert to occasion for utilizing information), and be disposed to act upon that information, before he or she can even initiate a sequence of intelligent behaviours.

Expertise as noticing

I hope it is evident by now that any form of expertise involves noticing, but, whereas in the beginner's mind there are many possibilities, in the expert's there are few (Zen proverb). The chiropractor cannot help noticing backs out of alignment as people walk down the street; the physicist notices the use of physical principles in sculptures and in machines; the mathematician notices the use of pattern and symmetry in design and how it is also broken; the mathematics teacher notices how counting provides a starting point for learning a new language; the family doctor notices symptoms in friends and colleagues; the pharmacist notices signs of distress both psychological and medical; the musician notices rhythm and tones; the educator notices ways in which adults give each other instruction; the architect notices structures behind the surfaces of buildings; the landscaper notices the shape of land and the use of plants; the sociologist notices types of interactions between people; and so it goes on. Expertise is sensitisation to notice, coupled with techniques for analysis of, use of, or enquiry into, that noticing.

Researching is itself a form of expertise, and so becoming a researcher, means, at a superficial level, becoming sensitised to the problems of enquiry, to the asking of questions and the warranting of proposed answers or findings or refinements, in their domain. The expert researcher is practised in responding to novel situations. In the middle of an observation, an interview, a task-exercise, they are able to respond to what happens, creatively, rather than simply following habitual or trained behaviours. This sensitisation comes about through engaging in actions which are at the very least similar to, if not identical to, the practices described earlier as parts of the Discipline of Noticing. For example, while preparing oneself for an interview, one might make use of mental imagery to prepare oneself to ask follow-up questions, and to stay alert while listening or watching. One might keep a notebook of striking incidents as they occur so that they are available later for further reflection. I conjecture that where distinctions such as between account-of and accounting-for are not made, and where preparation is not undertaken as vividly as possible, then improvements could be made in the conduct of that research by doing so. In this sense, then, noticing is part of research, and systematic work on noticing could be of assistance.

Professional development of expertise

In the natural sciences, including mathematics, it is customary to focus on technical expertise. Scientists are concerned to become better and better at formulating problems, at modelling situations, at finding and expressing possible relationships, at modifying familiar techniques to resolve new problems, at developing new techniques, and at internalising new ideas from colleagues. Their focus appears to be on the content, on the science, and traditionally, there has been relatively little interest in the processes by which experts become expert, with, of course, some notable exceptions.

By contrast, other domains of enquiry have almost been forced to grapple with the issue of how one becomes expert, because that reflexively becomes part of the original enquiry. The sociologist starting out to study some aspect of society is eventually thrown back on considering the social implications of the form and nature of their enquiry, and how their theory applies to their theorising. The educationalist eventually is thrown back on to how people learn, which includes how they learn about how people learn. The psychologist is eventually thrown back on to psychological aspects of conducting psychological research. Socially oriented anthropologists–ethnologists are thrown back on to themselves and the community of researchers as both an object of and a component of, their research. The inter-relatedness of these domains of enquiry results in a flow of ideas, methods, and most of all, ways of describing, between different domains. The philosophical problems of trying to account for the common enterprise of enquiry, research, and warranting assertions are thus of common concern. More will be said about the problems in a later section.

Working within the Discipline of Noticing suggests that it is possible to work on developing one's expertise directly, not just through application of one's expertise, but through personal professional development. The fear of many creative people that their creativity might disappear or fade away if they try to examine it, or even if they acknowledge it too directly, suggests just how fragile apparent experts can be. There is an enormous difference between self-consciousness (ask a centipede how it walks and it will fall over) and self-awareness (the awakening of an inner witness). All it takes to start work on one's expertise is to try to notice, to try to catch oneself caught in a reactive habit which might fruitfully be turned into a creative response every so often. The Discipline of Noticing is designed to support the awakening of the inner monitor–witness, which is what makes an expert be expert.

Distinguishing phenomena and explanation

At the heart of noticing lies the distinction between accounts-of and accounting-for, of distinguishing the phenomenon to be explained and the explanation. This distinction may seem obvious to the natural scientist, to the researcher engaged in measuring, to the researcher for whom there is an external material world about which evidence can be gained or which can be manipulated. The distinction is not so obvious in other domains in which the phenomena are only distinguished through using language, so that there is a temptation to slide from descriptive to explanatory terms. I suggest that even in the case of researchers measuring in a material world there can be unintentional and slippery slides between the words used to describe the phenomenon, and the ways in which the phenomenon is accounted-for. Physics provides a good example of this, for although if pressed most physicists would admit that the existence of fundamental particles is deduced from the production of effects which themselves are either predicted by theories or cast in the language of theories, most of the time they talk and think of particles as real objects. Similarly, a label such as 'lazy' or 'bright' all too easily slides from being a short-form for particular observed behaviour into becoming a quality possessed by a child. Every profession has these labels which start as handy terms which everyone knows mean something else, but turn into categories which can trap everybody into unwanted behaviours.

The same thing happens in everyday speech, when metaphors which initially attract attention and comment, become frozen into the way of thinking. 'Delivering skills' is again an example. Using a label can quickly produce commitment to the label actually labelling something, as the controversy about IQ showed only too clearly. The notion of 'beliefs as determinants of behaviour' may be another instance in which the use of a term like 'beliefs' for what determines the actions people engage in, constructed so as to be able to talk about choices made, turns into an attribute which people possess. It may be that 'beliefs' only come into existence when someone asks you about them. It is not our preferences that cause problems, but our attachment to them (Zen proverb). For example, Harré (Harré and Gillett 1994) suggests that the construct of an 'I' and a 'me' may similarly be only a product of the language in which we are embedded, not an experience. He and other social constructivists (see Burr 1995) claim that we experience that which has been distinguished previously in language.

Now, how could this conjecture be tested? One way would be to look for ramifications of such a conjecture. For example one would expect as a consequence that people brought up in a language which has few or no personal pronouns would have different experiences to those brought up speaking English: but how could those experiences be compared when they are constituted by different discourses? Another approach would be to interrogate one's experience very closely, constructing and trying out task-exercises in which certain words were not used for a period, to see what substitutes arise, while trying to catch oneself using a word in order to get a sense of the import of the moment. Harré's conclusion about 'I' and 'me' fits well with discoveries made through disciplined use of self-observation (Bennett 1964b, Minsky 1988, Varela *et al.* 1992). As many writers have concluded, experience is at most provisional, since we construct and abstract it from experiences.

Observation and measurement as noticing

Extra-spective research studies phenomena external to the researcher. As such, any observation or account can be seen as a form of measurement (an observed response to a probe). But observation or measurement requires an instrument, which may be anything from a machine to a questionnaire to a trained panel of observers to oneself. For example, a ruler is a means for distinguishing between different lengths, and its sensitivity is in terms of the fineness of its scales and the user's ability to align those scales with the objects to be measured. Similarly a photon counter or movement detector makes distinctions, and the sensitivity determines the precision of the measurement data. Thus even a machine distinguishes between phenomena of interest and others, at some level of sensitivity-precision. The same holds for 'instruments' such as questionnaires, interview formats and observation schedules. In the end, the machine, the instrument, is an extension of the researcher's sensitivity to notice and distinguish. Derrida (1967) went further, suggesting that presence always contains absence.

For example, you cannot measure something without distinguishing your measurements from other things happening. I originally wrote that you cannot measure something without distinguishing what it is you are measuring from the background, but this apparently obvious remark is contradicted by a great deal of psychological research in domains such as IQ and personality traits, in which instruments are employed (questionnaires usually, sometimes observations) which are then statistically summarised in some way to produce some assertion, despite no direct access to what it is that one claims to be measuring. But then some physicists do the same thing: they look in a cloud chamber for the effects of some purported interaction between particles, and when they find a predicted effect, they assert that the phenomenon took place.

Even so, both physicist and psychologist sensitise themselves to notice the measurements arising from the incident, and they are further sensitised to look for pattern and structure in the measurements themselves. They use their measurements as a warrant for speaking about a phenomenon they cannot directly experience, and the speaking-about eventually induces a commitment to the objective existence of the phenomenon. In a later section this ontological move will be explored further as it lies at the heart of all research, indeed of language and experience.

Research as mirroring

If one takes seriously the contention that we notice what we are sensitised to notice then there is a curious problem about research. When someone reports an observation, what we can be confident about is that that person has a particular sensitivity. For example, when a group of people watch a video-tape of a class-room, and someone announces that they see differences between behaviours of females and males, we know that that person is sensitive to (at least certain forms) of gender differences. Unless we see the video-tape ourselves, we are not in a position to gauge the accuracy or appropriateness of the observation, tempting as it may be to align it with our own observations. It follows then that what we learn from an observation is something about the researcher, as well as, perhaps, something about the phenomenon.

We can even be semi-quantitative. The more details that the observer reports, the more we know about the degree of sensitivity of the observer to distinguish, to make distinctions. In physics the Heisenberg Uncertainty Principle says that of two linked parameters, the more detail you know about one parameter (the more accurate your measurement of it), the less you know about another related parameter (the less accurate you can be about its measurement). In observational research, it seems that the more detail you appear to be given about the phenomenon, the more you know about the sensitivity of the observer. Thus, whereas in physics the product of the errors in measurement is invariant (Heisenberg's Principle), in observation research, the ratio of the degrees of detail about the phenomenon and about the observer is perhaps invariant.

An extreme formulation might be that what we learn from other people's reported research is a lot about the researcher, but unless we have independent means of validation we can never be sure about the accuracy of the reported observations. For example, it is impossible to be sure about whether Carlos Castaneda, in his eight books about his experiences with the Shaman Don Juan, was writing a brilliant and gripping novel, or was reporting ethnographic research. As Campbell (1988: 69) put it:

> All we really know about the world is grounded in the consciousness of what might be called an Autobiographic Self. . . . an attempt to understand anyone else in particular or human behaviour in general is a common quest for what might be called the Biographic Other.

> Words and actions take their meanings out of the perceiving individual's personal field of experience, a construct of the individual's particular biographic store of episodic memories.

Korzybski (1941) expressed the same sentiment as:

> Every scientific discovery is in a sense the autobiography of the [person] who made it.

Storm (1972) cast it in a North American Native People's perspective:

> The world is a mirror for the people.

and novelist Italo Calvino (1983) expressed it as:

> The universe is a mirror in which we can contemplate only what we have learned to know about ourselves.

That is why the Discipline of Noticing suggests that the construction of task-exercises is the most fruitful form of research report, because it enables others to experience something of what the researcher claims to notice, and then to test it out in their own experience.

Summary of Chapter 10

I have suggested that refining their noticing is what researchers do, and that they have this in common with any expert. Consequently not only could the Discipline of Noticing be used to work on developing one's professional expertise, but aspects of the discipline could contribute to the conduct of research itself, including careful distinguishing of phenomena and their explanation, and the form in which research results are disseminated.

11 Noticing *AS* research

In the previous chapter I claimed that most research involves working on noticing in some way or other. This chapter proposes that the Discipline of Noticing itself constitutes a research method which is particularly suited to practitioners researching their own practice. In order to do this effectively, reliably and robustly, it is necessary to stress rather more some aspects of the discipline which have been under-played so far, particularly the use of task-exercises with colleagues as both report and validity check.

Noticing as research is designed to take as its domain of concern the locus and focus of attention: what am I attending to, and what is the structure of that attention (broad or narrow in focus, single or multiple in form, body or head or heart based, concentrated or diffuse in nature). Central to such a concern is the question of how to stimulate or entice others to attend to aspects and features which may be of benefit to them. This is the role of task-exercises in the validation process. Attention to noticing turns studies focused on other people and situations into studies which learn about other people and situations through learning about oneself. What makes some features salient and others invisible? What is the significance of what I find myself observing? What can be learned about what is not noticed, not marked, not recorded?

Noticing involves locating and offering to others opportunities to experience and test out alterations in the structure of their attention. This is done through providing experience of phenomena worth attending to in their professional practice. In a sense this is a Maslow-type approach (Maslow 1971), because instead of being interested only in what people have done or do do, one is more interested in development, in what could be, in what is possible and how that possibility might be actualised. The researcher focuses on useful sensitivities and effective actions (in their experience) *and* on how to make these available to colleagues so that they too can recognise them as potentially useful, and become sufficiently aware of possibilities to try them out in practice themselves. What constitutes usefulness may be decided on the basis of effects in practice, but may also be determined by my own inner experience and by whether others find it useful to them in some way. The process of refinement is then also part of the research, as people report back on what they have noticed in trying out what they saw as possibilities for them in their situation.

By 'own inner experience' I refer to the central focus of noticing, which is to be mindful, to be awake in the moment (spectively) so as to participate in an increasingly rich and productive range of options at any given moment. The idea has been around for a long time, as this verse from one of the Upanishads suggests:

> Two birds, close yoked companions,
> Both clasp the self-same tree;
> One eats of the sweet fruit,
> The other looks on without eating.

The image of two birds, one eating, the other watching pervades Eastern and Western art. One interpretation is that the two birds are forms of attention and the tree represents the material world of sensation. The eater is the part of us that gets caught up in doing, while the watcher is an internal monitor that observes without judging. The watching bird is an inner witness who observes, comments, but does not act. The watcher has also been likened to conscience, which needs to be awakened and developed. An alternative interpretation is that the tree is the tree of immortality, and that only some people eat of its sweet fruit while others do not. Those who are awake and mindful, like the seven wise young women with their lamps oiled and their wicks trimmed, experience time as moving more slowly, even stopping and so experience a form of longevity or immortality. Those caught up in the exigencies of simultaneous and rapid-fire activity, like the young women too busy to fill their lamps or trim their wicks, are not ready for opportunities when they suddenly arise. (An image is traditionally only considered potent if there are several interpretations with apparently conflicting values.)

Studying oneself in order to gain wisdom about the world has an ancient tradition. For example, the Sanskrit term *svadhyaya* means observation and study of oneself, as well as of literature, in order to provide self-knowledge. Furthermore, Eco (1994: 129) claims that the word *anthropos* (man) 'is the corruption of an earlier [term] meaning "the one who is able to reconsider what has [been] seen"'. Eco is but one of many philosophers who acknowledge imagery as a significant feature of human experience, and it is the power of mental imagery which is called upon and exploited in acts of pre- and re-flection, through which the past is integrated and the future influenced or informed. William Golding explores this theme in his novel *The Inheritors* (1955), in which he conjectures what it might have been like when people first became aware of the power of mental imagery to inform actions.

Awakening a second bird, an inner witness who watches and comments but does not interfere, comes about through post-spective reflection using accounts-of incidents to re-enter moments, switching these into pro-spective preparation by re-inforcing a strong mental image of possible action in the future. It comes about by labelling phenomena suitably in order to enhance the possibilities of metaphoric resonance and metonymic triggering. It comes about by seeking alternative actions to try in specific situations, and integrating these into one's preparation. In order to provide evidence and to blaze an efficient trail for others to follow, it is useful to keep accounts of this whole process. Most importantly, one looks for ways of testing out personal sensitivities, and this is done by constructing task-exercises through which to acquaint colleagues with the possibility of similar sensitivities.

Components of noticing as research

This section contains further repetition, but as André Gide (1891) observed, 'Everything has been said before but, since nobody ever listens, we have to keep going back and beginning all over again.'

In Chapter 10 I outlined the principal components of research. Here is how they play out in the Discipline of Noticing.

Questions asked	What am I attending to, moment by moment? What choices are available to me moment by moment? What possible acts could I initiate? What am I sensitised or attuned to notice and what other possibilities might there be?
Objects of study	My own actions, my choices, the structure of my attention.
Methods	See the summary in Part III.
Purpose of study	Principally, to awaken and enliven your own second bird, but through this, to enable others to do likewise. The researcher is the one who gains most; students stand to gain through the practitioner's increased sensitivity to the student's situation, and wider range of choices of actions. Initially, the research is trying to achieve a sense of freedom for the researcher through participation in moments of choice; this enables the researcher to act more effectively and sensitively, leading to enhanced experience for others. The audience is fundamentally the researcher, with knock-on opportunities for colleagues and for students. Students will gain from more effective interaction with the practitioner, as well as, perhaps, themselves coming to notice more effectively in their own domains. Colleagues are used to guard against solipsism and may themselves embark on some sort of related personal enquiry.
Data	Data consist of moments of noticing. These may be recorded as brief-but-vivid accounts-of incidents which are used to enhance future moments of noticing. What can be presented to others are accounts and, more generally, task-exercises, but these are not data: the data for them is what they notice or experience as a result of engagement.

Analysis   Analysis consist of examining accounts by looking for
                    grammatical actions, seeking significance, interrogating
                    experience, threading themes, scanning for scripts, propos-
                    ing principles, gathering gambits, etc., as described in
                    Chapter 7. Multiple interpretations are sought, and com-
                    pared with accounts and theories in the literature. All of
                    this analysis is in order to refine sensitivities to notice and
                    to construct task-exercises for others.

Claims   The only claims made are that there are certain things
                    worth noticing, certain phenomena which others may
                    wish to look out for, and certain actions which others
                    may wish to consider trying in some modified form. A
                    thesis consists of honed task-exercises situated with
                    respect to the literature and the practitioner's situation,
                    with descriptions of what may be noticed, what phenomena
                    may be identified etc. No claim is made that anyone will
                    necessarily notice what has been identified, or that some act
                    or action will have a specified effect, only that some people
                    other than the practitioner–researcher have also noticed
                    something.

Products   The product of noticing is increased sensitivity to notice,
                    and enhanced awareness of possibilities and choices in
                    the moment. Visible products are task-exercises, including
                    brief-but-vivid accounts of incidents, which offer others
                    access to similar noticing and informed choices. Reports
                    of incidents and experiences, of the research process itself,
                    are secondary.

Validation   Validation is something that happens in and through one's
                    own experience. It is specific to time, place, people and sit-
                    uation. Generality lies in whether future action is informed,
                    and whether readers are alerted to something they can test
                    out in their own experience. A thesis does not prove valid-
                    ity, merely offer the means for readers to check relevance for
                    themselves in their situation. Strong validation involves
                    others replicating similar enquiry, coming to similar notic-
                    ing, and seeking resonance in yet further colleagues. Weak
                    validation is satisfied with recognition in colleagues, at least
                    some of whom are from a broader community of practice.

Probably the most tendentious and non-standard components are the role
and form of reports, and validation, so these are discussed more fully in subsequent sections.

As indicated in Chapter 10, research methods, research questions and world
perspective are all intimately intertwined. Noticing in the sense being used here

is not needed in a world of absolutes in which there are facts to be objectively identified and tested by anyone at any time. But noticing makes a great deal of sense in a world in which what matters is sensitive participation moment by moment in a situation which may have some aspects of generality, but which is specific in many of its details. This is characteristic of caring professions generally, and of education in particular.

Validity and validation of noticing

If I am observing myself, how can I be sure that I am not fooling myself, much less convince someone else of this? Even the notion of account-of loses its bite when it applies to what I notice about myself.

Or does it? Self observation is not a simple matter of 'think aloud protocols' or narrative accounts of feelings and impressions, like poetry of the soul. Nor does self observation succumb to the use of logic about the pitfalls of trying to observe yourself. In fact it is an action in which an inner monitor or witness, a second bird, is developed. An expert somehow knows when things are going a bit wrong, and can deftly modify actions in mid-stream, as a result of their expert intuition, their expert sensitivities, their inner monitor. Experts have awareness that novices do not, and becoming expert means not just deftness with a variety of tools, but a certain extra 'sense' or awareness. Becoming expert requires education of awareness along with training of behaviour through harnessing emotions, and ways of supporting this is precisely what the Discipline of Noticing offers.

Robust and reliable results

Findings are considered to be robust if they are valid under specifiable changes in conditions, whether for the same or different researchers. In the natural science paradigm, this means indicating the possible ranges of parameters, and indicating which parameters 'are deemed to be held constant'. In order to tell someone else about quantitative findings, it is not sufficient just to provide the data and their analysis. It is also necessary to describe the conditions of the 'experiment' in sufficient detail that someone else can replicate it. The Discipline of Noticing takes as an integral part of its methodology working with others to highlight informative distinctions and appropriate gambits, not just by talking *about* them, but by offering direct experience *of* them through descriptions and exercises. Thus results are not really passed from one person to another, but rather sensitivities to notice are highlighted. But what is noticed depends on links made to past experiences, so the mere fact that similar labels are used cannot be taken for evidence of similar noticing until negotiation of meaning through the brief-but-vivid descriptions of incidents has been undertaken.

In researching people, not only are there usually huge numbers of parameters, few of which can be held constant, but the very basis of a mathematically expressed causal model with mutually independent parameters is highly questionable. Furthermore, what things one person can 'do' another cannot, and even if they try, the situation will unfold differently. Robustness in the Discipline of Noticing refers to the variety of conditions under which sensitivities inform action effectively, and the variety of people who recognise and resonate with proposed distinctions.

For example, working with a specific student or group of students over a period of time will inevitably result in certain localised practices: a nod here a wink there, a shared laugh, an ebb and flow of control and of concentration. A great deal depends on the relationship established. However as separate acts, these are unlikely to transfer to other situations. The important question for a practitioner is how such possibilities, such relationships, can be fostered with other groups of people. Thus robustness has to do with generalisability: what aspects can inform future actions with others. But instead of trying to locate and describe recipes, noticing aims to increase sensitivity to the subtle interactions with groups of people so that each person and each group are experienced and treated as special, not as 'other examples'.

Reliability is similar to robustness, but refers to the possibilities of repetition over time. When 'used again', 'results' should be similar. Again noticing aims not to repeat, but to afford opportunities to choose to act according to desires and principles, and a means for exposing and testing out those desires and principles.

That is why the Discipline of Noticing is built upon a conjecturing atmosphere in which all assertions are modifiable, all choices experimental, and upon constant resonance seeking and re-negotiation with others. An essential aspect of validation in the Discipline of Noticing is the seeking of resonance with others, whether with students or colleagues. It is essential to bring into question distinctions that have been fruitful in the past and actions that have been effective, precisely because of the tendency to automate.

Falsification

How can I be certain? How can I guard against being swept away on a tide of personal insight or charismatic emotion rather than rational sense? As mentioned in Chapter 6, this question has driven philosophers throughout history, and there is no certain answer to it. No one wants to be duped by a misguided leader; most people want to have somewhere to stand, something to be certain about.

Popper (1972) proposed that in order for a theory to be scientifically objective, it has to be able to be tested. In order to test it, there has to be something which could be false, and an experiment which decides between truth and falsity. If there is no edge, no specification of one thing over another, there is no substance to the theory, no content. For example, stating that '"this" may happen but so may other things' is pretty woolly, unlikely to be very informative, and certainly not testable (what if 'this' never happens: does it negate the claim?). Stating that '"this" or "that" will happen' is at least testable. Stating that 'there is something worthy of attending to, and sensitising yourself to notice it and to respond in such and such a way may inform your future practice' is closer to Popper's ideal but still problematic: if I don't find my sensitivities altered immediately, or even ever, is the claim falsified?

Popper's approach is based in a world of objective facts in which claims are either true or false, and once determined, they stay that way. But the world of human experience is not like this. Something which works today in one situation may not work tomorrow in another, and what works for me, may not work for someone else. Furthermore, the notion of some act 'working' is itself problematic, since it depends on the propensities, criteria, and hence world view of whoever is judging.

A sensitivity to notice cannot be universally falsified. It can only be deemed insignificant or ineffective for certain people at certain times in certain situations. Failure to recognise a distinction being offered does not indicate that the distinction is wrong or false, merely that it was not recognised. It may be that through refinement of examples and exercises, resonance can be obtained; it may be that the distinction offered is inappropriate for that time, place and those people; it may also be that the distinction is idiosyncratic, temporary or misinformed, and not useful.

How then might an assertion be challenged or falsified?

> If a colleague claims that they give equal quantity and quality attention to girls and to boys, then it is possible to conceive a series of observations (measuring length of time, collecting transcripts of interactions and analysing language patterns etc.) to verify or dispute such a claim.

But if it is done in an atmosphere of antagonism and challenge, then most 'findings' will be rationalised away, justified, or ignored. Overt falsification will be resisted unless the individual is genuinely themselves questioning. Some way has to be found to energise the colleague to want to investigate for themselves.

> If I claim that a particular gambit is working for me, or a particular distinction is useful to me, then it is possible to imagine a series of observations to test whether the claimed effectiveness is visible to an external observer.

Suppose an external observer fails to see what I claim to see. Suppose even that I am unable to persuade colleagues that something I am noticing is noticeable or fruitful, to them? Unlike mathematics itself where a counter-example forces reconsidering and either modifying or abandoning an assertion, there is always the possibility that colleagues are not oriented or in an appropriate state to notice what I notice. It may be that I am deluding myself; it may be that my attempts to point out what I see are not succeeding; it may be that such noticing is not appropriate for them at this time.

Of course, if I continue to fail to achieve resonance, to persuade colleagues that they too can see something of what I am seeing; if I increasingly find myself talking only to myself, then I may be presciently ahead of my time, or I may be deluding myself. That possibility is always present. Indeed, even if I can persuade colleagues that they can see what I can see, I may be deluding myself and them. That is where investigations into human experience differ from investigations into the experience of others. There are no guarantees of validity for the former; there are limited possibilities for success for the latter.

If a colleague claims that they are maximally effective in their present mode of teaching and not willing to contemplate any changes or variations, it is possible to conceive of an interventionist strategy, such as observing their practice, or drawing in external inspectors, which force the colleague to expose their teaching to outside observation.

But such an approach is bound to raise defensive postures. Much more effective is to enlist the colleague as a partner in investigation, even to the extent of seeking their support for your own investigation. Getting them to observe and comment on (giving accounts-of rather than accounts-for) some of your lessons can provide a point of difference, a disturbance which can grow into discussion and negotiation of meanings of words like learning, discussion, investigation, exercise, telling, etc., which may seem on the surface to be unproblematic.

One technique that is often effective is to ask people at the end of a lesson to record what they thought the lesson was about, and for the teacher to record their own answer, as well as a prediction of what the children will say. Getting several colleagues to do this (and doing it yourself) for a single class once or twice a week over two or three weeks produces plenty of material to generate discussion. It is rare that there will be unanimity!

The non-standard approach taken to validity is such a crucial element of the epistemology of the Discipline of Noticing that it bears repeating. If someone does not find their noticing enhanced, then there may be a number of different explanations.

- perhaps the feature is indeed irrelevant or even misleading;
- perhaps their sensitivity is not yet sharply enough attuned to become fully aware of what is being offered;
- perhaps they are fully occupied working on some other aspect of their practice, and lack the necessary available attention or motivation to work on what is being offered;
- perhaps they find no particular force in the noticing being offered, and are unable to make use of such noticing to modify their behaviour;
- perhaps they agree that the proposal seems promising, but feel that the exposition does not actually inform their behaviour;
- perhaps the presentation (task-exercises) does not speak directly to their experience.

Any of these could be taken as possible falsification, but only for some person or people, at that time. To move from the specific to the general conclusion that the distinctions being offered are false would be a mistake. For unlike mathematics in which a single counter-example disproves a conjecture, it may be that what you are noticing is inappropriate for others, whether in form, content, purpose or presentation. Like mathematics, in which a counter-example may lead to modification of the conjecture, lack of recognition, resonance or take-up may lead to working on any or all of the aspects listed above.

Resonance

Why, if we are researching ourselves, do we want others to recognise our accounts? The answer is that we need to be constantly on guard against fooling ourselves, seeing what we want to see, and leading ourselves into difficulties as a result. We need the communities of practice of which we are a part not only for stimulation and companionship on the long and sometimes lonely road of self-exploration, but as foils for checking that what we think we see is visible to others as well. Umberto Eco (1994) employs the metaphor of fiction as descriptions of walks in a wood in discussing the problems of including too much and too little detail as an author, and of over- and under-interpreting as a reader. At one point, after recounting how a friend accused him of describing the friend's uncle and aunt in one of his stories, Eco remarks that in fact he was drawing on an incident involving his own uncle and aunt.

> What had happened to my friend? He had sought in the wood something that was instead in his private memory. It is right for me while walking in the wood to use every experience and every discovery to learn about life, about the past and the future. But since a wood is created for everybody, I must not look there for facts and sentiments which concern only myself. Otherwise . . . I am not interpreting text but rather *using* it. It is not at all forbidden to use a text for daydreaming, and we do this frequently, but daydreaming is not a public affair; it leads us to move within the narrative wood as if it were our own private garden. (Eco 1994: 9)

Resonance seeking is not a simple matter of recognising or not recognising what someone is talking about. A strong adverse reaction at one time can be followed by an equally strong positive reaction later, while a weak acceptance at one time can evaporate in a short time. When people's first reaction is warm and positive but essentially passive acceptance, it is often the case that they have not actually recognised the distinction being offered, but rather that they have subsumed it into their own categories. No further effect can be expected because no energy has been released and no transformation has occurred. On the other hand, an initial adverse reaction to a suggested distinction or gambit is often a sign of someone beginning to work on an idea, and there may be some noticeable effect subsequently, making use of released energy.

How can one check for true resonance? Might not colleagues appear to agree with what you say for various psychological and social reasons, while not actually making much sense of what you are checking out with them? Self-conning is just as easy as conning others, and just as impossible to eradicate. Asking people directly whether they recognise what is being pointed out is a form of probe and as such is subject to socio–cultural–psychological effects and influences, or, put another way, is not terribly reliable or robust! Less direct means involve the use of prompts with varying degrees of directness to jog people into re-marking about something they have noticed. The most desirable form of validation is the largely or wholly spontaneous utterance which indicates that someone has noticed something freshly and meaningfully for themselves. The more sponta-neous the evidence of resonance, the more confident one can be that the resonance is real and not imagined.

Failure to obtain resonance may mean that what I think I am noticing is just my construction and has no validity beyond my immediate experience. It may also mean however that the task-exercise through which I introduce the noticing, is ineffective. It may also mean that the people with whom I am seeking reso-nance are not prepared, or are otherwise preoccupied and so do not recognise what is being offered.

Rigour

Theories arising through the Discipline of Noticing are just as rigorous as Popperian theories, but in a different way. If a distinction, sensitivity or gambit generally fails to find resonance, there is no incentive, no reason to hold or pursue it, and so it will atrophy and/or be ignored. The fact that a noticing might atrophy and be ignored does not mean that there is no potential in it, just that it is not appropriate at that time and place. If on the other hand, some people find the distinction makes sense, find it sharpens their noticing, enables them to read a situation freshly, and thereby informs their practice, then for that time the theory is meaningful and valid for those people.

A standard objection to any framework which cannot be tested independently of its practitioners is that since all observation is theory laden and theory cir-cumscribed, the practitioners simply see what they are looking for. There is no objectivity in what one person notices which are to be preferred to those of another. The methods employed under the banner of the Discipline of Noticing acknowledge this, and turn it to advantage. Instead of trying to circumvent the inherent subjectivity of experience, objectivity is achieved by working through the subjective (personal observation) to achieve objectivity in resonance and confir-mation with others. The objectivity gained is not external and analytic, but rather internal and synthetic.

Evidence that such a position makes sense is available in sessions when par-ticipants find that during a workshop aimed at professional development, something that is said resonates with their experience. It is common for practi-tioners to prefer to attend workshops run by practitioners or recently ex-practitioners, precisely because they believe strongly that these are the people who understand and appreciate their problems, who can speak to their experi-ence, and hence someone whose suggestions are tried and tested and trustworthy. By dwelling in what you notice in your own experience, it is possible to 'speak to experience' through offering tasks and descriptions which resonate with them. It is not, however, useful or possible to remove the need for each practitioner to test out acts and ways of describing them in their own experience.

Knowledge is validated not through logic, though logic may be helpful in ruling out some apparent possibilities; not through accumulation of claims of success from others, though these may stimulate people to investigate for them-selves; not through statistical studies though again these may provide stimulation.

Knowledge is action. Knowing is acting effectively. But effectiveness of action is not determined through external criteria based on five criteria: it is based on a sense of flow, of consonance, of appropriateness, tempered with a constant dissatisfaction and scepticism. Once these latter disappear, we are no longer in growth, no longer sensitive instruments, but have become wilful agents who are in danger of doing damage.

This brings new force to the quote from Bacon (1605: 49) concerning knowledge: 'So knowledge, while it is in Aphorisms and observations, it is in growth; but when it once is comprehended in exact Methods, it may perchance be further polished and illustrated, and accommodated for use and practice; but it increaseth no more in bulk and substance.' Put another way, those who seek objective, external criteria to measure success will be disappointed with noticing, because it offers no such certainty. The reason is, that such certainty is illusory in any domain based on human interactions and hence human will. No specific action can be guaranteed to have a specific effect, even if all conditions could be exactly replicated, which they cannot.

Single and multiple interpretations

There are of course, potential dangers in seeking objectivity through shared experience, through potentially idiosyncratic and solipsistic behaviour. But these dangers are present even in the most objective of sciences, and furthermore, because extra-spective research assumes that it is not biased by subjectivities, these are all too easily overlooked. At least in noticing one is constantly aware of the issue. These dangers are in fact faced by everyone each day, as we all try to justify our actions and share with others what we notice. One of the major dangers lies in unquestioning acceptance of language patterns, which is why Chapter 6 emphasised a variety of ways of probing the language of description of accounts.

Where language patterns are used to justify behaviour, there is a danger of biases being reinforced, as when a politically extreme group meet and rehearse language patterns which justify their perceptions and actions. But if what is rehearsed refines noticing, then it can be of positive benefit. The only antidotes to reinforcing habits of mind and body are remaining in question, seeking resonance in an ever-widening circle of colleagues, and constantly looking for alternative interpretations or readings.

Here, as elsewhere, we come close to the paradox of objectivity and subjectivity. Picking up labels, picking up ways of speaking about or describing certain situations can have positive and negative consequences. The negative ones are to do with reinforcing stereotypes, and becoming yet more sensitive to perceived slights. The positive ones are to do with extending the range of incidents to which one is sensitive, and extending the range of fresh responses to such situations. Noticing does not and cannot distinguish between these. But the Discipline of Noticing does call upon each practitioner to seek resonance with wider and wider groups of colleagues. It is not enough to find a group of like-minded individuals and rehearse one's prejudices with them. Equally, there is no method which offers guarantees against prejudice and blindness.

What distinguishes the enquirer from the bigot is not sensitising to notice, but the desire to encounter and take on multiple interpretations. Whereas the bigot is locked into a single perspective, a single perception, the enquirer seeks to accumulate different ways of reading and different ways of responding to what appears to be the same situation. The bigot tramples their way along their path, the enquirer dances along and across multiple paths. By intentionally holding alternative, even conflicting interpretations, you remain flexible and sensitive to alterations and variations, whereas, when you select a single interpretation you become blunted and chunked (in the sense of de Bono, see p. 36), insensitive to subtleties and unprepared to change.

Dwelling in multiplicity has all the dangers and conflicts of full democracy: people may choose to limit their freedom, so somehow their freedom to re-choose liberty needs to be preserved. So too, multiplicity of interpretations appears to be indecisive, wishy-washy, and unconfident. If no single account-for is taken as paramount, then how do you justify any action? The answer is that you remain in a state of conjecture, of experiment, of trial. By being aware that you are only conjecturing, not certain, your sensitivities to notice effects are sharpened, and you are disposed and oriented to modifying your actions and your conjectures. While the bigot has a single aim, the enquirer experiments with variety.

Reporting noticing

Some research has as its intended product a description of what was done, of the analysis, and of conclusions drawn, as if somehow the logic of the enquiry and the analysis would convince others, whether through logic of reasoning (using verbal data) or through logic of calculation (using numerical data), or some combination of these, that the conclusions were valid and should be taken up and applied. Yet most people on reading conclusions either deny them ('my situation is different!') or affirm them as obvious ('Any practitioner knows that!').

It is rare to be convinced simply by reading a report of someone else's activity, and even rarer to change your practice simply on the assertions of a report. What is much more usual is that you respond to what you read. If the report fits with your expectations or opinions then you may feel justified in continuing, possibly making adaptations and modifications informed by the reading; if something in the report does not fit with experience, you are more likely to ignore the findings, or to challenge them. Either way, you may find yourself embarking on your own investigation, stimulated by what you have read. In that sense, 'noticing' begets 'noticing': noticing something in a reading or seminar or professional development session which you think you could adapt or which you disagree with, can lead to noticing more sensitively for a time. Bohr (1920) said that every sentence uttered must be understood not as an affirmation but a question, and this is usefully applied to any research report in any research paradigm. The Discipline of Noticing exploits this observation about how people respond to encountering 'results' of other people's research, and integrates it into its reporting phase. What is maximally important is that opportunities are offered to others to investigate for themselves.

The first requirement of appropriate reporting is that what has been noticed is described or communicated (perhaps on tape) in some form which is recognisable to others. They then have a fresh stimulus to investigate for themselves. They might try to re-produce the phenomenon for themselves, or they might find themselves sensitised to notice what previously they had not noticed. The important features are *reporting* to others so as to enable them to investigate for themselves.

Reporting is not just important for the access it provides to others to validate what is asserted in their own experience. The very act of organising and giving accounts, and making claims based on that experience, helps to refine and clarify, to organise and simplify that experience. The act of externalising, of formulating (literally seeking to put into form or formula) is perhaps the most important feature of moving from being embedded in practices, to working on practices.

Research reports in the Discipline of Noticing can have several components:

- descriptions of assumptions, philosophies, perspectives, approaches etc. to teaching and learning which support the work undertaken or which came to the surface and were questioned;
- accounts of incidents which seemed significant at the time and issues abstracted or generalised from them;
- comments and reflections on those incidents (making connections between them, locating similarities and differences with accounts from other researchers) made at different times;
- connecting accounts-of and issues abstracted from them to general principles and issues in the research literature;
- presentation of tasks-exercises, accounts and transcripts which highlight or illustrate particular noticing;
- descriptions of actions taken in connection with noticing and possible alternatives;
- identification of labels which have proved useful;
- reports from colleagues of what they have noticed in connection with suggested noticing.

If the work being reported is a study of changes and developments in an individual or group, then a chronological account, with multiple layers of reflections at different times may be in order. If the study is linked to a particular topic or pedagogical theme, then the report might be structured around issues or distinctions that emerged from the work.

The purpose of the report is not to prove or persuade, but to suggest potential, to provide access for the reader to notice similar situations in their own practice, and to demonstrate the range of work undertaken in order to reach the proposals being made.

Criticism of such a report can draw attention to particular assumptions or perspectives that seem to be implicit but are not explicitly acknowledged. It can draw attention to prolepsis, scripts, metaphors and metonymical gaps in accounts, not to say implicit or explicit value judgements, justifications, explanations and the like. It can criticise the clarity, effectiveness and the brief-but-vividness qualities of accounts, and it can draw attention to places where accounting-for intrudes on or displaces accounts-of. It can comment on how readily or not similar noticing is generated in others and the ways in which it informs their practice. Attention can be drawn to other literature which deals with similar or related issues, or which adopts a different perspective.

Criticism can also contribute to further development by offering alternative explanations for observations made, alternative actions which could be taken and alternative task-exercises for accessing noticing. In the final analysis, validity of work pursued in the Discipline of Noticing lies with individuals who find that, at least for a time, their sensitivity is sharpened and their access to alternative behaviour is enhanced.

Epistemological foundations of noticing

The Discipline of Noticing as a method of research is based on a world-view which includes positions on what it means to know, and how knowledge is validated. This section summarises implicit and explicit assumptions about what really matters to practitioners enquiring into and developing their practice, which form the foundations for the Discipline of Noticing, but, at the heart, the important thing is not to stop questioning (Albert Einstein 1916).

The whole point of professional practice in education and allied areas such as the caring professions is that students (as a generic term for those being supported and cared for), get more effective care and attention. In education particularly, the whole point of teaching is that students learn; the whole point of nursing is that patients have the support and context which supports their recovery and coping. In both cases it is up to the student–client to change or develop. The teacher cannot do the learning for the student, and the nurse cannot heal the patient. What professionals do is try to create settings and situations which enable and promote development.

It follows then that the best test of improvement must reside in the experience of the student–client. However, it is dangerous to assume identifiable cause-and-effect chains between professional practices and changes in student–client opinion or feelings. Even where you can show correlation, you must justify a connection, which leads into story-spinning in order to account-for what may be spurious connections. When you probe for causes (of success or failure, enjoyment or dislike, etc.) it is also dangerous to expect that students or patients are even aware of what it is that has contributed to their success, failure, enjoyment etc. These links are at best tenuous. At worst, they lead to surveys and market research which proposes practices based on immediate likes and dislikes rather than professional support which is effective in the long term. It may even lead practitioners into engaging students and clients in mechanical and repetitious acts which may produce a minimal change, but which ultimately deaden everyone involved.

The Discipline of Noticing is designed to overcome the difficulties inherent in working with people, by focusing attention where it really matters, on what each person can actually do, namely, to work on and develop themselves, to enhance their sensitivity to notice and their range of choices in which to participate.

Thus, the Discipline of Noticing is founded on an epistemological stance in which knowing is seen as a dynamic process not a static state. Various practices such as post-spective reflection and pro-spective anticipation are used in order to increase the likelihood of being awake to a possibility in the moment when it occurs: waking the second bird. Furthermore, we come to know, or rather our access to knowing develops through increasing our sensitivity to notice, through having a growing range of different actions to call upon, and through having those possibilities come to mind in the moment. We *can* learn from being told things, but only if we are able to integrate what we hear; we *can* learn from experience, but only if triggers are set up to alert us in the future; we *can* learn from others, but only what we mark and try out for ourselves.

The following elaboration is only one attempt to bring to expression a view of how knowing comes about, which both underpins and is informed by the Discipline of Noticing.

- As functioning organisms, we are embedded in fields of experience. Present experience consists of sense impressions together with a state which consists of integrated thinking, feeling and acting in the moment. These are coupled with the present effects of resonated and triggered experiences in the past, however abstracted and re-formulated.
- Our sensory and cognitive functioning is based on making distinctions, supported by, but not totally dependent upon language. We experience tensions, even disturbances, and we attempt to resolve these, either by isolating the poles, by adopting one or other pole, or by turning the energy locked in the tension into awareness.
- We participate in actions which constitute sense-making (making sensible and sensate), such as having past experiences juxtaposed by a present experience with a result of re-inforced opinion and belief, and having present experience act upon past experiences through exercise of desire, intention and will, to suggest new insights and actions.
- We engage in activity with the intention of facilitating particular actions in ourselves and in others, known as professional development, teaching and learning.
- We seek to enlarge and develop access to potential in the future, for ourselves and others, with others.

We do this effectively by being present in the moment, through the structure of our attention as we participate in the moment by moment flow of unfolding events.

Aspects of the Discipline of Noticing can be used, as suggested in Chapter 10, without accepting these assumptions, and the Discipline of Noticing can be used to explore these assumptions to test their validity and relevance for you in your situation.

As an example of the intricate interweaving of observation, enquiry and influences of other perspectives, here is a list of some observations and connections with other methodological and epistemological positions. These come from reading and observation and have been tested in my experience using the Discipline of Noticing. It is inappropriate here to try to provide a collection of task-exercises to offer direct experience, so you will have to examine them for yourself, perhaps with the assistance of Chapter 13. The point of the collection is to suggest that even though the many different elaborations of positions which have been written about may arise partly in order to distinguish one position from another, to try to be distinctive, underlying many apparently different positions are some rudimentary commonalities.

- An event consists of the experience resonated by reference to 'that event', that is, the dynamic web of memories, connections and associations triggered in participants and in others who encounter descriptions (*cf.* phenomenology, Macann 1993; Smith and Woodruff 1995; Patocka 1996).
- An event consists of the stories we tell (the accounts-of we render): radical constructivism (*cf.* von Glasersfeld 1995).
- A phenomenon consists of accounts in agreement with a sense of generality: radical constructivism (*cf.* von Glasersfeld 1995).
- Knowing is acting and acting is knowing (hence reduce accounting-for and collect accounts-of; preparing oneself to act in the future): enactivism (*cf.* Varela *et al.* 1992).
- Doing ≠ Construing.
- Acting out of habit is inert knowing: (*cf.* Whitehead 1932).
- Investigating what it is like to . . . or to be . . . as a means of sensitising oneself to the experience of others: phenomenology (*cf.* van Manen 1990; Smith and Woodruff 1995; Patocka 1996).
- What is real is lived experience: phenomenology and narrative enquiry (*cf.* van Manen 1990; Smith and Woodruff 1995; Patocka 1996).
- Maintaining complexity through holding multiple interpretations rather than seeking one 'true' account: (*cf.* postmodernism, Anderson 1995; Zizek 1999).
- Recognising that to express is to over stress and that I cannot speak the richness of my experience.
- Necessity of agreeing the phenomenon before accounting-for it: scientific method (*cf.* Galileo ref, Roger Bacon 1268 in Thatcher 1901).
- 'All sciences are vain and full of errors that are not born of experience, mother of all certainty, and that are not tested in experience' (Leonardo da Vinci in Zammattio *et al.* 1980: 10).
- 'It is my intention first to cite experience, then to demonstrate through reasoning why experience must operate in a given way' (Leonardo da Vinci in Zammattio *et al.* 1980: 124, 141).
- 'My subjects require for their expression not the words of others but experience, the mistress of all who write well. I have taken her as my mistress and will not cease to state it' (Leonardo da Vinci in Zammattio *et al.* 1980: 131).

- A succession of experiences does not add up to an experience of that succession (*cf.* Immanuel Kant's *Critique of Pure Reason*).
- Validity (truth) is local to people, time, place and situation: (*cf.* Sufism, Shah 1964).
- Everything must be tested in experience (*cf.* Leonardo da Vinci: 'Avoid the teaching of speculators whose judgements are not confirmed by experience' in Zammattio *et al.* 1980: 133, also Galileo, Francis Bacon etc.).
- Read, mark, learn, and inwardly digest (Book of Common Prayer, 1662, Collects, 2nd Sunday in Advent).
- To be awake in the moment to a possibility, and to make the most of each opportunity that is recognised (*cf.* Omar Khayyam's *Rubaiyat* as translated by Fitzgerald: 'awake, for morning in the bowl of night'; Gregorian chant: 'that awake we may be in Christ'; Buddhism: mindfulness; see also Langer 1989).
- Anything which has positive potential also has negative potential; what seems good can be used for ill.
- We are each made up of multiple selves, themselves comprised of multiple strands (*cf.* Bhagavad Gita Chapter 14, Samkhya philosophy, see Raymond 1972, Bennett 1964a).
- In education and professional development, something asserted which is often true, also has its converse true sometimes (Tahta, private communication).
- Observing oneself impartially intraspectively (from an inner witness) not introspectively conjecturing and hypothesising.
- Actions are prepared, undertaken and evaluated as in action research, but the evaluation is not offered as evidence to others.
- Knowing is knowing-to act in the moment drawing on past experience whether by repeating a relevant fact (knowing-that), acting in some way (knowing-how), appreciating principles (knowing-why) or discoursing about it (knowing-about, knowing-when) (*cf.* Ryle 1949).
- Experience is recalled in fragments; experience is fragmentary (*cf.* James Stewart 1983).

Noticing in relation to other forms of research

There are very many forms and variants of practitioner research, some of which share at least some of the orientation of noticing. Here I consider two of these: action research and grounded theory. The differences between them and noticing are helpful for shedding light on noticing.

Action research

The Discipline of Noticing can be seen as a form of action research, which itself has become a label for a form of research with many different interpretations in practice. For example, *action research* itself has an enormous literature and a wide range of detailed methods of implementation, whether for socio-political critique or for effecting change in some complex situation; *phenomenology* is less action oriented and more observational, less committed to making change and more committed to understanding and appreciating; *narrative enquiry* focuses on the individual making sense through constructing and refining stories about their experience; *phenomenography* works to reveal a range of types of experience in order to appreciate the lived experience.

McKernan (1991) summarises the articulation of approaches taken over the last hundred years to research which involve action and change in many domains including education and professional development (see also Carson and Sumara 1997). In the diagram he offers his own elaborated version of a cycle of activity common to most authors, in which a problem is identified, clarified, plans made and implemented, evaluation undertaken, and modifications made as a result.

As a description of what experts seem to do, such cycles can be informative, especially as a source of inspiration when things get sticky or complicated and you feel in danger of losing your way. However, no more can be expected from mechanically following such a description like a recipe than can be expected from simply behaving naturally but unsystematically. What is missing in summaries of cycles and sequences is probably the most important aspect: the changing awareness and sensitivity of the participants to their situation in relation to their aims and expectations.

Flexibility is vital. If in the midst of doing what you planned, something develops which you hadn't expected, you do not run home and get advice, you act; if you suddenly find something else come to mind that seems appropriate, you can choose to stick to your plan despite the insight, or you can act upon your insight and try to make a note of what you did and why you thought it would be a good idea. Participating in moments of choice is central. Being systematic can be misinterpreted as rigidly following some pre-arranged format, when it merely means intentional use of devices and practices such as those suggested in Part III.

In contrast to many manifestations of action research, noticing *as* research emphasises the same person doing the planning–preparation, the experimenting, the observing of effects, the evaluation of results, and the reflecting with the support of colleagues, all through monitoring their own participation, through developing their inner witness. Furthermore, validation lies not so much in external measures of improved performance of others, but rather in the development of ways of working which enable others to take up and try something similar for themselves: the education of awareness which enables relevant action to come to mind as an option in the moment. To be open and creative requires a constant struggle against the mechanical. Indeed the whole point of the Discipline of Noticing is to break out of habitual and mechanical acts, to strengthen awareness, and to awaken oneself to possibilities.

Suggestions and possibilities can of course come from any source, but at the heart of activity lies the individual, using whatever support the discourse, culture and local community of practice can provide.

Even where the practice involves and has impact upon other people, the focus of noticing *as* research is on oneself. Others are used not as validators of what you observe about yourself, though this might be possible in some circumstances, but rather as sources of evidence that *their* noticing is enhanced. Thus a teacher working on her/his practice focuses on self, but looks for evidence that students' sensitivity to notice is enhanced in some domain or direction. Someone leading professional development looks for enhanced noticing and informed practice. Someone educating novices to become practitioners does likewise. But changes in sensitivity to notice and act, and development of informed practice, are not usefully or consistently evaluated by study. They are evaluated consistently through the self-same action of checking out with others that they too notice something and are informed to act in the future.

What is essential is to be engaged in enquiry, to be sceptical, to be difficult to satisfy, as has been suggested so many times over the centuries; as it is supposed to say on the tomb of Socrates in Delphi, 'Know Thyself'.

Grounded Theory

Strauss (Glaser and Strauss 1967, Glaser 1978, 1993, Strauss and Corbin 1990) proposed Grounded Theory as a means of systematising the desire to begin with observations, from and through which categories and theories might gradually emerge. Since observation is acknowledged to be theory laden, why not use observation to reveal, challenge and modify those theories, not as an external activity, but within practice. The discipline required lies in recording as carefully and rigorously as possible any organising and structuring theories which arise or emerge, and the development of these as more and more observations are made. There is deliberate search for similarities and for differences in what has been observed. As themes, classifications and stories to account-for observations emerge, there is a deliberate process of making more observations looking for differences. Observation and analysis continue until a point of saturation is reached, in which, despite attempts to find new features, wrinkles, or aspects, everything being observed is already described in the unfolding theories. Typically, observations are in very fine detail, and all new observations are carefully examined through the current categories for fit and non-fit. This puts more weight on the observations as data than in noticing, where observations or accounts are seen as access to experience which constitutes the data. Setting oneself to look out for features which contradict or complexify what has been noticed so far, is also part and parcel of discipline of noticing.

One of the tenets of Grounded Theory is that theory is not the formulation of an external truth or reality but rather that *truth is enacted*.

> Theories are interpretations made from given perspectives as adopted or researched by researchers. (Denzin and Lincoln 1994: 279 quoting Addelson 1990)

All interpretations are acknowledged to be provisional and hence both subject to modification and limited in time and context. Theories are embedded in history and hence in culture. There is common ground here with noticing, where events consist of the memories triggered by accounts. But noticing places less emphasis on analysis of accounts than does Grounded Theory, which aims to uncover and espouse theories about those events. Noticing aims to uncover theories held by the researcher, but analysis of accounts is for revelation and for providing access to experiences for oneself and for others.

Grounded Theory depends on developing and maintaining multiple perspectives, so that no one theory is allowed to dominate. The objects of Grounded Theory are minute details of ongoing observations. The object of research is to generate theories which account for patterns detected, and which generate that pattern detection. Those patterns are then tested against the observations of other participants to see whether they also accord with their experience.

Summary of Chapter 11

Whereas in Chapter 11 noticing was found to be at the heart of most approaches to research, in Chapter 12, the Discipline of Noticing is put forward as a research paradigm in its own right. It forms an epistemologically well-founded method of coming to know and of validating that knowing in a reliable, robust and generative manner. While in common with every other research paradigm it is unable to offer certainty, it provides a self-consistent way of working through which the practitioner can take responsibility for remaining in question rather than committing themselves to a single interpretation. As a method of research, it applies to practitioners developing their own expertise.

In the next chapter, some of the practices of noticing are applied to making use of personal experience to inform response to questions about people. Then it is developed into a form of personal development, called *researching from the inside*.

12 Researching from the inside

In Chapter 3 I quoted an observation quoted by Tripp (1993: 18–19):

> John didn't finish his work today. Must see he learns to complete what he has begun.

which led through interrogation of underlying assumptions to questions such as the following:

> Why did (does) John not finish his work?
> Why should he finish it?
> How does he see the tasks demanded of him?
> Are the tasks of the right kind, quality, and quantity?

Let me assume that I am the teacher and that I have made the observation. In order to examine the issue of finishing it may be tempting to ponder what John is doing and thinking, but it makes sense to probe more deeply, to try to get inside what it might be like not to finish. I can of course question John, even lead him towards personal psycho-analysis. But this is both intrusive and even potentially dangerous if I am not suitably trained and experienced. It also focuses on John, whereas the problem resides at least as much in me, because John's not finishing is an issue for me, and not, apparently, for John. The obvious thing to do is to interrogate my own experience for examples of 'not finishing', and perhaps even to 'ask around' for examples from colleagues of 'not finishing'. That way I can get a taste of different aspects of 'not finishing' while at the same time trying to locate in myself why it is an issue for me.

Another example is drawn from the work of Olive Chapman (1999: 201–16) who uses a narrative approach to teacher development. Typical is a set of three tasks:

> Write a story of your experience of a . . . class as a student in which you encountered a new idea for the first time. It should describe a complete lesson from beginning to end and provide details of what the instructor–teacher did and said, what you did, said, and thought, how the content was presented and dealt with, what other students did and said during the lesson.

Rewrite that story in the first person, with the same detail, from the teacher's point of view.

Rewrite the story as a description of how you intend to teach a lesson in the future.

Abstracted from this we could get a more general exercise:

- Give an account of an incident in which you felt at odds with what was happening.
- Rewrite your account from the point of view of someone with whom you disagreed.
- Rewrite your account from the point of view of either you or the other, in the way that you wish the incident had happened, or how you would like to act differently in a similar incident to happen in the future.

The move from a straightforward account of an incident to trying to get inside it, to acknowledge the possibility of multiple perceptions and interpretations, is typical of moving inward in your enquiry, moving from blaming or basing the incident in others, to considering how to change what you can actually change: yourself.

Interrogating your own experience is both common and insightful, as Lao Tsu said around 500 BC, 'How shall I know the way of all things? By what is inside me.' This forms the heart of practices adopted by the Discipline of Noticing but which are applicable in any professional practice. This is developed in the first section. Once you start to attend to your own noticing, it becomes more attractive and more important to move from researching other people or other things (instruments, objects, people's behaviours, attitudes, intentions etc.) to researching yourself. Interrogating your own experience can become the cornerstone of personal development, or what I call, *researching from the inside*. As Lao Tsu also said, 'Knowing yourself is wisdom.'

The idea is as follows. The Discipline of Noticing offers activities which support the broadening and deepening of sensitivities to notice selected attributes of professional practice. In a practice such as education, and more generally in professions centred on people, it is vital to continue to work at sensitivity to the people with whom you work: students and colleagues. One way, but for me a fundamentally important way to re-vivify sensitivities to the experiences of others, is to re-awaken similar experiences in myself.

Professionals have a healthy disrespect for those who offer advice and comment without 'having been there themselves'. They demand that people who offer alternative practices be able to show that they can themselves 'cut the mustard', for example, by having done similar jobs in similar institutions. But shared experience is neither sufficient nor even necessary. It is not sufficient, because many colleagues who do share experience are of little help in probing beneath the surface of practices; it is not necessary, because what really matters is being able to speak to the experiences of others. The more assertive one is, the more dubious the audience is likely to be. Constantly referring to 'when I was teaching (practising) in . . .' may impress the audience, but even so what really matters is that what is suggested rings true to the audience, opens up images for them of how they could act themselves. You will not have read this far in the book unless you have felt that what was being said spoke in some way to your experience. What matters is that what you read, or what you hear from someone, strikes a chord with you.

Researching from the inside involves more than simply going through the motions of being a student or of returning to the shop-floor. It requires being committed to act as a student while simultaneously being awake to noticing what it is like; being involved in exploring or encountering new topics or new aspects of familiar topics, while at the same time being aware of how you go about exploring; engaging in the processes of thinking in your discipline, while at the same time being awake to notice the use of those processes, perhaps even to notice the way in which you use your powers.

Just as the Discipline of Noticing can be seen as a collection of practices which can be used in most forms of enquiry-research, so Researching from the Inside can be seen both as a collection of practices to employ when it seems appropriate, and also as a field and method of research in and of itself. The principle question such research addresses, is 'What is it like to . . .'?

After exploring the question of 'what is it like to . . .?', this chapter offers some simple practices under the heading *Interrogating experience*, concerned with making sense of what other people are saying and asking, in any domain of enquiry. The rest, and largest part of the chapter is concerned with researching from the inside as an on-going practice of personal enquiry, under the heading *Researching experience*. Here the domain of enquiry is your own experience. The idea is to probe beneath the usual words and phrases into which we have been enculturated and from which we have constructed our own way of explaining ourselves to ourselves and to others, even to enquire into the foundations of noticing itself.

What is it like to . . .?

The notion of researching from the inside was inspired by formulating questions such as 'what is it like to think that way? . . . to do that? . . . to make that mistake? . . . not to know to . . . ?'. These questions arose for me from noticing that at every workshop I gave, someone at the end would ask me where my accent was from, so that I began to wonder what participants were actually attending to during sessions. Alerted to the notion of attention, what came to mind was a bevy of reports from teachers and researchers who had had opportunities to listen to children and to discover that when a child said something which seemed unusual or wrong, it was often because they were attending to something quite different, not because they were being awkward.

For example, Hoosain (2000) reports that in response to the question

A baker used two-thirds of the flour that he had to make a cake, and two-thirds of the remainder to make bread. If he then had two-thirds of a pound left, how many pounds of flour did he have at first?

two 13-year-old students gave responses of

$$2/3 + 2/3 + 2/3 = 2 \times 3 = 6 \text{ and } 2/3 \times 2/3 = 2 \times 3 = 3 \times 2 = 6.$$

Of course the 'working' shown makes no sense without some sort of commentary, but since the answers are correct, there may be more going on below the surface than is immediately evident. For example, a student who intuits an answer may try to offer the teacher what the teacher asks for (being constantly admonished to 'show your working') in order to justify an answer found in some other way. Only by finding out what the students are attending to, how they are seeing things, can you begin to form a judgement as to the quality of their thinking.

I soon found that trying to work out what someone else was attending to was very difficult. All there is to go on are a few bits of overt behavioural detritus which strike me. In the example above, all I have is a correct answer and incorrect arithmetical calculations. I can ask probing questions, but I then have the difficult problem of how much credence I give to the responses. I found that what I *could* do was to ask myself what I was attending to. I could try to locate what it was that I was overtly and covertly stressing when expressing myself (including physical, emotional and cognitive dimensions). And I could try to put myself in the place of others by seeking, not identical, but similar experiences. From this sort of personal enquiry was born *researching from the inside* (Mason 1992). In relation to the example of the cake, I can try to catch myself launching into explanation for something I sense intuitively, and I can tackle problems which are difficult for me to reason my way through but about which I have some intuitions. Others who have adopted aspects of this approach include Williams (1989), Chately (1992), James (1993), Ollerton (1993), Hewitt (1994), Wilson (1994), Tahta (1995), Bills (1996).

As a relative expert I may not be able literally to put myself in the experience of students, colleagues, or clients who do not know what I know, but I *can* do two things which help. I can suspend a lot of what I know, and I can put myself in analogous positions where I really do not know. In the following section I will suggest that you can actually come close to experiencing what others experience, but that there are significant obstacles regarding validation.

Suspending knowing

When students are working on routine exercises, teachers' first thoughts are that they themselves should know how to do the question: how to write such an essay, at least how to find out relevant historical or geographical facts, how to do the experiment, which treatment to apply, which technique to use. But the trouble with having your knowledge at the surface is that if a student asks for assistance, it is very difficult not to respond in terms of seeing a gap between 'where they are' and 'where they should be', and then giving them directions, literally, to get back on track. Sometimes it is extremely pertinent to make a focused remark which alerts a student to their straying from a path, or correcting some error that they have started making. But if the expert always corrects and re-directs, then students will quickly learn to wait until they get specific instructions (for example Account 41: *Pressing buttons*, p. 135). The didactic tension is ever-present.

An alternative strategy is to suspend knowing about answers and to focus on what students are attending to. Instead of trying to be in a state of 'being in question' about answers or about techniques to find those answers, the teacher can be in question about what students are thinking. The teacher can then ask genuine questions about 'Why did you do or think this?', 'What prompted you to do that?', 'Talk to me about what you are doing', 'Read me this bit . . .' or 'Wry and tell me in your own words'. As Casement (1985: 34) observes: 'empathy is the capacity to share the experience of others as our own'. And as the proverb has it, 'there is no room in an already full cup'. If you want to be open to what others are experiencing, you have to be able to suspend identification with your own experiencing, as well as with desires about what students 'should accomplish'. Casement puts it as 'experiencing the ego free to move from self to patient, from thinking to feeling'. He recommends (in the context of psychoanalysis) an *unfocused listening* in which you let go of trying to follow every detail and try to be inside what they are saying, immersing yourself in their saying, so that you can be sensitive to gestures and postures, to what is not said as well as to what is said. At the heart of such listening is a suspension of the primacy of your own experience in favour of trying to feel what it is like to be speaking and acting as the student does.

Putting myself in analogous positions

The best way to resonate with other people's experience is to try to keep awake to your own experience, to put yourself in situations in your own discipline deliberately which parallel, if not duplicate, experiences of your students. For example, as an English teacher handing out essay topics, I could every so often undertake to write an essay from a list composed by someone else (my students, other students, colleagues, etc.). It is not the essay writing itself that matters, but the discipline of submitting to the requirements of someone else, and attending to the flux of emotion around not wanting to write on that particular topic or not wanting to do the task at all; wanting to rephrase the topic; wanting to write more, or less, than required; and so on. Similarly, a geography teacher would do well to go out on expeditions led by someone else, not just to see how other people do it, but to experience again at first hand what it is like to be led around. Teachers who take children to museums could benefit by actually carrying out a collection of observation tasks set by someone else. Mathematics teachers benefit enormously from returning to the state of studenthood themselves to learn something in topics they have forgotten or never knew. Science and technology teachers benefit similarly from having to design experiments in a new topic domain, as well as having to carry out fully an experiment or design challenge devised by someone else.

As an experienced practitioner, it is very difficult to experience what it is like for a novice. For example, as a mathematics teacher it is very difficult to put myself in the position of 'not knowing how to add fractions'. But what I can do is seek out opportunities to study further mathematics, to work on mathematical problems, and to attend workshops on topics I know little or nothing about so as to re-experience the not-knowing which characterises the experience of students. This is why it is so important as a teacher to find a group of colleagues who are willing to work together on a subject discipline, exploring new topics and new problems as well as revisiting more familiar topics through unfamiliar explorations. To remain alive as a teacher it is essential to keep refreshing the heuristics, the sensitivities and awarenesses which make up that discipline, in order both to be stimulating for students, and to be sensitive to their experiences.

For example, pharmacists dispense drugs according to prescriptions. But they also know a great deal about drugs and how they interact. They are the front line for detecting inappropriate repeat prescriptions, side-effects, and symptoms of drugs interfering with each other. They can also contribute to encouraging patients to take the medicines prescribed. In one programme, pharmacy students are prescribed a collection of pills (in the form of candies) with different times or conditions in which they are to be taken. Students report that 'they forgot', 'they didn't like the taste', 'they lost some when opening the packet', 'the dog ate some' and so on. Curiously they don't always recognise without explicit attention being drawn to it, that this is exactly what patients do with prescriptions. By experiencing as closely as possible what it is like, they can be more sensitive to the patients they will serve. This is an elementary version of *researching from the inside*.

Interrogating one's own experience

One particular practice connected with researching from the inside is to approach any question by using one's own experience, and to treat any assertion as a conjecture which has to be tested out in experience. The idea arose when I became aware that whenever someone raised an issue or posed a question about the teaching and learning of mathematics, my natural response is to quietly interrogate my own experience. Where a matching experience is not easy to locate, I look for some situation or context which might be analogous. I then put myself through the experience (as a task-exercise) in order to gain some insight into the issue. This is no more than what everyone does naturally most of the time, but it is often overlooked or suppressed in an attempt to conform with imagined standards of research objectivity.

For example, when asked about students forgetting what they seemed to have learned only days or weeks before, I inspect my own experience to locate a recent event in which I failed to use some technique with which I was familiar. This led me to distinguish between knowing-how and knowing-to. Labelling enabled me to recognise many more instances in the following weeks, and so gave me some insight into what it might be like for students. A famous case of this emerged when a senior doctor suddenly found himself on the receiving end of the health care for which he was responsible. The 'insight' he gained was put to immediate use in transforming doctor–patient relationships. For a teacher, it is salutary to put oneself in the position of being taught in your own discipline for exactly the same reason.

Addressing questions

A question arises, perhaps from my own enquiry, perhaps from someone else. It can arise from someone reporting an incident, or asking an opinion. How do I respond? An immediate reaction may come to the surface. Before giving vent to it, I try, when I can catch myself, to put it to one side, in order to probe more deeply. Each of us constitute a wealth of experience, so it seems odd not to make use of it. The first thing I do is to ask myself whether I recognise the question. Can I find any resonance with incidents or thoughts from the past? Things may flood into mind, or nothing may come to mind immediately. I find it useful to wait for a short while to see if anything will come. I do not alight on the first thing that comes to mind, but rather add it to the store of possible responses. I can also take the initiative, by actively seeking relevant situations or similar questions or contexts, and this I can do with varying degrees of commitment and discipline. A third thing I can do is to try to locate some experience which might be analogous. I can then choose from among the responses which seem most appropriate to the situation in hand, perhaps even by offering a task rather than an opinion. Situations and incidents are more likely to come to mind, to be resonated or triggered, if I have paid them some attention in the past, if I have noticed and marked, if not recorded them.

For example, I noticed when working on a mathematics problem that I was stuck for a while because I was having to write down subscripts of subscripts which referred to each other in what was for me a novel way. It occurred to me that this might be giving me a taste of what it is like for a student to be unconfident with ordinary subscripts. Subsequently, when I meet students struggling with subscripts, I can re-run the more complicated exercise for myself, in order to help me enter the world of the student. If someone asks me about the struggles students have with subscripts, I can offer them the task-exercise as a way of gaining some appreciation of what it might be like. It is not that the students will have exactly the same struggle, but there is a good chance (to be tested out in experience) that there will be some similarities. At the very least I will be sensitised to the fact that there may be a problem for students in what for me is normally completely automatic.

If the investigation turns into a research enquiry, I can look for similarities and differences with students' experience using observations and interviews, by setting them tasks and seeking resonance between their descriptions and my own, and by seeking further potentially analogous tasks for myself.

Testing assertions

Whenever an assertion is encountered, the enquirer treats it as a conjecture. We look for confirming instances in our experience, and for possibly contradictory experiences, for instances which raise problems with the assertion or about which the assertion is unclear, and situations in which the assertion seems to make sense. Whether one looks first for confirmation or contradiction is an indicator of the status afforded to the author of the assertion. If the assertion has been offered in a spirit of conjecturing, then seeking confirming examples is a useful initial mode of enquiry, in which everyone is seeking to reach an articulation which fits with and makes sense of past experience. If the assertion is strongly made, then seeking counter-examples may be a useful initial mode of enquiry.

To pursue the enquiry requires testing out whether the assertion helps to inform practice in the future. In other words, through employing some of the practices of the Discipline of Noticing, does the assertion sharpen a sensitivity to notice in the future? Does it help to make sense of new experiences as they happen?

Some things to try now

Select one or more accounts of particularly significant moments from your experience, moments which illustrate or highlight some issue, or some typical moment when you would like to be able to act in a certain way. Find some colleagues to whom you can describe these moments, and ask them if they recognise such moments, and whether they could describe some similar ones from their own experience.

Select something that you have become freshly sensitive to in your practice, and construct some task for colleagues or students which you think will focus attention on that sensitivity. It might be to do with generalising, or speaking in meetings, or something more detailed and technical. Invite people to undertake the task, and then, in discussion later, see if they recognise the sensitivity which has been of importance to you. If they do recognise it, then you might invite them to work at sharpening that sensitivity, and compare what different people choose to do in such situations. If they do not recognise it, then work at refining or altering the task, and at the same time, pay particular attention to further examples in your own experience, so that you are more sharply aware of that sensitivity. The whole cycle of observation and reflection, sharpening sensitivities, recognising choices, preparing and noticing, and validating with others begins again, for them and for you.

If possible, arrange with a colleague to observe each other, and to describe brief-but-vivid moments noticed. See whether you can reduce judgements and explanations and concentrate on specific phenomena of teaching. See whether you notice a heightened awareness when they are observing you, and whether that continues when they are not even there.

Researching experience

The Discipline of Noticing is conceived as a practice which can be increasingly precised and disciplined, turning professional development into research if that is desired. By working at your practice, you can find yourself liberated through having more choices available, or constrained because aspects of practice which previously seemed satisfactory become problematic. Usually it is a two way process. Self-esteem and personal confidence grow while certainty evaporates and questions become more common than answers. We move towards what Keats (letter dated 21 December, 1817) called *negative capability*, namely, being capable of being in uncertainties, mysteries, doubts, without any irritable reaching after fact and reason.

The discourse of this presentation of the Discipline of Noticing treats experience and description as different. Consequently those who believe that experience is only a language pattern, a way of speaking, are likely to find difficulty. But within the articulation offered here are possibilities to enquire into whether experience is indeed only the stories we tell. By being rigorous with oneself, and working with an enquiring community of colleagues, assertions like this can be held up to scrutiny. In the end, you cannot escape the language in which you talk to yourself. But it may be the case that there is something we could call experience which is not verbalised, not even perhaps enacted, yet somehow happens; something of which only aspects are ever spoken. As soon as we try to bring this to articulation we adopt fragments of established discourse and so position our account within one or more already articulated perspectives. But it is not always necessary to articulate everything, even in media other than words such as images and sounds. The challenge suggested by the Discipline of Noticing is to locate or construct task-exercises which highlight non-verbal pre-articulate experience without converting it into articulated expression. Failure to locate such task-exercises does not invalidate the enquiry, for it provides only absence of evidence, not evidence of absence.

The following subsections suggest domains of possible enquiry. Warning: research from the inside can be surprising, even upsetting. As one colleague said, 'I find myself discovering aspects of myself I didn't realise were there: hostility and negativity; desires and urges; in catching moments of choice I seem to be seeing "how I am" which is not how I like to think of myself'.

Experience

Is experience merely the story we tell, or is there more?

> Try to describe an experience, whether personal or shared with others as fully as possible, verbally or written. Can you in principal capture everything in language? Where does the language come from? Where does the languaging that you also experience come from?

Events

Something happens. How can that happening be captured, if at all? What does it consist of?

> Take opportunities to ask groups of people to report on some minor but shared incident, and compare their accounts. In what sense is there a shared event or shared experience?

An eye for an I

Throughout this book there has been a deliberate sliding between the pronouns I, you, we and one. The fact that people sometimes switch in mid-sentence even from using 'I' to 'one' often signals a desire to distance themselves from the remark. Pronoun use constitutes a fruitful domain of enquiry (Pimm 1987; Rowland 1999a), which can be pursued as researching from the inside by asking what constitutes 'I' when it is said.

What is being referred to when 'I' is being said, and is there any difference between the use of 'I' and of 'me'? Of course grammar often determines which is used, but are there any detectable differences in experiences of using these words? For example, very often the word 'I' is said very quickly and rather lightly compared to other words in the sentence. Might this be informative about the structure of attention of the speaker? When the speaker is dwelling in themselves, there is often considerable weight or stress placed on 'I'. Put another way, take a sentence such as 'I want to go out', and explore different impacts arising from putting stress on different words. What about the use of 'one' when referring to or drawing upon your own experience?

> Try to catch yourself saying 'I', and try to be fully present in that moment. This is a lot harder than it sounds. If it proves difficult, try training yourself to say 'I' to yourself every time you pass through a door, say, or every time you pick something up. Once you have caught some 'I' statements, try to examine the substance behind the assertion. Who or what is saying 'I' and to what does it refer?

Whose who

What is referred to by 'myself'? Is there a unique core self that is 'me'?

- What is the same and what is different about the person who sits down at their desk or enters a classroom in the morning, attends a meeting, arrives home, goes shopping, engages in a hobby or non-professional interest?
- What are you like as a householder (cleaning, washing, preparing meals), as a professional or as a consumer (shopping, seeking entertainment, . . .)? How do you change when you hear different people speaking on the other end of

the telephone? How do you switch from one to another? Can you catch the moment of transition?

- Try to catch yourself uttering an opinion in one context, and a contrary opinion in another.
- Imagine yourself carrying out some specific professional practice (opening and reading correspondence or email, entering a room in which you will do something pre-arranged, . . .). Now try to catch yourself actually doing what you imagined.
- As you leave the office, catch yourself preparing all the work you will do that evening, and the desire you feel. In the evening, try to catch the desire you have to do the work. In what way are the desires the same and in what ways different?

George Mead (1934, 1969), often referred to as the 'founder of sociology', presciently initiated social constructivism by proposing that 'the human self arises through [the] ability to take the attitude of the group to which it belongs' (1969: 33). 'The structure of society lies in social habits, and only insofar as we can take these social habits into ourselves can we become ourselves' (1969: 33). 'Through speech and acts we affirm ourselves insofar as we reflect the social views of us' (p. 36) so that 'what constitutes the self is the collection of internalised social practices' (p. 40). Thus 'a self can arise only when there is a social process within which this self has had its initiation'. All of these assertions warrant close investigation!

Choice choices

The Discipline of Noticing revolves around the issue of how and when choices are made. Can you catch a moment of choice?

> Try to catch yourself choosing to act. For example: can you catch the decision to get out of bed? To get into bed? To speak? To read (a cereal packet, a letter, a newspaper article)? To change from reading one line to reading the next? To turn off the TV? Even where there is lengthy deliberation, when is the choice made? What is it like at the moment a choice is made? Where does the choice come from and what conditions are required for there to be a choice?

Beverly MacInnis (private communication) described moments of choice as like being poised on a rock in the middle of a river crossing, with concern about slipping (you'd remember that!) but a smooth passage would not be remembered. The act of crossing is one of letting go of not-moving, and finding yourself on the next rock. Another version is that a moment of choice is like being perched momentarily on a knife edge, and the slightest twitch sends you down one side or the other. Yet another version is that it is like being present at a gathering of older and wiser people whose discussion you do not fully take in, and out of which some decision arises. Dewey (1933: 41–42) suggested a similar participative perspective with respect to having ideas:

the having of ideas is not so much something we do, as it is something that happens to us. Just as, when we open our eyes, we see what is there; so, when suggestions occur to us, they come to us as functions of our past experience and not of our present will and intention. So far as thoughts in this particular meaning are concerned, it is true to say 'it thinks' (as we say 'it rains'), rather than 'I think'. Thinking occurs.

Reacting and responding

Converting habitual reaction into informed response requires considerable effort.

- Try catching yourself being asked a question and pause long enough to allow an alternative response to come to mind before deciding what to say or do.
- Try catching yourself being caught up in a flow of negativity, and see what you can do to find a quick exit, or what it is like to allow the negativity to continue. Perhaps catch yourself responding inwardly when someone else gets caught up in negativity, and use this to sensitise yourself to your own.

Noticing noticing

- Try to catch the moment when you stop noticing something, stop being aware of a person, a notice, a movement, etc.
- Try to re-enter a moment from a meeting or a session, and catch yourself re-entering related or connected moments. What forms the boundary of individual moments?

Knowing knowing

- Try to catch yourself confidently knowing something. What is the basis of that confidence? How do you distinguish between confident and tentative knowing?
- Try to locate (in retrospect) incidents in which at the time you did not know-to do something, even though you do know how to do it. What is it like not to know to act even though you have the expertise?
- How do you come to know something new? A word or phrase, a new element of practice, a new interest? Try to catch the moment when you use or refer to something which is new for you and see how it feels.

Acts, actions and activities

I have been using these words in slightly different ways to refer to slightly different experiences.

- Try to identify participating in an action, in which something is changed or transformed, and contrast this with situations where nothing seems to change at all.

- Try to catch yourself initiating some activity by acting. Try to catch yourself responding to someone else's initiative by acting. Try to catch yourself enabling two other people to interact (more) effectively by acting. What is similar and what different about these experiences of acting?

Participating in an action, whether as initiator, responder or mediator, means that as a result of some initial and some consequent acts, something changes or is transformed in some way. Activity has direction or purpose and requires a means to be employed to pursue direction and purpose.

The mechanical and the mindful

> It is a profoundly erroneous truism, repeated by all copy books and by eminent people when they are making speeches, that we should cultivate the habit of thinking what we are doing. The precise opposite is the case. Civilisation advances by extending the number of important operations which we can perform without thinking about them. Operations are like cavalry charges in battle - they are strictly limited in number, they require fresh horses, and they must only be made at decisive moments. (Whitehead 1932)

A parent's admonishment to a child who has dropped a dish ('Watch what you are doing!') is too late and perhaps misplaced. What might be meant is that the child learn to use awareness for what it is for, for being mindful of the conditions and goals, but to leave the details of handling a dish to the automatic functioning of the body. As the Zen proverb says, 'When you walk, just walk.'

Gattegno (1970) put great emphasis on studying the ways that very young children automate fundamental actions (like standing, walking, running, speaking) in order to appreciate how people learn to subordinate their mental attention to their bodily movements, because much of mathematical competence involves a similar subordination of attention to routine. I get good at tables by withdrawing inessential attention. When exercises are assigned with the intention that pupils become practised, the exercises will be most effective when they draw attention away from the part that is to become habit.

I learn my tables and no longer have to 'think' about the answers, and this applies at all levels of schooling. It also applies to teaching. In order to survive I develop all sorts of automatically triggered coping strategies so that I can attend to more important matters. But as has already been suggested, not all habits continue to be useful. Some actually get in the way of developing sensitivity. The discipline of noticing includes techniques for bringing habits to the surface, questioning their effectiveness and perhaps augmenting or modifying them.

Experiencing the experience of others

It is often asserted confidently that we cannot know what someone else is thinking. The odd thing about this cliché is that we all have experience of the contrary. Everyone has had some experiences of knowing for an instant what it is like to be someone else. What is unusual is being sufficiently aware of the moment to recall it later, much less to be able to act upon it in the moment. As soon as we become aware that we are experiencing someone else's awareness, the contact disappears. Furthermore, if you try to confirm with them, almost always people will deny any link, perhaps because it is very threatening indeed to find that someone has literally 'gotten inside your head'. Yet we all crave others to be sensitive towards us.

> Try to catch a moment of harmony with partner, colleague or student. Try testing out whether they agree that you experienced what they experienced.

Summary of Chapter 12

The practice of interrogating your own experience in order to address questions or issues arising in professional practice was put forward as being both entirely natural and at the core of professional expertise. It is one example of using the practices of the Discipline of Noticing to research one's own practice, from the inside, that is, by becoming more aware and articulate about what it is like to have certain experiences. The bulk of the chapter consists of suggestions for enquires to undertake in order to learn more about oneself.

Researching from the inside is a complement to extra-spective research. Large-scale surveys of responses to questionnaires and tasks can highlight previously unsuspected commonalities, trends and phenomena which individual practitioners do not encounter very often or are unlikely to notice. Transcripts of interviews and interactions analysed in detail can reveal details of people's thought processes, behaviours and attitudes, which questionnaires cannot get at. Theoretical reflections and analyses can stimulate and inform. Working on noticing can bring about actual change, not by imposing from the outside or trying to convince through demonstration and reasoning, but by providing the requisite environment to foster and sustain personal enquiry. Outer research reports can be assertive, perhaps statistically, where as products of inner research tend to be stimuli to generate relevant experience. Neither is better than the other, for much depends upon purpose, and each can inform the other.

SUMMARY OF PART V

Part V opened with a discussion of what constitutes research, suggesting that even formulating a question involves commitment to a perspective with an expected form of answer. It then proposed a fourfold structure, in which noticing is seen both as a core component of all research and as a method of research itself. When applied to oneself, noticing provides a technique for interrogating one's own experience in the face of any assertion or conjecture, as well as a lifelong process of personal research and development.

Part VI

What about . . .?

Questions and concerns

It is natural and even an integral part of the Discipline of Noticing to have doubts and questions come to mind. This final part addresses the kinds of questions which have arisen for practitioners and for theorists, about issues which are inherent in practitioner research (Chapter 13), in qualitative research generally (Chapter 14) and in the Discipline of Noticing in particular (Chapter 15). Indeed, the thrust of Part VI is how the Discipline of Noticing addresses many of the problematic aspects of qualitative research, and, how, taking the bull by the horns, it breaks through epistemological and methodological barriers inherited from scientific methods and epistemologies. Summarised succinctly, in enquiry concerning human beings, the objective can be approached *through* the subjective, not by trying to circumvent it. Leonardo da Vinci (1500) noticed that, 'It is easier to be diverted to study data rather than to use data to study the phenomena of interest.' The Disipline of Noticing maintains from an experience and an informing future practice, rather than getting caught up in analysing data.

13 Questions and concerns about practitioner research

This chapter addresses some tensions in practitioner research which are endemic and inescapable. Sometimes they may even be experienced as debilitating. But if tensions are embraced rather than avoided, they can often provide access to useful energy and sensitivity, which in turn can be used to inform practice.

Professional practice involves seeing a large number of people (students, clients, colleagues) in similar roles, so it is very tempting to formulate generalisations which seem to help sort out and even predict behaviour. For example, I might form the impression that a particular person is not very adept at using diagrams in mathematics, or that someone else finds it difficult to pay attention to details when making arrangements, or that a group is boisterous and hard to handle. I might even link these to more general assertions such as that women tend to be less adept at diagrams, that men tend not to pay attention to details, and that the last lesson on a Friday is not going to be very productive. Of course these generalities are false, since there are evident counter-examples, but similar ones are tempting on the basis of experience, especially personal experience not tested against the experience of others. The trouble with 'experience' is that I may be discounting cases that disagree with my generality, and I am at best inferring generality from a few instances. Alexander Pope (1734) noted this:

> To observations which ourselves we make,
> We grow more partial for the observer's sake.

Despite being common, conscious and unconscious generalities block both personal development and effective practice. Uncovering these is the work of professional development and of research. They also pose logical, philosophical and ethical problems, which are raised in what follows. First, though, the fundamental problem of insufficient time and energy.

Energy and time

A major challenge for practitioner research is the sheer demand on energy that coping day-to-day makes. It is one thing to experiment a little when the opportunity arises, but quite another to undertake systematic enquiry. There is rarely enough time in the few breaks one gets as an active professional to make any sensible notes. Evenings are devoted either to preparation and marking or to recovering. Writing about the day is an added burden, while reading is a recipe for falling asleep. Yet there is a liberating and exhilarating effect from being enthusiastic about a new approach or new sensitivity, from participating in choice rather than mechanically getting through a session. Taking time and energy to record cannot only get researching under way, but can feed back into states of enhanced awareness with a feeling of being invigorated.

The Discipline of Noticing is conceived as a practice which can be made increasingly precise and disciplined as suits the individual, turning professional development into research if that is desired. By working at your practice, you can find yourself liberated through having more choices available. Of course, if you are overly ambitious and take on too much at once, you can feel overwhelmed when several aspects of practice become problematic which previously seemed satisfactory. Usually it is a two way process. Self-esteem and personal confidence grow, while certainty evaporates and questions become more common than answers.

In the project supporting teacher enquiry mentioned in Chapter 5, Jaworski (1998) found the teachers eager to talk about details of their practice. They went to sessions with questions they wanted to pursue, and with the desire to describe things that had happened or were happening. The pressures of teaching and administration make it virtually impossible for individuals, or even a small group, to initiate and sustain collective enquiry into their practices, yet when offered attention and support from two academics, the teachers were keen to engage, to the extent of having something to report at each meeting, discussing with each other between meetings, and carrying the activity into a second year.

Initial enthusiasm has to be transformed so that activity is sustained when novelty rubs off and reflection becomes part of your routine. But it is precisely at this point that new energy is available when you work against the natural tendency to give up.

Ethics

Any practitioner interested in developing and extending their practice is centred in the effects of that practice. The practitioner is concerned to support the people they serve, by being themselves more aware and sensitive. For example, teachers, nurses, pharmacists, and administrators all want to help the people they care for to become less dependent and more self-sufficient. There are two immediate issues:

- short-term desires may conflict with long-term goals; and
- developing practice may turn into experimenting on people.

Remembering that whatever you do affects other people, even to the extent of reporting what you interpret their actions to have been.

Short-term desires and long-term goals

There is an endemic tension when one person tries to do something for another: does the patient or student recognise that what is being done is for their own ultimate benefit? Where the patient relies on and trusts the carer, then caring can take place. Where students trust and respect the teacher, then teaching and learning can proceed. But increasingly, professionals are being required not only to act in the best interests of those they support, but to be able to justify those actions to them, in the short term.

For example, a teacher may know from experience that students need to get down and work hard practising for an examination, but students may resent being called upon to work so hard at that time, unaware of what they face. A patient may not appreciate being cajoled and urged to try harder to regain control of some function, when all they want is for the whole experience to go away. So practitioners are caught. Somehow the energies of the patient or student have to be mobilised and directed in order that recovery-learning can take place most efficiently.

So not only is there an endemic tension in any professional practice which has to do with the fact of working with other human beings, but that tension has additional ethical complications when there is constant pressure to develop and justify (whether coming from outside or from within the practitioner).

Developing or experimenting?

No one likes to think that they are being used as guinea pigs in some experiment, yet most people are pleased to know that those trying to help them are also trying to improve the form and nature of that help. There is a fuzzy area, therefore, between experimenting on people and striving to improve practice by making adjustments. In all cases it is a matter of maintaining the care you have for the individual while at the same time attending to the implications of changes that you try. In a sense, all practice is experiment, for no matter how typical the symptoms or how standard the diagnosis, each patient, each student, each client is an individual and deserves to be recognised and treated this way. The successful practitioner is the person who can retain both care for the individual while being informed by, and informing, the general.

One form of the tension between developing and experimenting manifests itself when in the midst of professional practice which you are also researching, you find yourself torn between acting as a researcher and acting as a practitioner.

Many people find themselves alternating between teaching and researching, whether through changing from one to another over a few years, over a few months, on a daily basis, or even moment by moment in the classroom. Forced in the moment to choose between helping a student and holding back as a researcher to see what will happen, the student's progress must be the first priority. Sometimes this tension can be useful, because the holding back might actually be of benefit to the student. Other times it can be frustrating because it is more important to provide professional help in the moment than to explore some fascinating aspect of what they are currently thinking and to wait to see where it will lead them.

A great deal depends on exactly what is being researched. If you are enquiring into what students are thinking or doing, in other words, if you are studying someone else, then you are susceptible to divided loyalties between teacher and researcher (Ainley 1999). But if you are enquiring into your own states, your own thinking, your own practice, then every moment of choice or tension you experience can be used as stimulus to make an observation about yourself or your practice. If you feel caught between intervening and not intervening, between making a direct and specific suggestion or trying an indirect prompt, between telling and asking, then you can enter fully into the moment, and try later to recall what was going through your mind as you followed your instincts. What matters for your practice is how possibilities come to mind and how one is selected. Working at being aware of such moments, and trying to prepare for them, is likely to extend the range of choices you have, and so the richness of the types of interaction you offer your students.

Justifying practices

Ultimately, validity for any process of professional development must be improvement in 'the service offered', so that those served become less dependent and more self-sufficient where possible. This is the long-term goal, and in most cases it is shared by the student, even if details differ. Thus students may feel they have no future, while the teacher sees potential; a patient may feel hopeless while the carer is confident that a condition can improve. In such cases, part of the professional practice is the harnessing of energies of those they work for, and with educating their awareness and even training behaviour where appropriate.

Ethically, then, any professional must be concerned to seek evidence for effectiveness of what they are doing. But effectiveness can only be judged in terms of stated aims, and the short-term desires of a patient or student may conflict with long-term goals. For example, for a researcher, effectiveness may mean clarity, impact and validity of their reports, and it may mean an improvement in the atmosphere or functioning of their own or others' practice. For a teacher, effectiveness may mean more students scoring higher grades on tests, and it may mean more harmonious lessons and both student and teachers feeling better about themselves, and each other. For a carer, effectiveness may mean more independence for those being cared for, and it may mean less frantic and more relaxed interactions and feeling of self-worth for the carer. Thus ethics and validity are intertwined.

The practitioner who becomes articulate about both short-, medium- and long-term goals is in the best position to justify their choices, and the practitioner who is aware of the choices they make, and works at being more and better informed, is in the best position to explain their actions.

Issues in reporting

The researching practitioner is interested in the people they serve, but also has some interest in making connections with a wider community outside of their specific practice, and possibly outside the institution, and this is another source of ethical tensions.

When reporting incidents to other people there are ethical problems of identification. Analysis may not cast the person in a fully positive light as possibilities emerge of which they were unaware at the time. Yet as a researcher, on the one hand, you want to retain access to people's real names so that you can re-enter the situation as necessary, but on the other hand it is considered unacceptable to report incidents involving other people without explicit permission from them, because they may change their view or they may not want others to know what they said. Many people use initials, and where that is too obvious, they change the initials according to some private code. Some people prefer to use names, and so develop pseudonyms for those involved in accounts to be reported. This can make it hard to remember who the original person was, so it is probably wise to make the switch as early in the analysis process as possible!

Self-observation

I can observe what is happening (as far as I can tell) in some situations, and I can observe myself through becoming aware of propensities and habits, judgements and emotions, swings of mood and shifts of attention, alterations in intention and desire, and so on. As a practitioner trying to observe my own practice, I can get myself into all sorts of logical and philosophical tangles. How can I observe myself, since I am simultaneously observed and observer? If the two can be separated, can I not also observe the observer and observe the observer observing, in an endless sequence of increasing complexity?

Furthermore, even observing as an outsider, such as shadowing a colleague or client, can significantly alter a situation, much in the way that a visit by an inspector alters the state of the people being inspected. Will not any attempt to observe myself severely interfere with what I am doing? Is it philosophically possible to observe one's self (Cassam 1994)?

These are legitimate and significant concerns, but they arise from confusing self-consciousness and self-awareness. Self-consciousness refers to that dysfunctional state when you feel larger than life, when your feet seem to be slightly off the ground, and when you have tunnel or restricted vision. It is typically generated when you are called upon to expose yourself to others, perhaps being called upon to address a large audience or otherwise become the centre of attention of a large group. For example, whereas the presence of an inspector can generate a state of panic, of tunnel vision and tension which is essentially dysfunctional and corresponds to being self-conscious in the awkward sense, the presence of an esteemed colleague can generate quite a different state, in which you experience heightened awareness and sharpened sensitivity because of their presence. This latter is self-awareness or 'being awake', which is a positive state of heightened awareness and sensitivity to what is happening. Instead of tunnel vision you feel you can see more than ever; instead of feet off the ground you feel grounded and confident.

Consider the following experiment:

> As you sit (presumably) reading, become aware of the fact that you are sit-ting and reading. You might begin to attend to the sensation of your feet on the ground, of the sensation of your body on the chair, of the scanning movement back and forth of your eyes. If you work at strengthening this awareness, you will probably find that you are no longer reading! Your attention is elsewhere and at best the words are passing by.

This shows that observation can certainly interfere with the action being observed. But if you are less ambitious, if you permit the awareness of sensation to emerge without focusing on it, you may find that you can develop an aware-ness of sensation and yet still read. While continuing to read, you can also become aware of yourself specialising to your own experience, agreeing or dis-agreeing, or applying the ideas to some other context, all without having to stop reading. This observation is properly the work of the second bird, referred to in Chapter 11. When ordinary consciousness tries to observe at the same time as participating, there is the kind of interference experienced in the exercise on reading, often called self-consciousness, which can be debilitating and de-sta-bilising. But if this function is undertaken by the inner witness, it does not interfere. It can then be referred to as self-awareness, which informs and improves practice, and makes possible the ancient injunction to 'know thyself'.

Avoiding interference

One of the requirements of a master-driver qualification is to be able to make a running commentary while driving. But to achieve this state of simultaneous action and articulation requires considerable practice and is perhaps not unlike the sports commentator or the news broadcaster who has to be able to hear someone talking to them in one ear and yet keep talking to the audience. What is required is an inner separation, and this requires training. Indeed, such a sep-aration is the ultimate aim of the Discipline of Noticing.

Without training, what people report while they are engaging in their practice is highly unreliable, as indeed early introspectionist psychologists found (see Gardner 1985). For example, attempts to get people to verbalise their thoughts as they work on mathematics problems rarely produces convincing data, because they have not had the requisite training. The same is true when you try it on yourself. To try to maintain a running mental description to yourself or to some-one else usually diverts attention into what you are saying and away from the action (try it as you prepare a meal or take a shower!).

But if when you 'come to the surface', when you get stuck, or get a new idea, you take time to use some of that energy to move from marking into recording, to make the briefest of notes of the fact of being stuck or uncertain, of the current conjecture and assumptions, of what you are about to try, you will find that at the very least when you look back you can see what you were doing. So often, people get stuck because they have lost touch with what they were doing. Making notes as you go makes it much easier to write up a neat and succinct report, and you can use the notes to re-enter moments mentally and recall what it was like: the frustration of being stuck, the enthusiasm of a new possibility, etc. (Mason *et al.* 1982).

By refreshing the experience and imagining yourself acting in a positive and effective way you can set up possibilities for the future. You may find that you begin to 'think' of strategies spontaneously, like try a simpler example, generalise, draw a diagram, or admit ignorance and let some symbol stand for the unknown. Some people report that they begin to recognise a little voice, almost a person on their shoulder, who every so often asks questions like 'Is this going anywhere?', 'What has this got to do with the task?' and which seems to know when to go back and check actions and calculations. Other people report merely that ideas suddenly come to them. In either case there is an some part of you which is watching and monitoring. Schoenfeld (1985) referred to this as an *executive*, and Mason *et al.* (1982) referred to an *inner monitor*. Once this starts working, your sense of self-observation changes markedly. You are no longer trying to look from outside, but rather work from an inner participant observer who augments and enhances rather than interferes.

The Discipline of Noticing is primarily a means for producing functional rather than dysfunctional participant observation that contributes to the situation. George Mead (1934), one of the founders of sociology, claimed that 'I' (ego) can observe, be aware of and think about 'me' (alter ego), and that the growth of this separation marks an important transition in a child's experience. A similar transition is possible within professional practitioners, and is both the aim and the essential mechanism for researching from the inside.

Confusion between self-consciousness and self-awareness can also confuse objectivity and subjectivity. The notion of objectivity is based on an image of a neutral white-coated scientist peering at dials and bubbling test-tubes which proceed independently of her presence. But this is not only an inappropriate image of scientific enquiry, but totally inappropriate when applied to work with human beings.

Objective and objectively-subjective observation

The notion that experiments can be observed objectively is problematic and questionable even in science, where it is an important part of the method that the experiment can be described in sufficient detail for others to replicate it. Whenever specified chemicals are placed in a test-tube in specified proportions, observers will agree that there is or is not a precipitate of a specified colour, mass, etc. . . ., and it is part of scientific assumptions that the same result will always occur. However, when studying people, the mere fact of observations, whether asking questions or administering a questionnaire, or even just watching, influences the thoughts if not the behaviour of the people being studied. To see this, try filling in a questionnaire for someone doing a survey, and observe how the fact of the questions you are being asked directs you to thoughts you would probably not otherwise have had. Similarly when a colleague visits a session, or even when you imagine that a colleague may visit your session, your awareness and your participation changes, as already mentioned above.

Instead of trying to withdraw, to maintain an extra-spective separation between observer and subject, it is possible to obtain a degree of objectivity by fully embracing the necessarily subjective. Objectivity is after all judged by whether what is observed fits with other people's experience, and can be observed by them. Replication may have an extra-spective form in which all essential conditions are specified so that someone else can arrange for those conditions and can follow the given recipe. But replication may have an inter-spective form in which experience is generated and reflected upon communally, with negotiation of interpretation, meaning and significance. Here objectivity emerges where there is negotiable agreement. Replication can even take an intra-spective form in which experience is generated and insights integrated into practice. This latter process of course runs the risk of self-delusion, which is why it is essential in the Discipline of Noticing to seek resonance in the experience of others.

When a community have developed a shared vocabulary from intra- and inter-spectivity which speaks richly to their experience, there is a sense of objectivity which is every bit as powerful as objectivity based on extra-spection. Through consonance of experience, an experiential objectivity can be reached which is validated through synthesis rather than through analysis, through the effectiveness of action taken which is made possible by noticing.

Summary of Chapter 13

A practitioner's first responsibility is the person with whom they are working, the activities in which they are engaging, their professionality. Research and personal development have to take second place. But when the enquiry is focused on your own practice (rather than on studying what others are doing etc.), then every professional act can become data for your enquiry. It does require energy and time to do more than simply practise one's profession, but to be fully professional requires constantly striving to improve one's practice, to become yet more professional and in the process, to define what 'being professional' means.

14 Questions and concerns about qualitative research

All research is problematic, precisely because there is no guarantee of truth. Research concerning human beings cannot guarantee truth because the notion of truth is itself problematic when desires and will, attention and intention, are involved. A Chinese proverb put it as, 'Every sect has its truth, and every truth its sect.' Being problematic does not mean that we have to throw up our hands and give up, however. The whole point about research methodology is to discuss and elaborate on disciplined and systematic procedures which are accepted, and to develop within a community of practice a so called 'paradigm' or accepted way of working. This chapter elaborates on some of the inherent problems of qualitative research, with responses to those problems offered by the Discipline of Noticing.

Describing as a methodological issue

Description is a cornerstone of all research. Any description is based on making distinctions and drawing attention to relationships, through the process of stressing some features and consequently ignoring or down-playing others. In some research, description provides data for analysis, the description becoming a substitute for 'the real thing'. Description also serves as a means for reinforcing membership in a local culture through linguistic consonance: a group of people will develop certain ways of describing, and hence certain aspects that they tend to describe will become prominent. For example, one group may stress gender differences while another focuses on alienation. The description acts as data, not for analysing what is described, but for revealing and rendering available for analysis what marks it, makes it salient, and what actions might proceed in the future as a result of the distinctions made.

The problematic issues raised in this section are as follows:

- If what we perceive is what we are prepared to perceive, and what we are prepared to perceive is what we have perceived in the past, how then do we ever come to perceive anything new?
- Data is a construction by a researcher: how do I know I would construct the same record in the same situation again?
- Data is only a summary presentation of some richer experience: how do I know that what is presented is a faithful record?

- Observation, description and analysis all involve selection; how do I know that the researcher has not been highly selective?
- Analysis creates data, and in the process tempts the researcher into confusing the data for the originating experience; how can I keep in touch with the original phenomenon?
- Description (observation) involves interpretation, so the observer is caught up in, is even part of, the data, as well as the analysis; where then is objectivity?
- Description involves making distinctions and labelling; how can I be sure that distinctions are 'really there', and that labels are appropriate?
- Given these problems, how then can any reliable generalisation be obtained?

As soon as I set out to describe a situation, I am caught in the conceit that there is *a situation* to be described. Yet reflection on the nature of events, particularly after watching video recordings, leads to questioning what it is that constitutes 'the event'. My own position is that events consist of the experiences triggered by reference to a label for 'that event', and that these are often confused with the stories we have to tell about them, which become elaborated and attenuated over time. I say 'confused with' because there is a tendency for the story to become the experience. For example, parents repeat certain stories of what their children did when very young, and the children grow into adulthood with these stories becoming part of their experience. Thus there is a complex interplay between story and experience. Where I part company with the extreme social-constructivist perspective is that whereas they tend to identify experience with language, I acknowledge experience as being broader than language: I can (attempt to) say only a small part of what I experience, but differentiating experience is assisted by language which is social and all encompassing, rather the way water encompasses a fish.

Instead of bemoaning the fickle features of memories which generate novel details to past events through the telling and retelling of stories, research from the inside grasps the nettle and approaches stories as constituting selves; as framing how the world is seen. Recalling the Talmudic saying: 'We do not see what is there; we see what we are', the role of the researcher is not to declare what did take place, but to suggest what could take place, to share awareness of awareness so that each individual can construct and reconstruct their own selves. Thus tasks are not difficult or easy, nor are classes boring or interesting. Rather, a person in a particular state at a particular time finds a task difficult or easy, a class boring or interesting.

Instead of seeing an event or incident as absolute, with different observers approximating to some invariant reality, each participant can be seen as engaged in 'eventing': in mutual determination and self-construction. The event consists of the stories that participants (and others) come to tell of it, and the being of the participants incorporates (literally) their story of the event. Events might then be seen as unstable elements for research, but stability comes from the developing being, the wisdom, sensitivity to notice, and insight of the individual.

Bohm (1980: 17) suggests that distinctions are inevitably taken as divisions, implying separate existence of terms:

We have thus to be alert to give careful attention and serious consideration to the fact that our theories are not 'descriptions of reality as it is' but rather, ever-changing forms of insight, which can point to or indicate a reality that is implicit and not describable in its totality.

Maslow (1971: 155–7) put it more strongly:

> The world can communicate to a person only that of which he is worthy, that which he deserves or is 'up to'; that to a large extent, he can receive from the world, and give to the world, only that which he himself is.

> We express what we are. To the extent that we are split, our expressions are split, partial, one-sided. To the extent that we are integrated, whole, unified, spontaneous, and fully functioning, to that extent are our expressions and communications complete, unique and idiosyncratic, alive and creative rather than inhibited, conventionalized, and artificial, honest rather than phony.

Maturana and Varela (quoted in Bauersfeld 1993: 141) consider the function of language itself:

> So long as language is considered to be denotative it will be necessary to look at it as a means for the transmission of information, as if something where transmitted from organism to organism . . . when it is recognised that language is connotative and not denotative, and that its function is to orient the orientee without regard to the cognitive domain of the orienter, it becomes apparent that there is no transmission of information through language.

What is important in qualitative research in general, and in researching from the inside in particular, is not the validity or accuracy of the description, but the effect, the action that that description sets up inside others.

In Chapter 8 the question arose about an apparently paradoxical circularity regarding perception:

> what we perceive is what we are prepared to perceive, and what we are prepared to perceive is what we have perceived in the past. How then does one ever come to perceive anything new?

One approach is to try to break the circle of cause-and-effect and to declare one place as the initiator. But another approach is to embrace the circularity and to invoke a hermeneutic perspective such as that of Maturana (1988, von Glasersfeld website) in which instead of seeing a cycle of cause-and-effect we see co-emergence. Perception and preparedness to be able to perceive emerge together as the result of perceiving and preparing to perceive. This may not be a satisfactory answer to someone committed to locating mechanisms, but it works well when experience is interrogated closely.

How do we perceive anything new?

To address this question in a scholarly manner, one reads the experts across the ages in order to find out what they said and what rings true with us today. To address this question in an enquiring manner, one interrogates closely one's own experience, and juxtaposes that with what others have said.

Let me begin with the scholarly: Goodman (1978: 96–7) exploits his world-making metaphor and extends Hanson's (1958) observation that 'facts are theory-laden' to:

> (facts) are as theory laden as we hope our theories are fact-laden . . . facts are small theories, and theories are big facts.

Wheeler (1986) saw it as a paradox:

> If I have to construct my knowledge for myself, how do I come to know something new?

Pascual-Leone (1980) called this the 'learning paradox', which Bereiter (1985) put succinctly as:

> If one tries to account for learning by a means of mental actions carried out by the learner, then it is necessary to attribute to the learner a prior cognitive structure that is as advanced or complex as the one to be acquired.

Bereiter suggests that Piaget (1977a, 1977b, 1978) spent the last years of his life trying to resolve this paradoxical circularity, and the Meno dialogue of Plato addresses the same question.

A variety of answers have been offered through the ages. From the Vedic:

> we are all part of a single will, or come from a single soul-pool, hence what we know is what we contact in that universal pool,

through Plato:

> the soul is immortal and learning consists of re-collecting what we already know or have known in previous existences,

and Aristotle:

> we are persuaded by one who knows through logic; we need only think rationally to uncover what we already know,

and in Islam:

we all have access to many worlds including a world of forms, from which we learn,

and Francis Bacon:

we need to make nature reveal herself through active experimentation,

to draw on just a few. Every philosopher has elucidated their own take on this question, precisely because it lies at the heart of questions about how we know what we think we know, whether what we think we know is valid or true, and how we manage to learn something new. Dewey (1933) summarised these in three images:

Pure reasoning is like a spider spinning a web out of itself: orderly and elaborate, but only a trap;

Traditional empiricism is like an ant busily collecting heaps of raw materials;

Baconian enquiry is like a bee, collecting material and transforming it.

A post-modern social-constructionist stance (Burr 1995) suggests that

to be a person is to be constituted by and immersed in discourse (all there is is language).

From this perspective, learning is a process of developing facility in the use of particular words, phrases and narratives. Language does not express experience, but rather experience is what we say. One consequence is that we can only perceive what language permits us to perceive.

A phenomenological–phenomenographical position is that learning consists of extending variations of which we are aware (Marton and Booth 1997), which in the discourse of situated cognition might be rendered as learning consisting of reducing the situatedness of what we know and perceive. An enactivist view of learning is that action *is* knowing, so learning is extending the range and scope of actions (Maturana 1988; Davis *et al.* 2000). As a result of pursuing the Discipline of Noticing, my view is that learning consists of becoming more sensitive to making distinctions, developing awareness of connections and inter-relations amongst those distinctions, broadening the range of resources one calls upon and the tasks one undertakes in order to pursue aims and goals which are more precisely articulated, and increasing the scope and nature of possibilities and potential we recognise, because our present moment (Bennett 1964a) is extended.

Whatever eclectic position we try to forge for ourselves, it is useful, nay essential, to engage in personal enquiry. We try espousing various positions to 'see how it feels'; we listen to positions espoused by others and try to distinguish between the elements we find fitting and the elements which do not seem to fit with experience. As it says in the Book of Job (34:3),

The ear trieth words as the palate tasteth meat.

Above all we consider what seems to inform future actions and we extend and develop that, leaving the rest behind. This is a natural approach, a practical approach, and a pragmatic approach. As long as it is pursued critically and reflectively, it is also sensible.

For me, the answer to how we come to 'know' or perceive something new lies in a development of sensitivity. Undifferentiated experience provides the ground or substance which serves as a component of an action involving subsequent experience, which acts as the core for further discrimination, and hence a sensitivity to notice. At first I do not see. I do not make distinctions. Then, through the construction of my brain and supported by social practices (particularly language), subsequent sensations sufficiently similar to past experience are linked or connected together. My brain accumulates apparently similar sensations (using all senses and corresponding associations and thoughts), organises these into networks of connections and through labelling, provides metonymic access in addition to the metaphoric access of resonance. These bodily–mental–affective processes then inform action and activity.

Lakoff (1987) and Johnson (1987) demonstrate linguistic elements of how this happens in the more sophisticated stages. Helmholtz (1896) formulated a similar response in terms of seeing meanings as built inductively from many 'similar' instances. This position assumes that the brain does have a rich mental structure or rather, complex powers of attention focusing, diffusing and splitting, generalisation (through stressing and ignoring) and specialisation, among others.

Maturana and Varela (1972, 1988) coined the term *autopoesis* or *self-making* to describe the way in which out of a chemical bath such as a primordial ooze, a cell emerges. A cell marks a distinction (Spencer-Brown 1989) which is co-determinant with its non-self, since prior to the emergence of what can be distinguished as 'cell' there is no distinction. The distinction of inside and outside which distinguishes the cell from the chemical bath, and which is marked by the cell boundary, is the mark of a self-constructed Leibnizian monad. Cells show by analogy how autopoesis operates at all levels of coming-to-know, from the micro to the macro. Thus the self (or selves) which George Mead described as arising through such constructs as the significant other, are similarly autopoeitic. Gattegno (1975) pushed this a stage further by declaring that 'I made my brain', thereby drawing attention to an action through which the body and all its powers (together with emotions and intellect) is constructed conjointly from genetic blueprint and interactions with the environment, autopoeitically.

If I am curious and actively construing, then new impressions act upon old ones, mediated by my intention, to activate discrimination and distinctions. These evolve through purpose and effect. Alternatively, I may be passively construing, and so current impressions mediate between disparate past experiences to produce yet more dissociated experiences. Gurdjieff (1950: 1167) disparagingly called the latter reason-of-knowing, in contrast to the former action which produces reason-of-understanding. Coleridge (1829: 115) makes what is for him a fundamentally important distinction between reason and understanding:

understanding is the faculty of reflection; reason of contemplation.

Dewey (1933: 41–42) spoke in a similar vein when he spoke about 'it thinks' rather than 'I think'.

Data construction

A measurement is not the thing measured, only an indicator. It stresses some aspect but ignores many others. Thus the length of time someone waits between hearing a student respond and then responding to that response ignores what else the teacher and the students are doing, the tones of voice, postures, gestures, eye movements, and so on in and around that gap. The same is true for a transcript, a recording on audio or videotape, for field notes, as well as for crafted accounts and honed task-exercises. All are records of observations, and as such, are distillations of aspects of much richer experience. But different observers can see different things:

Account 53: Seeing differently

A number of colleagues were gathered at a restaurant for lunch. Sitting side by side were two Koreans, a young woman and an older man. Two North Americans were also among those present and observed the following:

A: I saw a plate set before the young woman who immediately passed it to the Korean man beside her. There was at most the very slightest movement of eyes to acknowledge receipt of the plate. I read this as the custom of honouring those who are older.

B: I also saw a plate set before the young woman who immediately passed it to the older man, and interpreted it as a typical action of the self-effacing and shy young woman.

C: (one of the Koreans) at the time said that it was the custom to serve older people first. Later she said that the plate given to her was not what she ordered!

Just as law courts find different witnesses rendering very different, even contradictory accounts of what they recall, so the whole notion of observation is actually highly problematic.

If accounts are to be used as evidence for something happening in the particular which is then to be analysed, then it is vital to get agreement about the incident, so some form of triangulation (Elliott and Adelman 1976) is necessary. That means, negotiation between different observers, is an essential component of data collection, which in the case of noticing, means negotiating accounts so that they consist only of what people agree they noticed.

If different observers can disagree, how do I know I would notice the same things, or construct the same record in the same situation another time or in a different context? It seems even more problematic to accept someone else's crafted accounts: how do I even know that the incident ever took place at all? This is the issue of fidelity.

Fidelity

How do I know that what is presented is a faithful record?

Suppose for example that I am offered a transcript. How do I know that it records in print what can be heard on the tape? What about voice tones, or pauses? What about people talking over each other? If I have the actual tape, I can in theory 'check' for myself, but even with a videotape there is much that is not recorded (for example I am shown faces but can't see hands, or vice-versa), and making transcripts is much more difficult than people imagine before they start, for when I do check, I bring my own sensitivities and propensities to bear and these may differ from person to person.

Fidelity to some 'actual event' is a highly contentious and problematic issue, since for most events, all that remains afterwards are stories told by participants, which are bound to be selective. Even where there is audio-recording or video-recording, there is only a partial record, and in any case there is inevitable selection amongst all that could have been recorded from different angles etc. There is almost always room for ambiguity or disagreement. Once the analysis has been achieved, there is bound to be the question of what the analysis achieves: if it indicates how analysis might be carried out, then fidelity is not actually important since attention is on how the analysis is done; if it is intended to make some final statement about a particular event or incident, then since the incident is now past, the analysis can have no effect on the future so fidelity is of little consequence; if the analysis is intended to inform future action or to illustrate a theory or perspective, then fidelity is again of less importance than the sensitivity to notice and act which results.

The Discipline of Noticing addresses fidelity by treating experiences as data, not the accounts which give access to that experience. Fidelity is taken as fidelity to experience, not fidelity to some imagined incident. It does not matter whether a crafted account really did take place, or whether it is a figment of imagination. What does matter is that it speaks to other people's experience, affords them entry into their own experience, and that they do not take the account itself, or the experience it triggers, at face value, but continue to enquire into the assumptions being made, the sensitivities and predispositions being exercised, and so on. If an account serves that purpose, then it functions adequately. In that sense, all accounts are fictions, and the degree of fictionality is not the issue. Rather, in common with literature, the criterion is whether readers recognise something in their own experience, and whether this leads to informing future practice. One of the features of the Discipline of Noticing is that there are no final answers, only ongoing development and enquiry.

This is no mere sophistry but an important epistemological move. Instead of aiming to 'capture' an event, accounts record what struck the person rendering the account, and are used to afford re-entry to those memories, to that situation and to others 'like it', in order to inform practice.

Selection

When someone puts forward descriptions of events, or even tapes and transcripts of what has been said and done, they have purposes and intentions. Almost certainly the 'stuff' that turns into data when it is analysed, was collected for a reason. Some of it was purposely selected for analysis, but the reasons for selection are likely to be pragmatic, and hence different from the reasons for collection in the first place. Of the many possible interpretations of the data, some have been selected and others ignored. Of the many possible theoretical perspectives that could be employed, one, or some combination, are selected, and others not.

The recipient of data is in quite a different state. They know little or nothing about what has not been selected, so it is rather like looking at holiday snaps. When you look at your own photos you can see beyond the frames, you can re-enter the situation and hear and smell as well as see. They function as memory triggers. When you look at someone else's pictures, you can only see what is framed, and you have to interpret that in terms of what you can see and what you have yourself seen. You have to fill in beyond the frame. So in research, the recipient has either to take what is presented at face value, as stimulus for their own enquiry, or to try to ask questions about what has been omitted, what has not been reported, what has not been considered.

Each act of selection is an act of focusing for the person selecting, but therefore in itself can be revealing to recipients of the results, who enquire as to what has not been selected. Thus it is valuable to attend to acts of selection, and to offer comments about what has been rejected, as aid to the recipient.

Keeping in touch with experience

When you set out to research some question, some types of incident or phenomenon, you have to make observations, to summarise the rich field of experience with words and numbers. But once collected, records run the danger of becoming the sole object of attention, displacing the phenomenon which they purport to re-present or summarise. The researcher ends up saying plenty about the records, without saying very much about the original phenomenon, or else asserting too much about it through having only analysed the summary records. So an abiding issue is just what constitutes the data.

A record becomes data only when it is constructed as such by someone. For example, a description in words of an incident is no more than ink on paper. It emerges as data as and when someone treats it *as* data. It is only when someone interprets, contextualises, sees them as particulars illustrating more general principles, and so on, that records turn into data. Thus analysis of data is part of creating data out of records. Data do not possess significance, nor do they imply conclusions. It is people who, acting upon records, locate significance and implications. Thus significance and implications are a product of, and hence tell us about, the person who engages with the records.

For example, the recorder must have had some purpose, some focus, some reason that what was recorded was recorded, and what was not was not. They may have had some intention, or been responding to a suggestion or to instructions. Unless statements about these accompany the record, the record remains an un-situated object.

Some methodologists, especially those engaging in methods based on grounded theory (Glaser and Strauss 1967; Glaser 1978, 1993) advocate immediate interpretation and analysis so that subsequent data collection is informed by sensitivities being sharpened. Other methodologists engaged in naturalistic enquiry (Lincoln and Guba 1985; Owens 1982) try to 'collect everything possible', recognising that this is literally and metaphorically impossible, before analysing the corpus. One disadvantage of the latter is that enormous numbers of records can be hard to turn into data, hard to make sense of and find structure in. The sheer volume can be very daunting. The disadvantage of the former is that records collected under one aegis, for one purpose, may not be adequate for some other purpose which arises later (Watson 1998).

Wimborne and Watson (1998) also distinguish 'vertical' or 'deep data' which try to capture as much as possible about one or more incidents, and 'horizontal' or 'broad data' which provide accounts in the form of personal histories which perhaps come together in one or more shared incidents and then diverge again. To appreciate the incident requires appreciating the forces and influences, the horizontal stories which coincide for a brief period. Note the analogy with metaphor (deep structure, inter-relatedness of aspects) and metonymy (surface structure, multiplicity).

Patterns and distinctions may emerge during data analysis, but insight usually emerges because the researcher is able to look through the data rather than just at it, in a manner analogous to Account 34, p. 109.

Interpretation

Observing and describing necessarily involve interpretation by the observer–describer. Indeed, the describer is in fact part of the description, the observer part of the observation. This is true of any attempt at expressing some thought or awareness, which is why the distinction between accounts-of and accounting-for is necessarily fuzzy: all language involves interpretation, involves stressing some aspects and consequently ignoring others. This is the mechanism of generalisation and abstraction, which is why language and hence in particular, describing, tempts authors away from particulars. It requires specific and dedicated effort to counteract this natural flow. Furthermore, the act of stressing some features implies, or is often taken to imply, a disregard for those not stressed ('What about the . . .?'). Thus speaking stresses and so also ignores, while at the same time appearing to imply priority and importance. Put succinctly, 'to express is to over stress', for expression constitutes selection of what to stress, and this downplays what appears to be being ignored. Finding a way to retain complexity while still saying something useful is extremely difficult.

In Eco and Sebeok (1983), the case is put for salience due to particular intentions, illustrated with examples drawn from doctors, art-validators, psychologists, and even fictional detectives. Through a thorough analysis of the methods Conan Doyle attributes to Sherlock Holmes, and extensive deconstruction of sources and influences, they make strong connections with Peircean thought (Peirce 1935–1966) concerning induction (what actually or usually is), deduction (what must be) and abduction (what may have been). It all flows from the aphorism 'The devil is in the detail'.

As Conan Doyle put it (quoted in Eco and Sebeok 1983: 145), '"I cannot think how I came to overlook it," said the Inspector [referring to a match that Holmes had found]. "It was invisible, buried in the mind. I only saw it because I was looking for it."'

Through abduction we prepare ourselves for what we expect, so that we are 'looking for something' (Eco and Sebeok 1983). It is impossible to simply open oneself to a situation because each observer uses themselves, their sensitivities and their predispositions as instrument. Adopting Sherlock Holmes's tendency to seek to explain the odd details rather than the principle features requires the sort of effort which the Discipline of Noticing is designed to release and support. In the rush to collect and analyse video, audio and transcripts, we may instead be reinforcing Dr Watson's tendencies to see nothing. Thus selectivity, discrimination, distinctions and, above all, expectation play a vital role in enquiry. Steinbring (1993) raises similar questions for mathematics lessons.

Interpretation is a very complicated matter, and has been much studied over centuries, starting with religious texts and broadening into literary criticism more generally. The term *hermeneutics* originally meant the study and elucidation of religious texts but is now used to refer to the theory of the interpretation of texts. At issue is whether meaning can be said to reside within text (for text read also *data*), whether meaning is something constructed when a reader reads, or whether meaning is a social phenomenon mediated through and residing in language, independent of the individual. In other words, do authors 'mean', do texts 'mean', do readers 'mean', do languages 'mean'?, or is it some combination of all four, in which case, how can we ever come to agreement?

In order to make sense of a whole text, it is necessary to make sense of the components, but sense made of components is based on one's sense of the whole, so the two develop and change together. This inescapable *hermeneutic circle* presents a problem for those trying to uncover *the* meaning of text or data. At least with a text you have a sense of an author of the text, an 'author-ity' who selects and structures words, phrases, sentences and paragraphs in order to mean something. Numerical data give the appearance of being 'from the book of nature' so that the 'author' is an objective structure to be located within the data. Descriptive data have both an implied author (the situation) and an actual author (the describer). In all cases, trying to discover 'what the data say' assumes that there is something being said, and ignores the fact that interpretation requires an interpreter, who has desires and prejudices, sensitivities and propensities.

Recognising that interpreters bring propensities and sensitivities which incline them to stress certain features and hence to down-play or overlook others, implies that when analysing data we reveal as much about ourselves as we do about the data, as described in Chapter 10. Locating meaning-making as a process depending on language in general and on the idioms and metaphors of the times, displays interpretation as a social act, especially when one tries to get agreement from others. Italo Calvino (1981: 185) addressed this fundamental tension in his post-modern meta-novel *If On A Winter's Night A Traveler*:

> I believe that she has read [my books] only to find in them what she was already convinced of before reading them.
>
> I tried to say this to her. She retorted, a bit irritated: 'Why? Would you want me to read in your books only what you're convinced of?'
>
> I answered her: 'That isn't it. I expect readers to read in my books something I didn't know, but I can expect it only from those who expect to read something they didn't know.'

This captures a fundamental tension in text, between 'what the author intends to say' and 'what the reader interprets the author as saying'. I take Calvino's point to be that no matter how strong an author's intention, the reader approaches the text with their own perspective, intentions, desires, etc. Consequently they read into it what is possible from their own experience. This same sentiment is expressed by Marcel Proust (1927): In reality, every reader is, while he is reading, the reader of his self.

What you can read into a text, what you can see beyond a 'frame', depends on your own experience. Consequently what you stress by expressing, and consequently what you ignore by not expressing, says as much or more about you as it does about the situation.

As mentioned earlier, if, during an enquiry, you assume that there is an actual objective event that took place, then description and transcription are seen as approximations to that absolute situation. But the situation includes, for each participant, unspoken, even unconscious, thoughts and dispositions that remain below the surface. If instead you assume that events are essentially subjective, that each event consists of participants' memories together with the experiences they have resonated and generated by the stories they subsequently tell, then description and transcription are triggers to fragments of experience. That experience consists of memories and reconstructions of an incident, enriched by connections with other memories and sensitivities. Unfortunately, because we are so immersed in language, we all too readily identify accounts with the experiences they trigger. Consequently descriptions and transcripts become the components constituting or comprising the event. Each re-telling alters both emphasis and memory, and 'the event' turns into a collection of changing accounts.

If you assume that events are manifestations of language-based social practices, then each event achieves its identity from the socio-cultural history of the language used explicitly and in the heads of participants derived from participating in other prior events. The meaning of the event is then located as much in the socio-cultural–political forces which have led up to the particular playing out of standard scripts as in the intentions of an individual.

Depending on your approach to the nature of data, what it means to analyse and work with data will vary considerable. For objective events, the purpose of analysis is to reveal what 'really' happened. For subjective events it is to contribute to interpretation by investigating surrounding circumstances, to shed light on motivations, and to become more aware of oneself as 'reader'; for social events it is to reveal the culturally transmitted practices and defining forces, and to expose these to questioning and analysis.

In each approach the very intention to analyse requires a standing back or separation from participation in the event. The objective stance takes this metaphor almost literally, that there is something 'there' to observe and analyse when standing back has taken place. The subjective stance takes it as a metaphor, in which it is *as if* one stands apart from (separated in space and time from) the event itself and looks back at it. This metaphoric standing-back is at best an approximation to the development of an inner monitor or witness which observes without comment, just like the second bird which 'looks on without eating'. The social stance takes standing back as yet another example of a language-based practice, a manner of speaking, which has to be enculturated in each individual freshly and which shifts the individual from a participant into a social commentator. Every situation, every text, every incident is interpreted, and the interpretation is based on experiences, propensities and social factors.

A further step is to suggest that interpretation reveals as much about the interpreter as it does about the interpreted. I can learn about my sensitivities by juxtaposing my interpretations with those of others, not to determine which reading is correct or even most apposite, but rather to locate where my interpretation agrees with and is different from others. In this way I become aware of alternative ways to stress aspects that perhaps I do not currently stress. The aim is not to change other people's stories, and not even to change my own story, but to open myself to alternatives and multiplicities. Interestingly, the etymological roots of *interpretation* are *to act as agent between two values*, as in mediating a bargain. Interpretation could be 'interpreted' as a mediation between alternative accounts for an event, looking for and holding on to the notion that accepting a multiplicity of interpretations is more likely to enable me to be sensitive to a situation than a single dominant interpretation.

The objective stance has roots through Galileo and Descartes to Plato and Aristotle, the subjective stance has roots back through Heidegger to Indian and Chinese sources, while the social stance seems to be of relatively modern origin, developed in response to political authoritarianism in Marxism and studies of other cultures (e.g. Margaret and George Mead). Gadamer (1975: 268–269) takes a strong position:

To acquire an awareness of a situation is, however, always a particular difficulty. The very idea of a situation means that we are not standing outside it and hence are unable to have any objective knowledge of it. We are always within the situation, and to throw light on it is a task that is never completed.

Heidegger argues that there is no objective place to stand; that all observation involves standing somewhere, and that this therefore influences what is seen. So it is impossible ever to make all our implicit beliefs and assumptions, theories and practices explicit, although we can of course make some progress at peeling back a few layers! Meaning is seen as fundamentally social, bound up in vocabulary and patterns of speech accommodated from a community of practice.

In introducing his book on researching lived experience, van Manen (1990) brings these notions into present day thinking, arguing that the research which he espouses, and which is very similar to noticing, is based on and depends upon the notion of experience. The trouble is, experience is itself not a clear notion. He points out the fundamental tension which drives much of present-day philosophising, between language as the creator of experience, and experience as only partially or inadequately captured by language (p. xii–xiv).

Objectivity

At the heart of objectivity is identification of the issue, the phenomenon to be theorised or analysed. In order to be able to critique the analysis it is essential to be clear on what it is that is being analysed, and this in turn leads to separating the phenomenon being analysed from the analysis. The distinction between accounts-of and accounting-for is intended to assist in this necessary separation. Although it may sound like a relatively easy thing to do, it is not. It is very hard to do when the data objects are accounts, transcripts, audio and video recordings of the behaviour of human beings. For through these media, behaviour is all that can be agreed by independent viewers.

Beliefs, motivations, emotions, cognitions, thoughts and reasoning are all imputed processes. Despite the commitment to them as objective phenomena merely because they are formulated in language, many of them may be constructions of observers trying to account for observations. For example, it is common to speak as though beliefs drive behaviour. But beliefs may in fact be a construction by researchers in order to enable them to speak about and account for observed behaviour. An alternative approach might at least be agnostic concerning whether beliefs 'exist', and may go so far as to describe beliefs and behaviour as at best co-emergent (behaviour enacted generates inner-chatter which is taken as belief, and inner-chatter encourages corresponding behaviour), or one might even go so far as to challenge the very construct of belief, and try to locate an alternative language of description which fits experience more closely.

Labelling

Human interaction is further confounded by the problem of premature labelling, and of labelling of people rather than of specific behaviour.

Suppose you observe an apparent pattern in student behaviour in certain sessions. It may be tempting to generalise the conjecture by labelling the students with some descriptive adjective (such as slow, bright, inquisitive, bored, lazy, hard-working, hypochondrial, insensitive, etc.).

This kind of labelling already alters the status of the observation in two ways: it moves towards an assertion, and it extends the domain of application. The behaviour observed may in fact be highly context dependent, influenced by the time of day, your presence, a particular phase of personal development, a particular event, and so on. It is never wise to label the person, but it can be helpful to label behaviour, because it makes that behaviour more noticeable in the future.

However, there are positive and negative aspects to this effect of labelling. Once someone else's behaviour has been labelled, there is a strong tendency to notice that behaviour and to ignore its non-occurrence, just as earlier it was noted that when you become aware of something new such as a brand of car, a holiday destination, or a new word, you tend to notice it everywhere.

As William Wordsworth put it (*The Borders*, Act IV):

We are praised, only as men in us
Do recognise some image of themselves,
An abject counterpart of what they are,
Or the empty thing that they would wish to be.

Consider for example a teacher who has formed the impression that one student, Ann, is very bright, while another, Marilyn is not (or a researcher who has formed a conjecture about one or more people). When Ann makes a mistake or struggles to understand, the teacher sees this as a minor slip or momentary lapse, whereas if Marilyn makes the same mistake it is taken as further evidence to support the teachers' opinion. Similarly, if Marilyn gives an insightful response, it is likely to go unmarked, or to be seen as an aberration, while if Ann makes it, it is seen as confirmation. Labels, especially labels applied to people rather than to specific behaviour at a specific time, is one of the ways in which teacher and student, researcher and researched mutually construct each other, supporting and reinforcing the behaves which led to the labelling in the first place.

Furthermore, it is often difficult to recognise how a relatively small change in conditions (a different teacher, a different time of day, and a different emphasis) can alter behaviour patterns which seemed to be fundamental to the character of a person.

If the behaviour is associated with a single person, then that person is effectively labelled. The result is that an unconscious force develops in that person to fulfil (or sometimes to counteract) that label, thus distorting the situation completely. If a particular behaviour is detected in one person, it is quite likely that it exists elsewhere, so it is worth looking out for it in others.

Labelling the behaviour of others also tempts your enquiry away from yourself and onto others, which can then lead to a switch from studying your own practice to studying the behaviour of others. As long as behaviour of others is an indicator or symptom for what you are studying in yourself, then you are less likely to be caught up in the potentially pernicious aspects of labelling.

Generalisability

Case studies, descriptions of a few individuals or of a small group all raise questions of generalisability for small scale but intensive qualitative research. How can what one researcher observes concerning a few students or patients inform choices for others in different situations? What constitutes the range of robustness or applicability?

In the first instance, qualitative research offers exemplars of enquiry which others may use to inform their own enquiry. Second, qualitative enquiry intends to probe more deeply into the details of a situation, in the expectation that this may inform the design of other large scale studies in the future. Third, the findings in one situation at least indicate a range of possibilities for others involved in similar enquiries, and may lead to refinement of distinctions or to questioning the efficacy of distinctions made in previous studies. Noticing tackles the issue directly by seeking generalisability in the awareness, in sensitivity to notice and opportunities to act, not in the applicability of assertions.

Summary of Chapter 14

Qualitative research finds it hard to justify general assertions, because it is difficult or impossible to specify the precise conditions under which conclusions might apply. There are serious problems with acts of selection at every stage of the research process, for selecting (consciously or unconsciously) consists of omitting things, which someone else may consider to be important. Furthermore, each act of description involves interpretation, selection and discrimination. As long as the researcher is concerned to say something objective about what they are studying, these problems will remain significant. But once you accept that this sort of enquiry is as much about yourself as it is about some external situation, that it is at least partly about improving your own practice through sharpening your awareness and through extending the range of ways of acting from which you can choose, then these problems become much less significant.

15 Questions and concerns about noticing

This final chapter addresses some of the questions and concerns which people have raised about the Discipline of Noticing when it is considered as a method of research in and of itself. The principal problems people have identified lie in the unusual aspects of what constitute data, what constitutes a research finding and what constitutes validity. The questions addressed here are the following:

- How do you decide what to notice?
- How do you select which incidents to recount, to transcribe, to study?
- How can you remove all judgement and interpretation from brief-but-vivid accounts?
- Since memory is fallible, how can anything based on memories be reliable?
- How is communication of selected meaning possible if priority is given to subjective experience?
- What makes something salient or significant?
- How do you distinguish between salience and emotional commitment or prejudice?
- How do you know that your 'sensitivity' is helping the student–patient–client?
- Does not similarity between accounts reside in the reader not the accounts?
- How can anything of value to others be revealed by using yourself as the instrument by means of which you probe phenomena?
- How can you protect yourself against being misled by a charismatic presentation?
- Why can't you just tell me what steps to take, rather than bother with all this uncertainty and imprecision?
- What values underpin the Discipline of Noticing?
- Is the individual the sole source of confidence and validity, and hence is the individual promoted at the expense of the community?
- How can you detect or measure effects and influence without being trapped back into a quantitative extra-spective paradigm?

Throughout it is helpful to bear in mind the Chinese proverb: 'Only those who pick the roses feel the thorns.'

How do you decide what to notice?

You can choose to try to notice something, you can even orient and prepare yourself to notice, but in the moment, noticing is not something that you choose to do at any conscious level. Rather, you participate in the act of noticing. A moment of noticing focuses attention and makes you (relatively) alert. Concentration then diminishes, whether gradually or quickly, until attention is suddenly alerted again, and the old is overlaid or displaced by the new. These ebbs and flows of attention produce the fragments of experience which constitute memory and experience. While the practices of the Discipline of Noticing are designed to transform desire to notice into actual noticing in the moment, we are subject to the workings of our organism. We work to try to enhance noticing, perhaps even to notice certain things, but this can only be preparation.

That said, you can indeed, as proposed in earlier chapters, set yourself to notice some feature or behaviour, whether triggered by an internal state (of mind, emotion or body, perhaps via some label), or something external such as something someone says, or associated with a particular place etc. However, people do tend to find that what they think they want to notice is not always what they actually notice, which is why it is worthwhile keeping accounts and looking back over them in the ways suggested in Chapter 7.

What is meaningful, important, salient or significant will be accessible to intentional re-entering. Put another way, what I can reconstruct is mine; the rest falls away in time, perhaps to be re-vivified by some new event, perhaps not. But all of the work is directed to the development and enrichment of one's being.

How do you select which incidents to recount, to transcribe, to study? How do you select which details to include?

The importance of these questions depends on purposes. If you are trying to illustrate a generality, perhaps some recurring feature you have noticed, then you want to capture incidents which focus attention as sharply as possible on the issue at hand. Bearing in mind that accounts are not the data, but rather the experiences triggered by accounts (and other task exercises) in others, you look for accounts which serve this purpose.

If on the other hand, you are offering accounts as data against which someone else is going to validate your conclusions, then you have quite a different problem. If you feel drawn to switching into a semi-quantitative mode by demonstrating how often you notice something, or by showing that some behaviour happens frequently, then you have switched research paradigms, and you will have to abide by other disciplines. You have to keep records of the specific incidents which you have identified, including what features struck you as relevant and as irrelevant to your particular study. Then you have to offer readers access to those data so they can judge for themselves.

As a student once reported 'I notice so many things, what am I to record?'. The answer is that what you find yourself recounting to others obviously has some importance for you; if when you sit down to record incidents, you feel daunted by the plethora of possibilities, then you need to focus attention on some issue or concern. There is a natural self-feeding cycle or perhaps co-emergence between 'being in question' and 'noticing', in the sense that if you have some questions, or at least if you have experienced some disturbance, then you are likely to attend particularly to details which seem to be relevant to those questions; and questions arise from noticing something(s) which may be disturbing. One common version of this is the difference between reading the literature to see what people are writing about, and reading the literature to gain some insight into a topic of particular interest to you. Questions are a response to disturbance, disturbance arises from noticing (not necessarily consciously), and noticing is the way in which people transform disturbance into possible action.

A related question to 'How do you select?' is 'How to you decide what to leave out?'. If you are trying to prove that some phenomenon is common, then you have to provide all the data so that others can judge for themselves. If you want to illustrate some phenomenon, then you select brief-but-vivid accounts of incidents which serve your purpose best, and task-exercises which seem to be effective in resonating with others. In noticing, what matters is that the incident affords you, and the people with whom you are working, access to relevant experience and that it informs future practice. You therefore choose the ones which prove to be most effective in providing access to past experience, and you let go of the others.

How can you remove all judgement and interpretation from brief-but-vivid-accounts?

The aim of an account-of an incident or part of an event is to afford other people access to something similar. To afford access to the event-as-experienced by the person rendering the account would require such a rich description that the reader would be overwhelmed, yet would never be able to suppress their own reactions in favour of the description. This is the sort of conundrum tackled by Marcel Proust in his monumental work, and by Laurence Sterne in *Tristam Shandy*. A completely full and faithful account would require real time, just as a map with scale 1 to 1 would be indistinguishable from what is mapped. The whole point about a novel, or a map, or research, is to summarise, condense, and distil, by making distinctions and being selective, without losing contact with what you consider to be the essence of the original.

As has been repeatedly stressed, the essence of an account is that it resonates with experience, providing access to experience which can then be similarly recounted, and assisting negotiation of meaning through identifying similarities and differences, leading to the identification of phenomena. Identification is of course only one side of the coin, for it is necessary to have alternative practices to use when a situation develops.

The very fact of a label like *brief-but-vivid account* suggests that there is some objective event being recounted, but this runs counter to the perspective on which the Discipline of Noticing is based. Accounts are cues to personal experience; events are made up of the experiences that they spawned, and they become identified with the stories that are told about them.

Since memory is fallible, how can anything based on memories be reliable?

Memory is notoriously unreliable. When there are several witnesses to a crime, it is often very hard to work out what is common between their descriptions. Not only do we interpret what we see and hear, and use that interpretation to access the memory, but we confuse the seen and heard with the imagined, and to compound this difficulty, memory proves to be selective over time. In one study, people recorded an actual and a fantasised event each day over a long period. Later they were asked about the validity of different accounts, and nearly half of the fantasised events were recalled as actual! A colleague described two incidents in a meeting, one truthfully, one manufactured: someone arriving late and a cup of water being spilled. Two weeks later he could not recall which one had actually happened and which had not.

Where then does truth lie? How can I be sure that what I am observing is real? One approach is to find various means for confirmation, such as arranging for a colleague to observe as well, arranging for audio or video recordings, and asking other participants for their versions. This can be done by asking them to initiate descriptions, or to validate descriptions you provide. The process of obtaining several different viewpoints or perspectives is known as *triangulation*, based on the method of surveying land which breaks the region down into triangles each of which is measured. By making redundant observations it is possible to check the accuracy of the surveying. Similarly, if three different perspectives all report similar observations, then some confidence can be placed in the event as described. But if there is disagreement, does that invalidate the observations?

Disagreement might easily be due to confused recall of similar events, but it could also be a matter of interpretation, evidence for the rich complexity of human existence, because over time, memories alter in accord with current ways of describing and accounting-for them. These stories we tell are part of the fabric which constitutes our being, the floor-coverings, the wall-hangings and the ceilings of our personal worlds of significance, occasioned by experience. Some would even say that they *are* experience.

If the aim is to give a factual and agreeable account (in the sense that others present recognise it and agree), then triangulation may be helpful, but it will be vital to stick to descriptive accounts-of and to avoid all extra interpretation and accounting-for. If the aim is to learn about the situation and others like it, then attention can be focused not on fidelity of observation but on evidence of recognition by colleagues and pupils (what does it matter, as long as people recognise the sort of situation described?). Instead of trying to prove that something happened, I can invite colleagues to see if they recognise what I am talking about and whether they can offer similar instances of their own. I can ask them to report back about future incidents in which they find themselves noticing along the same lines. And I can work at devising task-exercises which will highlight specific noticing for others. Here fidelity is to past, present and future experience, not to a specific situation at a particular time in a particular place with particular people.

A more radical approach is to call into question the whole notion that there is a single event, or even any actual event at all with objective qualities and characteristics. Rather, 'the event' can be seen to consist of the (augmented) memories and associated accounts of the individual participants (including those who only come to hear of the event). Validity lies then not in the match between description and some past event, but in whether the individuals gain something for the future. A virtue of this approach is that there is no background assumption of objectivity, only the possibility of negotiating some degree of commonality of the basic phenomenon (the account of). Offering a brief-but-vivid description with a minimum of interpretation and judgement maximises the possibilities of others recognising the incident themselves (because they were also there) or the flavour and tenor of the event (because they have been in similar situations). The more judgement and explanation that is allowed to creep into the description, the less likely people are to be able to agree.

How is communication of selected meaning possible if priority is given to subjective experience?

Although there are no guarantees, it is possible to hone task-exercises, particularly collections of accounts, through which people can gain access to specific experiences. You need, however, to test noticings and gambits against new experience, and with an ever widening group of people. A disciplined approach to negotiating meaning-use of technical terms is badly needed, and the Discipline of Noticing offers a way of doing this though task-exercises, negotiation of labels for what is noticed, refinement and honing of task exercises, location of alternative acts (gambits), and preparatory pro-flection to enhance the possibility of noticing and acting differently in the future.

What makes something salient or significant?

Locating what constitutes salience, criticality and typicality, is really the working out of a research programme. It is almost the essence of research itself. As you keep and look back over brief-but-vivid accounts of incidents, you begin to find structure and pattern, threads in what you are attending to, and this leads into further and more precise questioning. It helps to have colleagues who remind you that those patterns and threads, those significances, are largely particular to you. They are what need questioning, and challenging, as much as anything else. To notice what sorts of things are salient is sufficient for professional development; to mark what is salient facilitates collaboration with colleagues; to record what is salient enables participation in academic research.

How do you distinguish between salience and emotional commitment or prejudice?

When some incident or aspect of an incident sticks in your mind, then its very salience means that you are likely to mark if not record it. But salience could be due to some hidden assumption or bias. The only way to guard against prior commitment (including its extreme form, prejudice) is to practise 'being in question'. But you cannot constantly question everything! That is why the Discipline of Noticing advocates constantly seeking resonance with others in an ever-expanding community, because it is through the questions of those who are ideas that you can be reminded to go back and re-question.

In the final analysis, of course, there is no guarantee. It probably takes only a few moments to recall incidents in which some dispute or disagreement arose, only to find later that someone made an assumption which seemed obvious and natural at the time. In matters to do with people, the more certain one feels, the more likely it is that there is some hidden assumption or undetected bias towards the current interpretation.

How do you know that your 'sensitivity' is helping the student?

As was suggested in Chapter 11, overt short-term help may be visible, even quantifiable. But much of the help given to students by teachers, by educators to teachers, and more generally by carers to their clients, is subtle and hidden. The truly supportive practitioner works in such a way that the people being supported are more aware of their independence than of their dependence. Furthermore, the more sensitive you are to noticing details, the more tempted you are likely to be to act responsively, perhaps freshly. But these innovations may easily cut across established habits, which is quite likely to be disturbing and may not be appreciated in the short term.

For example, a student reported that his chemistry teacher was very unhelpful as there were virtually no notes, and the tasks set were obscure. A year later, that same teacher was described as his best teacher, because he had been made to think, to work things out for himself.

Noticing is not about change for the sake of change. It is about using disturbance to locate the ideals and desires which are reacting to the current situation, and probing those situations more fully in order to find alternative ways of acting which contribute to the ideals and desires. If others are affected by your practice, then it is vital that you 'keep them with you' by discussing what you are doing and why when it seems appropriate. You can even go the whole hog and invite them to engage in a parallel investigation of their own.

No matter how much a practitioner focuses on the person they are working with or supporting, there is always an element of personal gain, of 'doing it for oneself'. This may range from using students in order to learn more about yourself in order to be more useful to them, through to striving to be more useful to students and finding that the best way to do this is to develop yourself. Recall the motto of noticing:

I cannot change others; I can work at changing myself.

Does not similarity between accounts reside in the reader, not in the accounts?

What one person sees as similar between several accounts or incidents may not strike someone else as similar, because each person stresses and ignores according to their own propensities: that is the nature of perception. We see and hear what we are prepared, literally and figuratively, to see and hear. This means that incidents are just incidents, and accounts are just accounts. Similarities reside in how incidents are described and accounts rendered, and hence are as much a property of the person rendering the accounts and of the language employed in description, as of the accounts themselves. What then is the point of investing time and energy in seeking threads etc. amongst accounts?

The answer is that the process of seeking similarity (and difference) is part of enquiry, for you are learning about yourself as well as about the situations summarised by accounts. Similarity does indeed lie in the eye and ear of the beholder, not in any external or objective world, but it is through becoming explicit about what is beheld that the beholder learns about their beholding, about their own practice. It is through checking similarities out with others that you are led to be precise and pointed about what you think you notice and how that informs practice. This in turn enables you to seek resonance with others as well as to be more sensitive and able to respond more freshly in the future.

If similarities are in the eye of the beholder, then what is the status of the patterns perceived when seeking common threads in accounts of incidents accumulated over time? In the Discipline of Noticing perceived patterns do not actually matter, though they are useful along the way. What matters is becoming aware of the stressing and ignoring which constitute or generates those patterns. For it is the stressing and ignoring which will generate recognition of similarity in future noticing, with concomitant possibilities to act differently. Similarly, labels are not the subject of analysis, merely the means to sensitise and offer choice in the future. So the question of whether perceived patterns are 'really there' or are imagined, whether labels are bringing phenomena into perception merely by virtue of being labels, is only of concern to those who are building up a corpus of incidents and analyses of those incidents in order to produce some definitive statements about the past. The Discipline of Noticing in firmly directed to the future.

In one sense, then, there is an objectivity about brief-but-vivid accounts, for they speak to many people's experience. But the objectivity does not lie in verisimilitude to some 'objective event'. Rather it lies in its recognition by so many people. The Discipline of Noticing is not about the labels employed, which are arbitrary. Rather it concerns experience which can be provoked and evoked through the use of well chosen labels.

How can anything of value to others be revealed by using yourself as the instrument by means of which you probe phenomena?

All observation involves using yourself as instrument, whether in reading dials or in making distinctions and writing accounts of what you notice. By being explicit about *what* you are noticing, and by offering accounts to others, you can become aware of automatic behaviours which may not be entirely helpful, and of hidden assumptions and theories which may be driving these. By digging in your past experiences you may become aware of sources of those behaviours, as well as alternative ways of acting. Only when you become aware of those behaviours, assumptions and theories can you examine them critically to see if they are helping you to achieve what you want to achieve.

The principal difficulty with using oneself as the instrument is guarding against the natural tendency to leap to judgement and to at best tinker with that judgement in the face of disconfirming evidence. Effective mathematicians disbelieve their conjectures and spend time trying to see whether a counter-example might be constructed as well as trying to prove it. For trying to see what might be wrong can be as informative as trying to see why it is right. Researchers more generally can seek out examples which challenge or contradict generalities asserted by themselves and others for exactly the same reason: seeking counter-examples illuminates hidden conditions and structure. In trying to imagine what disconfirming evidence might or could look like, you either see flaws in your argument-perception, or you encounter finer details or a broader sense of the topic.

Judgements, especially about people, tend to be local (immediate to a situation and then forgotten), medial (middle term applicability) or deep-seated long term opinions. The more open opinions are to being expressed and challenged, the less likely you are to become caught up in your own beliefs and to wander from what can be agreed with other people based upon their experience.

How can you protect yourself against being misled by a charismatic presentation?

What do I know? How do I know it? Can I be sure that it is valid or true? Will it always hold? These sorts of questions are of constant concern. Everyone wants to avoid being taken in, to avoid making mistakes when possible. With examples of brain-washed cults only too common, it is important to have confidence in what we know, and to stop ourselves from being swept away by a charismatic speaker.

Attempts to outline how 'true' knowledge is obtained, and to specify methods that can be carried out so that error is eliminated or at least reduced have occupied people throughout recorded time. There are no easy answers. Different proposals reflect different social and cultural orientations as much as anything else.

Western science and its epistemological methods are based on certain requirements of robustness, generality and confirmability. Science (etymologically based on *scientia* = knowledge) is primarily concerned with *knowing about* external phenomena, and being able to state that knowledge in a manner which is person, place, and time independent. The phenomena have to be external, and readily recognised by any trained observer. Assertions have to be robust not only against variations in the conditions but also have to be independent of the particular observer. Ideally they include a statement of permissible variation of stated factors, within which the assertion is valid. The benefits of such an epistemology are visible all around us, but perhaps so are the costs. To be scientific means to be detached and uninvolved, yet this attitude has led to the exploitation of scientific knowledge without concern for the larger ecological picture, thus putting the earth and ourselves into crisis.

An alternative approach, emergent in Western writing under headings such phenomenology, experiential learning and action research, and often associated with Eastern traditions, concentrates on *knowing through* experience. But what experience, and how? Detailed answers to these questions require time and experience (*sic*) to assimilate, just as do detailed answers to questions about how scientists work when they observe, seek patterns, conjecture and verify.

The Discipline of Noticing accepts that:

- validity is always going to be a relative notion;
- what is valid in these conditions now, may have to altered when conditions change;
- it may not be possible to delineate what constitutes 'these conditions', because it is important to retain and work with complexity rather than reduce it to isolated simplicities; and
- validity is an individual matter based in resonance between description and experience and in finding future practice informed, moderated by predisposition to other epistemological positions, and mediated by the strength of intention brought to bear upon the enterprise.

Validity resides not in the ratification of an assertion, but in a confluence of assertion, person and circumstances, in which what matters is the sensitivity of the person to the circumstances, informed by the assertion. This is the force of seeking invariance in the midst of change. Changes may be taking place on many scales and levels and it is impossible to hold them all fixed without reducing the invariant to stupidity.

Accepting that validity is relative to time, place and people, it is natural to want to ensure that the time, place and people are as broadly defined as possible. Thus, knowing something that is appropriate only for a few hours or days, in one location, with one or two people, is not as informative as knowing something that seems to resonate for a few years, in many classrooms, with a wide variety of people.

Why can't you just tell me what steps to take, rather than bother with all this uncertainty and imprecision?

You can seek simplicity by reducing a problem, ignoring its complexity and ignoring aspects which are troublesome. This is what a simple sequence of acts would achieve. Noticing is an integral part of the functioning of every human being, and human beings are complex organisms. Therefore it does no one any favour by trying to reduce that complexity. On the other hand, dwelling in chaos for the sake of it, refusing to make distinctions or to try to reach beyond the particular to general themes and phenomena, also denies the way human beings operate in the world. The Discipline of Noticing aims to tread between the Scylla of simplicity and the Charybdis of chaos.

What values underpin the Discipline of Noticing?

The Discipline of Noticing values individuals practising within a community of colleagues. It values on-going enquiry into and questioning of practices. It values struggle against habit. It values increasing sensitivity and discernment. It values testing everything in your own experience, not just initially, but frequently, and also in other people's experience as well. It is concerned with the authentic nature of lived experience. The Discipline of Noticing places the onus for educating awareness in the individual, but it offers structure and practices for supporting individuals through the collective presence of others who are also working in a similar way, and of those who are more expert in some way. Each individual is ultimately responsible for their own awareness and for the structure of their attention.

The Discipline does not provide 'better things to notice' or 'better ways to choose to act'. Such value judgements come from the practitioners orientation to their practice and their professionalism. The Discipline can be used to question and critique practices from the point of view of whether they enhance the growth of awareness of practitioner or student–clients.

Like any other approach to human beings, the Discipline of Noticing can be abused by ideologues of any persuasion, because the values espoused in noticing will be those accepted and reinforced by the community within which one operates. If that community is restricted or curtailed, and especially if the practices of the Discipline of Noticing are not employed by all members of the community, then bigotry and prejudice can flourish. The possibility of negative uses is necessary if there is to be any possibility of positive uses.

Is the individual the sole source of confidence and validity, and hence is the individual promoted at the expense of the community?

The individual is responsible for testing practices and assertions against their own experience, seeing whether it helps to make sense of the past and/or whether it informs future action. Colleagues are very helpful in pursuing these enquiries, and essential for grounding noticing in a wider community. It usually requires some sort of disturbance to be awaked to the potential for enquiry, and colleagues are a good source of alternatives and disturbances!

Whether or not there are colleagues in the same institution engaged in similar investigations, it is important to locate colleagues from other institutions, such as at annual or local meetings of associations of colleagues, with whom you can try out ideas and with whom you can exchange accounts of significant moments.

Without this sort of network there is a danger that what seems like great progress is self-delusion and fantasy.

Summary of Chapter 15

This chapter has endeavoured to address the principal issues raised by practitioners and colleagues concerning the Discipline of Noticing as a research method.

SUMMARY OF PART VI

This final part has raised and addressed some of the problems associated with qualitative research in general and the Discipline of Noticing in particular. I make no claim to have 'argued' the case well for noticing as a collection of practices or as a research method. Certainly I neither expect nor wish anyone to be convinced through reading this book. Rather, I have offered some task-exercises, through which I hope some moments of noticing have occurred which fit with some of the descriptions I have offered. If some of those practices prove fruitful in the future, then the enterprise has been justified.

Epilogue

This book began with practical suggestions and examples of phenomena associated with personal professional development. If you have recognised some aspects of your own experience in the examples or descriptions, then the validation of the theory for you, now, will lie in the extent to which you find yourself developing sensitivity to notice in your practice, and whether you are thereby able to choose to act differently (if you so wish) in standard situations where previously you might not have noticed such possibilities.

Specifically, if you begin to see as-if-through some of the vocabulary of noticing, and more importantly, if you find that as you become accustomed to this perspective, you are able to modify your behaviour, or to account for what you observe in satisfactory ways, then noticing will be useful to you at that time.

It could be instructive to revisit the personal inventories in Appendix A mentioned in the first chapter, to see how your views have changed, deepened, developed. One of the most curious things about change is that we are often unaware of significant change because it is organic and part of our lived experience, and we often think we have changed when others are unaware of any significant differences.

> Knowing others is wisdom;
>   Knowing the self is enlightenment.
> Mastering others requires force;
>   Mastering the self requires strength.
>   (Tao Te Ching c. 300 BC)

Appendices

A: Self-inventory

The aim of this personal inventory is not to 'get answers' and then be evaluated in some way, but rather to use the various probes as stimuli for reflection, for re-entering past experiences. It is the actions which are initiated that matters, not the answers as such. Consequently if you that find a particular probe does not stimulate recollection, then pass on to another (but later it may be worth pondering why there was no immediate response!).

For each of the following, imagine yourself in a typical situation and try to find some simile, some analogy that captures at least some aspect of your experience. Returning at other times and adding other analogies can be most instructive as the point is to gain access to the composite complexity of experience of professional practice, not to distil the complexity down to a few simplistic summaries.

I see myself primarily as a . . .
The people I serve (teach, train, work with, support, care for . . .) are primarily. . . .

Use the role and the people you have chosen as your first source of incidents through which to access typical situations in order to respond the following probes. If a probe seems irrelevant, either transform it or leave it or consider a different aspect of your professional practice.

My principle professional activity is like . . .
(e.g. teaching mathematics is like. . .

Being on the other end of my professional practice is like . . .
(e.g. learning mathematics is like . . .)

What I like most about what I do is . . .

What I like least about what I do is . . .

_____

For me, the least important part of what I do is . . .

_____

For me, the most important part of what I do is . . .

_____

Whereas I used to . . .
I have recently begun to . . .

_____

What I do is important in the institution because . . .

_____

What I do is important socially or culturally because . . .

_____

What I liked most about being trained (becoming professional) in what I do was . . .

_____

What I liked least about being trained (becoming professional) in what I do was . . .

_____

What I look for in professional development opportunities now is . . .

_____

In each of the following diagrams, place a point in the triangle which represents your view as a combination of the three aspects expressed at the corners. The central dot represents a balance of all three components.

Stimulation for my professional practice comes from . . .

Picking up ideas as and
when I notice them

Actively seeking
better ways
of working

Being advised
what to
work on

My attitude to professional development is . . .

Growing in wisdom
and experience

Eagerly seeking
new approaches

Maintaining
competence

My response to suggestions for changing the way I do things is . . .

Reflecting,
considering

Trying things
out for
myself

Sticking with
the tried
and tested

My professional life is a source of. . .

Inspiration

Opportunity

Income

For each of the sentence starters on the side, place the corresponding letter in the triangle so as to indicate roughly the relative strengths of the three aspects in each case. You may feel the need to justify (to yourself) why there are differences or variations!

Preferred ways of working

I learn best myself from . . . (L)

The people I serve do best by . . . (S)

Supporting the professional development of colleagues is best done by getting them . . .
(P)

Reading, thinking

Participating

Being told
or shown

Issues of control and direction

Are told what to do
and guided in doing it

The people I support are served best when they . . . (I)

The people I support prefer it when they . . . (T)

My supervisor prefers it when the people I support . . . (S)

The colleagues who work with me prefer it when the people I support . . . (C)

Are advised and
then left to do things
for themselves

Have things done
for them and to them
by professionals

Strengths and weaknesses

In my profession,
　my principle tasks involve . . . (T)

　my biggest difficulties involve . . . (D)

　my greatest successes involve . . . (S)

　my greatest pleasures involve . . . (P)

　my greatest strengths involve . . . (S)

　my biggest weakness involves . . . (W)

Thinking

Doing　　　　　　　　　Feeling

I have organised my workplace so that . . .

The best advice I could offer someone newly qualifying in my profession is . . .

When I am successful, it is usually because . . .

When I am not successful, it is usually because . . .

I want the people I serve (teach, support, care for, etc.) to experience . . .

I can influence colleagues best by . . .

___

I can have the biggest effect professionally by . . .

___

B: Other inventory

Addressed to those whom you support or work with

What do you like most about sessions with me?
What do you like least about sessions with me?
Do I give you as much attention as others? Who do you think gets the most attention, who the least?
Would you like more or less attention?
You and I interact in various ways (one-to-one, in a small group, in a large group). Which of these do you prefer, under what circumstances, and why?
How many different types of session are you aware of? Please describe or characterise them!

Addressed to colleagues

If you came into one of my sessions, what would you expect to see happening (organisation, forms of interaction etc.)?
What do you think is most important about my practice for me?

Bibliography

Addelson, K. 1990, Why Philosophers Should Become Sociologists (and vice versa), in H. Becker and M. McCall (eds) *Symbolic Interaction and Cultural Studies*, University of Chicago Press, Chicago.

Ainley, J. 1999, Who are You Today? Complementary and conflicting roles in school-based research, *For The Learning Of Mathematics*, 19 (1): 39–47.

Anderson, W. 1995 (W. Anderson, ed.), *The Truth about the Truth: de-confusing and re-constructing the postmodern world*, G. P. Putnam's Sons, New York.

Armstrong, M. 1980, *Closely Observed Children: the diary of a primary classroom*, Chameleon, London; Writers and Readers, Richmond.

Bacon, F. 1609, reprinted 1851, *Of the Proficience and Advancement of Learning*, William Pickering, London.

Bartlett, F. 1932, *Remembering: a study in experimental and social psychology*, Cambridge University Press, London.

Bateson, M. 1994, *Peripheral Visions: learning along the way*, HarperCollins, New York.

Bell, A. and Purdy, D. 1986, Diagnostic Teaching, *Mathematics Teaching*, 115: 39–41.

Bennett, J. 1964a, *Energies: material, vital, cosmic*, London: Coombe Springs Press.

Bennett, J. 1964b, *A Spiritual Psychology*, Coombe Springs Press, Sherborne, Glos.

Bennett, J. 1976, *Noticing*, The Sherborne Theme Talks Series 2, Coombe Springs Press, Sherborne.

Bereiter, C. 1985, Toward a Solution of the Learning Paradox, *Review of Educational Research*, 55 (2): 201–226.

Bills, E. 1996, *Shifting Sands: students' understanding of the roles of variables in 'A' level mathematics*, unpublished PhD Thesis, Open University, Milton Keynes.

Bohm, D. 1981, *Wholeness and the Implicate Order* (revised edn), Routledge & Kegan Paul, London.

Broekman, I. 2000, The Use of Narrative and Biographic Methods in Mathematics Education Research, *Proceedings of 8th Annual Conference of the South African Association for Research in Mathematics and Science Education*, University of Port Elizabeth, South Africa, pp. 74–79.

Boud, D., Cohen, R. and Walker, D. 1993, *Using Experience for Learning*, Society for Research into Higher Education, Open University Press, Buckingham.

Boud, D., Keogh, R. and Walker, G. 1985, *Reflection: turning experience into action*, Kogan Page, London.

Brookfield, S. 1995, *Becoming a Critically Reflective Teacher*, Jossey-Bass, San Francisco.

Brousseau, G. 1997, *Theory of Didactical Situations in Mathematics: didactiques des mathématiques, 1970–1990*, N. Balacheff, M. Cooper, R. Sutherland, V. Warfield (trans.), Kluwer, Dordrecht.

Brown, L. and Dobson, A. 1996, Using Dissonance: finding the grit in the oyster, in G. Claxton (ed.) *Liberating the Learner*, Routledge, London.

Brown, S. 1981, Sharon's 'Kye', *Mathematics Teaching*, 94: 11–17.

Burr, V. 1995, *An Introduction to Social Constructionism*, Routledge, London.

Calvino, I. 1981, *If On A Winter's Night A Traveler*, Picador, London.

Calvino, I. 1983, *Mr Palomar*, W. Weaver (trans.), Harcourt Brace Jovanovich, San Diego.

Campbell, J. 1988, The Quality of Biography, in R. Sherman and R. Webb (eds) *Qualitiative Research in Education: focus and methods*, Falmer Press, London.

Carson, T. and Sumara, D. 1997, Action Research as a Living Practice, *Counterpoints 67, Studies in the Postmodern Theory of Education*, Peter Lang, New York.

Casement, P. 1985, *On Learning from the Patient* , Tavistock, London.

Cassam, Q. (ed.) 1994, *Self-Knowledge*, Oxford University Press, Oxford.

Castaneda, C. 1968, *The Teachings of Don Juan: a Yaqui way of knowledge*, University of California Press, Berkeley.

Chapman, O. 1997, Metaphors in the Teaching of Mathematical Problem Solving, *Educational Studies in Mathematics*, 32: 201–228.

Chapman, O. 1998, Metaphor as a Tool in Facilitating Preservice Teacher Development in Mathematical Problem Solving, in A. Oliver and K. Newstead (eds) *Proceedings of PME XXII*, University of Stellenbosch, Stellenbosch, SA vol 2, pp. 176–183.

Chapman, O. 1999, Reflection in Mathematics Education: the storying approach, in N. Ellerton (ed.) *Mathematics Teacher Development: International perspectives*, Meridian Press, Perth, pp. 201–216.

Chatley, J. 1992, *The Use of Experiential Learning Techniques in Mathematics Education: a personal evaluation*, Unpublished MPhil thesis, Open University, Milton Keynes.

Chevellard, Y. 1985, *La Transposition Didactique*, La Pensée Sauvage, Grenoble.

Cohen, L. 1976, *Educational Research in Classroom and Schools: a manual of materials and methods*, Harper and Row, London.

Cooney, T. 1988, Teachers' Decision Making, in D. Pimm (ed.) *Mathematics, Teachers and Children*, Hodder and Stoughton, London, pp. 273–286.

Corwin, R. and Storeygard, J. 1995, Talking Mathematics, *Hands On!* TERC, 18 (1) (see TERC website, *Hands on!* archive).

Davis, B. Sumara, D. and Luce-Kapler, R. 2000, *Engaging Minds: learning and teaching in a complex world*, Lawrence Erlbaum, Mahwah.

de Bono, E. 1972, *Po: beyond yes and no*, Penguin, Harmondsworth.

de Bono, E. 1977, *Lateral Thinking*, Penguin, Harmondsworth.

Denzin, N. and Lincoln, Y. (eds) 1994, *Handbook of Qualitative Research*, Sage, London.

Dewey, J. 1933, *Experience and Education*, MacMillan, New York.

Doyle, W. 1997, Heard Any Good Stories Lately? a critique of the critics of narrative in educational research, *Teaching and Teacher Education*, 15 (1): 93–99.

Earle, W. 1972, *The Autobiographical Consciousness*, Quadrangle Books, Chicago.

Eco, U. 1994, *Six Walks in the Fictional Woods*, Harvard University Press, Cambridge.

Eco, U. 1983, Horns, Hooves, Insteps: some hypotheses on three types of abduction, in U. Eco, and T. Sebeok (eds) 1983, *The Sign of Three: Dupin, Holmes, Peirce*, Indiana University Press, Bloomington, pp. 198–220.

Eco, U. and Sebeok, T. (eds) 1983, *The Sign of Three: Dupin, Holmes, Peirce*, Indiana University Press, Bloomington.

Edwards, C. 1995, Supporting, Piloting or Scaffolding: patterns of interaction in mathematics classrooms, *Proceedings of BCME 3*, Manchester, pp. 192–199.

Eliot, G. 1874 (1986), *Middlemarch*, Clrendon Press, Oxford.

Eliot, T. S. 1964, *Knowledge and Experience in the Philosophy of F. H. Bradley*, Faber and Faber, London.

Elliott, J. and Adleman, C. 1976, *The Ford Teaching Project*, Cambridge Institute of Education, Cambridge.

Eraut, M. 1994, *Developing Professional Knowledge and Competence*, Falmer Press, London.

Fenstermacher, K. and Hudson, B. 1997, *Practice Guidelines for Family Nurse Practitioners*, W.B. Saunders, London.

Fisher, P. 1998, *Wonder, the Rainbow, and the Aesthetics of Rare Experiences*, Harvard University Press, Cambridge.

Franklin, B. 1758, *Poor Richards Almanack, being the choicest morsels of wit and wisdom* reprinted 1961, Taurus Press, London.

Gadamer, H. 1975, *Truth and Method*, Seabury Press, New York.

Gardner, H. 1985, *The Mind's New Science : a history of the cognitive revolution*. Basic Books, New York.

Gattegno, C. 1970, *What We Owe Children: the subordination of teaching to learning*, Routledge and Kegan Paul, London.

Gattegno, C. 1975, *The Mind Teaches the Brain*, Educational Solutions, New York.

Gattegno, C. 1987, *The Science of Education Part I: theoretical considerations*, New York: Educational Solutions.

Glaser, B. 1978, *Theoretical Sensitivity: advances in the methodology of grounded theory*, Sociology Press, Mill Valley.

Glaser, B. (ed.) 1993, *Examples of Grounded Theory: a reader*, Sociology Press, Mill Valley.

Glaser, B. and Strauss, A. 1967, *The Discovery of Grounded Theory: strategies for qualitative research*, Aldine, Chicago.

Golding, W. 1955, *The Inheritors*, Faber, London.

Goldman, E. 1994, *As Others See Us: body movement and the art of successful communication*, Gordon and Breach, Lausanne.

Goodman, N. 1978, *Ways of World Making*, Harvester Press, Hassocks.

Hanley, U. Hardy, T. and Wilson, D. 1995, Using an Enquiry Research Paradigm with Practitioners in Mathematics Education, *Chreods*, 9: 29–36.

Hanson, N. 1958, *Patterns of Discovery: an enquiry into the conceptual foundations of science*, Cambridge University Press, Cambridge.

Harré, R. and Gillett, G. 1994, *The Discursive Mind*, Sage, Thousand Oaks

Helmholtz, H. 1896, *Handbuch der Physiologischen Optik*, Leopold Voss, Leipzig.

Henry, C. and Kemmis, S. 1985, A Point-By-Point Guide to Action Research for Teachers, *The Australian Administrator*, 6 (4) 1–4.

Herbert, G. 1633 (N. Ferrar, ed.), *The Temple: sacred poems and private ejaculations*, Buck and Daniel, Cambridge.

Hewitt, D. 1994, *The Principle of Economy in the Learning and Teaching of Mathematics*, unpublished PhD dissertation, Open University, Milton Keynes.

Holly, M. 1993, Personal and Professional Learning: on teaching and self-knowledge, in G. Plummer and G. Edwards (eds) *Dimensions of Action Research: people, practice and power*, C.A.R.N. Critical Conversations: a trilogy, Book 2, Hyde Publications, Bournemouth, pp. 58–86.

Hoosain, E. 2000, The Need for Interviews in the Mathematics Classroom, *Humanistic Mathematics Network Journal*, 22: 16–18.

Jackson, P. 1992, *Untaught Lessons*, Teachers College Press, New York.

Jakobson, R. and Halle, M. 1956 (1980), *Fundamentals of Language* (4th edn), Janua Linguarum 1, Mouton, The Hague.

James, L. 1993, From Anecdote to Action, *Chreods*, 6: 35–38.

James, W. 1890, reprinted 1950, *Principles of Psychology*, Vol 1, Dover, New York.

Jaworski, B. 1991, in R. Underhill and B. Jaworski, *Constructivism and Mathematics Education: A Discussion*, Centre for Mathematics Education, Open University, Milton Keynes.

Jaworski, B. 1995, The Critical Nature of Teaching Decisions, *Mathematics Teaching* 150 (March): 26–30.

Jaworski, B. 1998, Mathematics Teacher Research: process practice and the development of teaching, *Journal of Mathematics Teacher Education*, 1 (1): 3–31.

Jaworski, B. and Watson, A. 1994a, *Mentoring in Mathematics Teaching*, Mathematical Association and Falmer Press, London.

Jaworski, B. and Watson, A. 1994b, Mentoring, Co-mentoring, and the Inner Mentor, in B. Jaworski and A. Watson *Mentoring in Mathematics Teaching*, Mathematical Association and Falmer Press, London, pp. 124–138.

Johnson, L. and O'Neill, C. (eds) 1984, *Dorothy Heathcote: collected writings on Education and Drama*, Stanley Thornes, Cheltenham.

Keats, J. 1817, Letter to his brothers, December 21, see http://www.geocities.com/Athens/Parthenon/4942/negcap.html

Korzybski, A. 1941, *Science and Sanity: an introduction to non-Aristotelian systems and general semantics*, The International Non-Aristotelian Library Publishing Company, Lancaster.

Kuhn, Thomas 1970, *The Structure of Scientific Revolutions*, University of Chicago, Chicago.

Kvale, S. 1996, *InterViews: an introduction to qualitative research interviewing*, Sage, London.

Lakoff, G. and Johnson, M. 1980, *Metaphors We Live By*, University of Chicago, Chicago.

Langer, E. 1989, *Mindfulness*, Perseus Books, Reading.

Lave, J. 1988, *Cognition in Practice: mind, mathematics and culture in everyday life*, Cambridge University Press, Cambridge.

Lave, J. and Wenger, E. 1991, *Situated Learning: legitimate peripheral participation*, Cambridge, MA: Cambridge University Press.

Lerman, S. 1994, Reflective Practice, in B. Jaworski and A. Watson, *Mentoring in Mathematics Teaching*, Mathematical Association and Falmer Press, London.

Lerman, S. and Scott-Hodgetts, R. 1991, in F. Furinghetti (ed.) *Proceedings of PME XV*, Assisi, Vol II: 293–300.

Lincoln, Y. and Guba, E. 1985, *Naturalistic Enquiry*, Sage, Beverley Hills.

Macann, C. 1993, *Four Phenomenological Philosophers: Husserl, Heidegger, Sartre, Merleau-Ponty*, Routledge, London.

MacIntyre, D. 1993, Theory, Theorizing, and Reflection in Initial Teacher Education, in J. Calderhead and P. Gates, *Conceptualizing Reflection in Teacher Development*, Falmer Press, London.

Marton, F. 1981, Phenomenography: describing conceptions of the world around us, *Instructional Science*, 10: 177–200.

Marton, F. and Booth, S. 1997, *Learning and Awareness*, Lawrence Erlbaum Associates, Mahwah.

Maslow, A. 1971, *The Farther Reaches of Human Nature*, Viking Press, New York.

Mason, J. 1992, Researching Problem Solving from the Inside, in J. Ponte, J. Matos, J. Matos and D. Fernandes (eds), *Mathematical Problem Solving and New Information Technology: research in contexts of practice*, Nato ASI Series F No. 89, Springer Verlag, London, pp. 17–36.

Mason, J., Burton L. and Stacey K. 1982 (3rd edn 1998), *Thinking Mathematically*, Addison Wesley, London.

Masters, R. 1972, *Mind Games*, Turnstone, London.

Maturana, H. 1988, Reality: the search for objectivity or the quest for a compelling argument, *Irish Journal of Psychology*, 9 (1): 25–82.

Maturana, H. and Varela, F. 1988, *The Tree of Knowledge: the biological roots of human understanding*, Shambhala, Boston.

McKernan, J. 1991, *Curriculum Action Research: a handbook of methods for the reflective practitioner*, Kogan Page, London.

Mead, G. 1934 (ed. C. Morris), *Mind, Self, and Society: from the standpoint of a social behaviourist*, University of Chicago Press, Chicago.

Mead, G. 1938 (ed. C. Morris), *The Philosophy of the Act*, University of Chicago Press, Chicago.

Mead, G. 1969 (ed. A. Murphy), *The Philosophy of the Present*, Open Court, LaSalle.

Mead M. 1928, *Coming of Age in Samoa: a study of adolescence and sex in primitive societies*, Morrow, New York.

Middleton, J. 1998, The Self-in-the-Task: modelling as adaptive thought, in *Introductory Texts for the International Conference on Symbolizing and Modelling in Mathematics Education*, Freudenthal Institute, Utrecht.

Minsky, M. 1988, *The Society of Mind*, Touchstone, Simon and Schuster, New York.

Nias, J. 1989, *Primary Teachers Talking: a study of teaching as work*, Routledge, London.

Ollerton, M. 1997, Constructions of Equality in a Mathematics Classroom, unpublished Masters thesis, Open University, Milton Keynes.

Orage, A. 1930, *Psychological Exercises*, Janus, New York.

Owens, R. 1982, Methodological Rigor in Naturalistic Inquiry: some issues and answers, *Educational Administration Quarterly*, 18(2): 1–21.

Pascual-Leone, J. 1980, Constructive Problems for Constructive Theories: the current relevance of Piaget's work and a critique of information processing simulation psychology, in R. Kluwe and H. Spada (eds) *Developmental Models of Thinking*, Academic Press, New York, pp. 263–296.

Patocka, J. 1996 (E. Kohak, trans., J. Dodd, ed.), *An Introduction to Husserl's Phenomenology*, Open Court, Chicago.

Peirce, C. 1935–66, Collected Papers of Charles Saunders Peirce, C. Hartshorne, P. Weiss and A. Burks (eds) 8 vols, Harvard University Press, Cambridge.

Perry, W. 1968, *Forms of Intellectual and Ethical Development in the College Years: a scheme*, Holt, Rhinehart and Winston, New York.

Piaget, J. 1977a, *The Development of Thought: equilibration of cognitive structures*, Viking Press, New York.

Piaget, J. 1977b, *The Grasp of Consciousness*, Routledge and Kegan Paul, London.

Pimm, D. 1987, *Speaking Mathematically*, Hodder and Stoughton, London.

Pimm, D. 1993, From Should to Could: reflections on possibilities of mathematic teacher education, *For the Learning of Mathematics*, 13 (2): 27–32.

Polanyi, M. and Prosch, H. 1975, *Meaning*, University of Chicago Press, Chicago.

Polya, G. 1937, *How To Solve It*, Princeton University Press, Princeton.

Polya, G. 1945, *How To Solve It*, Princeton University Press, Cambridge.

Prestage, S. and Perks, P. 1992, Making Choices (part 2): '. . . not if you're a bear', *Mathematics in Schools*, 21 (4): 10–11.

Raymond, L. 1972, *To Live Within*, George Allen and Unwin, London.

Rice, M. 1993, Professional Development for Teachers: into the 1990s, in J. Mousley and M. Rice (eds) *Mathematics: of primary importance*, Proceedings of MAV 1993,

Mathematical Association of Victoria, Melbourne, pp. 189–195.

Rowland, T. 1999a, *The Pragmatics of Mathematics Education: vagueness in mathematical discourse*, Falmer, London.

Rowland, T. 1999b, Pronouns in Mathematics Talk: power, vagueness, and generalisation, *For the Learning of Mathematics*, 16 (2): 20–26.

Ryle, G. 1949, *The Concept of Mind*, Hutchinson, London.

Schank, R. and Abelson, R. 1977, *Scripts, Plans, Goals, and Understanding: an enquiry into human knowledge structures*, Lawrence Erlbaum, Hillsdale.

Schoenfeld, A. 1985, *Mathematical Problem Solving*, Academic Press, New York.

Schön, D. 1983, *The Reflective Practitioner: how professionals think in action*, Temple Smith, London.

Schön, D. 1987, *Educating the Reflective Practitioner*, Jossey-Bass, London.

Shah, I. 1964, *The Sufis*, Octagon, London.

Shigematsu, S. 1981, *A Zen Forest*, Weatherhill, New York.

Smith, B. and Woodruff, D. (eds) 1995, *The Cambridge Companion to Husserl*, Cambridge University Press, Cambridge.

Spencer-Brown, G. 1969, *The Laws of Form*, Allen & Unwin, London.

Sperber, D. and Wilson, D. 1986, *Relevance: communication and cognition*, Oxford: Blackwell.

Stewart, J. 1983, Interview in the *Guardian*, Saturday 3 December.

Storm, H. 1972, *Seven Arrows*, Ballantine, New York.

Strauss, A. and Corbin, J. 1993, *Grounded Theory in Practice*, Sage, London.

Tahta, D. 1972, *A Boolean Anthology: selected writings of Mary Boole on mathematics education*, Association of Teachers of Mathematics, Derby.

Tahta, D. 1995, Ever Present Affectivity, *Chreods*, 9: 3–9.

Thatcher, O. (ed.) 1901, *The Library of Original Sources, Vol. V: The Early Medieval World*, University Research Extension Co., Milwaukee. See also http://www.fordham.edu/halsall/source/bacon2.html

Tripp, D. 1993, *Critical Incidents in Teaching: developing professional judgement*, Routledge, London.

Valli, L. 1993, Reflective Teacher Education Programs: an analysis of case studies, in J. Calderhead and P. Gates, *Conceptualising Reflection in Teacher Development*, Falmer, London, pp. 11–22

van Manen, M. 1990, *Researching Lived Experience: human science for an action sensitive pedagogy*, Althouse Press, London, Ontario.

Varela, F., Thompson, E. and Rosch, E. (1992). *The Embodied Mind: cognitive science and human experience*. Cambridge: MIT Press.

von Glasersfeld, E. 1995, *Radical Constructivism*, Falmer Press, London.

von Glasersfeld, E. (n.d.), *Distinguishing the Observer: an attempt at interpreting Maturana* http://www.oikos.org/vonobserv.htm

Watson, A. 1998, What Can be Learnt by Selecting Anecdotes from a Range of Data? exemplifying 'noteworthy' mathematics with a small number of examples, *Proceedings of BSRLM*, February 1998, King's College, London.

Wheatley, G. 1992, The Role of Reflection in Mathematics Learning, *Educational Studies in Mathematics*, 23: 529–541.

Wheeler, D. 1986, Epistemological Approaches to the Study of Mathematics Education II, *Proceedings of PME 9*, London, pp. 23–33.

Whitehead, A. 1932, *The Aims of Education and Other Essays*, Williams and Norgate, London.

Wilder, T. 1938, reprinted 1975, *Our Town*, Avon Books, New York.

Williams, H. 1989, Tuning-in to Young Children: an exploration of contexts for learning mathematics, unpublished PhD dissertation, Open University, Milton Keynes.

Wilson, D. 1994, The Transference Relation in Teaching, *Chreods*, 8: 33–41.

Wimborne P. and Watson, A. 1998, Participating in Learning Mathematics Through Shared Local Practices in Classrooms, in A. Watson (ed.) *Situated Cognition and the Learning of Mathematics*, Centre for Mathematics Education Research, University of Oxford, Oxford, pp. 93–104.

Winnicot, D. 1971, *Playing and Reality*, Tavistock, London.

Zammattio, C., Marinoni, A., and Brizio, A. 1980, *Leonardo The Scientist*, McGraw-Hill, New York.

Zizek, S. 1999 (E. Wright and E. Wright eds), *The Zizek Reader*, Blackwell, Oxford.

Index of accounts

Index